Virginia Woolf's Women

Virginia Woolf's Women

VANESSA CURTIS

Foreword by
Professor Julia Briggs

The University of Wisconsin Press

The University of Wisconsin Press
1930 Monroe Street
Madison, Wisconsin 53711

www.wisc.edu/wisconsinpress/

1   3   5   4   2

Printed in the United States of America

A cataloging-in-publication record for this book is available from the Library of Congress

ISBN 0-299-18340-8

For Sue Fox, with heartfelt thanks for research,
inspirational friendship and shared enthusiasm

Contents

Acknowledgements

I would like to thank Angelica Garnett for permission to quote from her *Eternal Moment* and Henrietta Garnett, on behalf of the Estate of Vanessa Bell, for allowing me to reproduce quotations from both *Sketches in Pen and Ink* and letters sent from Vanessa Bell to Leonard Woolf. Anne Olivier Bell kindly provided a photocopy of *Stella Duckworth's Diary for 1893* (in her possession). Thanks also go to The Hon. Mrs C. Zielenkiewicz for permission to quote from a letter written by Ethel Sands, and to staff at the Lilly Library, Indiana University, Bloomington, who provided photocopies of the correspondence of Ottoline Morrell and granted permission to quote from the MacCarthy and Gathorne-Hardy manuscripts in their possession.

Dr Rosalind Moad at King's College Library, Cambridge, provided photocopied information and allowed me to quote from the King's College Archive, as well as granting permission to publish a photograph of Carrington from the E.M. Forster Archive. I would like to thank Dorothy Sheridan and her very helpful staff at the University of Sussex for providing access to the Monk's House and Charleston Papers, and the Society of Authors, as the Literary Estate of Virginia Woolf, for permission to include fragments of unpublished material held in the Monk's House Papers at the University of Sussex.

Staff at the Hulton Getty picture library assisted with the supply and reproduction of four photographs. Matthew Bailey at the picture library of the National Portrait Gallery, London, granted permission to publish photographs of Vanessa Bell, Ottoline Morrell and Julia Margaret Cameron. Jennifer Booth and staff at the Tate Gallery Archive supplied photographic illustrations from *Vanessa Bell's Family Album* and the Tate Gallery/Charleston Trust granted permission to publish them.

Joy Burden allowed me to quote from her *Winging Westward* and

8

provided personal recollections of Violet Dickinson. Karen Kukil and Barbara Blumenthal from the Mortimer Rare Book Room, Smith College, USA, supplied photographs from Leslie Stephen's photograph album and granted permission to publish them.

I should like to thank Frances Partridge for permission to quote from unpublished Carrington letters held at the Berg Collection, New York Public Library, and from her book, *Julia*. Richard Garnett granted permission for me to quote from *Carrington, Letters and Extracts from her Diaries*. Steve Crook at the Berg Collection, New York Public Library, has provided information and photographs relating to Violet Dickinson, and allowed me to study a copy of *Stella Duckworth's Diary for 1896*.

Sue Fox meticulously researched the lives of Julia Stephen, Violet Dickinson, Ottoline Morrell and Ethel Smyth. Adrian M. Goodman, as copyright holder for Ottoline Morrell, gave me permission to quote from her diaries and correspondence. David Higham Associates, as copyright holders for Dame Ethel Smyth and Osbert Sitwell, allowed me to quote from their diaries and correspondence. The Hon. Lord Sackville, Knole, as copyright holder for Eddie Sackville-West, granted permission to quote from a letter to Vanessa Bell.

Several people who have assisted in my research for this project are also friends. My thanks go to Jonathan and Caroline Zoob at Monk's House for their kind hospitality and enthusiasm. Nigel Nicolson has provided much useful information about Vita Sackville-West and has been endlessly hospitable. I thank Nigel for permission to quote from *Portrait of a Marriage*, *The Letters of Vita Sackville-West and Virginia Woolf*, *Collected Poems of Vita Sackville-West*, *Pepita* and his recent biography of Virginia Woolf.

A valued member of the *Virginia Woolf Society Reading Group*, Hilary Newman, offered books and information on both Violet Dickinson and Ethel Smyth. Sue and Nigel Bedford, during their years at Talland House, supplied both friendship and assistance with research – they will be sorely missed.

I am grateful and honoured that Professor Julia Briggs has contributed a valued foreword to this book. Sincere thanks must also go to Professor Katherine Hill-Miller for her essential help and advice during the formative stages of this project. Mr Jim Peers has kindly allowed me to quote from the late Rosamund Peers's PhD thesis on Virginia Woolf. Warm thanks go to Cecil Woolf for providing a short reminiscence of his 'Aunt Virginia' and for always showing such interest and support.

Jasmyne King-Leeder allowed me inside her private home at 22 Hyde Park Gate and provided articles and information about the Stephen family. Mary Cowin kindly provided clippings and much relevant information. My neighbour, Anna Parker-Rees, thoughtfully passed on relevant articles as and when she found them. As ever, my colleagues on the Executive Council of the Virginia Woolf Society of Great Britain have been generous enough to share their vast knowledge with me: Sheila M. Wilkinson provided copies of music composed by Ethel Smyth, Paul Evans kindly loaned books in his possession, Ruth Webb lent me her copy of *Vanessa Bell's Family Album* and shared her experiences of being a biographer, and Sandra Halsey helped with information relating to Carrington and Vita Sackville-West. Stuart N. Clarke, as always, has proved to be a walking encyclopaedia. I should like in particular to thank Stephen Barkway not only for providing a copy of *Friendship's Gallery* and useful information on Katherine Mansfield, but also for his quietly infectious enthusiasm for Virginia Woolf, which in turn helped me develop my own.

I would like to offer special thanks to my husband, Tim Cowin, for assistance with photographic reproductions and research. His willingness to traipse round all sorts of houses in inclement weather has been much appreciated. Also my family, David, Carol and Timothy Curtis, for their consistent encouragement and for instilling in me the love of books.

Finally, I should like to thank all the staff at Robert Hale for their constructive help and support on this project.

Foreword

by Professor Julia Briggs

Virginia Woolf published her earliest writings anonymously, yet although she disguised her gender beneath a genderless first person plural ('Mr Courtney, we think, feels some of this difficulty . . .'), her interest in the nature of women, what it meant to be a woman and, above all, what it meant to be a woman writer (or painter, or composer) is evident from the outset.

Visiting Haworth, she noticed Charlotte Brontë's shoes and her thin muslin dress, and the little oak stool that Emily took with her on 'her solitary moorland tramps'. Reviewing a male-authored book in *The Feminine Note in Fiction*, she wondered whether 'the adequate critic of women' might not herself be a woman. Her concern with women's creative powers prompted her to write of women as historians and novelists, as musicians and mathematicians. In 1910, at the instigation of her friend and tutor, Janet Case, she took on some voluntary office work for a universal suffrage society though she found it frustrating and not a little absurd. The First World War was to split the Women's Movement between those actively supporting the war effort and those opposed to it. Virginia Woolf was a pacifist, as were her family and friends. During the war years, the arguments of her *Three Guineas*, eventually published twenty years later, first took shape.

Although Virginia and her sister, Vanessa Bell, held the same views on pacifism, Vanessa (like their mother) took no interest in the Women's Movement. Virginia, with the artist's range of sympathies, could understand and imaginatively identify with the Victorian

11

fantasies of domesticity that located women at the heart of the family, while also recognizing how they shored up ideals of patriarchy, home and empire. At the centre of the great novels of the 1920s stand the controversial figures of Mrs Dalloway and Mrs Ramsay, heroines of an earlier age, torn between fulfilling their societies' expectations and needs of their own that they scarcely understand. For Woolf, a glow of romance hung over them, even though she could see precisely what had generated that romance and why it was self-deceptive. She could feel its appeal, while knowing that it had to be outgrown. As Woolf demonstrated throughout her life and her art, 'I often like women. I like their unconventionality. I like their completeness. I like their anonymity.' The rest of this book shows us her words in action.

Julia Briggs
January 2002

Illustrations

Between pages 96 and 97

17 Vita Sackville-West with Nigel and Ben at Sissinghurst Castle, 1924
18 Carrington and Lytton Strachey at Ham Spray, 1928
19 Ethel Smyth, 1901
20 Virginia Woolf, 1925

Picture Credits

National Portrait Gallery, London: 1, 13, 15. Mortimer Rare Book Room, Smith College: 2, 3. Tate Gallery Archive/The Charleston Trust: 4, 5, 6, 7, 8, 9, 10, 11, 14. Berg Collection, New York Public Library: 12. Hulton Getty Archive: 16, 17, 19, 20. King's College Library, Cambridge: 18.

Introduction

'Virginia Woolf's Women' is an unashamedly ambiguous title. It can be interpreted in a number of different ways, all of which have some relevance to Virginia Woolf and her relationships with the eclectic mix of women who passed through her life. It can be applied both to the female protagonists of her fiction and to the women who provided the love and care that she needed.

Virginia appreciated and treasured her friendships with women, confiding to her diary in 1924 that 'if one could be friendly with women, what a pleasure – the relationship so secret and private compared with relations to men'.[1] The women in her life gave her the stimulation, support, reassurance and maternal care that Virginia, deprived of her mother at the age of thirteen, craved relentlessly. Women came to mean many different things to her, but even as a writer of great eloquence, privileged enough to possess an army of words at her disposal, Woolf was unsure how to convey the importance of *being* a woman:

> I mean, what is a woman? I assure you, I do not know. I do not believe that you know. I do not believe that anybody can know until she has expressed herself in all the arts and professions open to human skill.[2]

Many women admired and were attracted to Virginia Woolf, finding irresistible the combination of her razor-sharp mind and vulnerable, sensitive beauty. Only a handful of these women weathered the storm, surviving Virginia's ruthless scrutiny to become her valued friends and correspondents. I include these women specifically in this book, otherwise it could have run riot with little or no order through the lives of too many people. I have selected only those few women who *notably* shaped and affected Woolf's life, her way of thinking, the women in her fiction or her sexuality. My intention is to reveal, through these unique and remarkable women, a side of Virginia Woolf that is perhaps not so widely seen. For this purpose also I have intentionally researched the lives of some women who are *not* usually considered to have been even cursory members of the 'Bloomsbury Group'.

It would be impossible, and unnecessary, to provide a full biography of each woman in the one short chapter that she is allowed, for with the exception of Violet Dickinson (who wrote her own history of the Dickinson family), the women I feature, Virginia included, are already the subject of, at the very least, several published essays, and in most cases, one or more full-length biographies. Therefore my aim is only to include each woman's essential biographical details in order to provide a solid background, before I concentrate more substantially on the development, nature and consequences of her particular relationship with Virginia Woolf.

Virginia's friendships with these selected women can be traced through correspondence (some of it not very well known or, in a few cases, previously unpublished), by analysing diaries, and also by studying the female protagonists in Virginia's fiction. Her reactions to the women closest to her were interesting and at times, extreme. Each of these women was able to extract different strands of Woolf's personality from the complex, multifarious web that was Virginia's mind. Some strands were appealing and brightly coloured, but others were considerably less attractive.

During the crucial, formative years of her youth, a string of unusual, enigmatic and occasionally tragic women shaped and influenced the young Virgina Stephen, from her pioneering photographer great-aunt, Julia Margaret Cameron, to her haunted, worn-down and beautiful mother, Julia Prinsep Stephen. The effect of Julia Stephen's early death on the highly strung and impressionable teenager was lifelong, resulting in phobias, insecurities and a constant need for maternal reassurance. The trauma of losing her mother rid Virginia, at the age of thirteen, of much of her natural flirtatiousness. The happy two-year-old, who had commanded so much of her father, Leslie Stephen's attention, lost her easy charm as soon as she became a teenager and was never to regain it fully. Hungry, even when Julia was still alive, for a mother's nurturing care and attention, she in turn learned to starve her own body as a means of staying in control, thus stripping herself of a healthy libido and limiting herself to flirtations that were rarely able to develop into full physical unions.

It was not only in death that Julia deprived Virginia of maternal comfort; she instilled a terrible insecurity in her little daughter by her frequent absences when caring for others or when she was caught up in seeing to Leslie's demands. The separation anxiety that Virginia had as a child, peering out from the nursery window to see if Julia was walking back up Hyde Park Gate, carried on into adulthood, with the result that she became extremely worried or depressed when parted for too long from her husband, Leonard Woolf, her sister, Vanessa Bell, or her close friend, Vita Sackville-West. Julia was a depressive who had suffered a similar lack of beneficial mothering from Maria Jackson. After her father's death, Julia had been a devoted nurse to the hypochondriac Maria who only dispersed tales of woe and warning, and not the unconditional motherly love that would have benefited Julia far more and enabled her to pass it on to her own daughter, Virginia. Unsurprisingly, both Vanessa and Virginia Stephen were to suffer depression and anxiety as a result of this lack of substantial maternal affection during their formative years.

Very early on in life, Virginia came to realize that being ill was the only way of assuring Julia's, and later on, Leonard's, undivided attention. Rosamund Peers summed up this addictive behaviour in her article 'Virginia Woolf and Food Imagery' (published posthumously as 'Virginia Woolf's Treatment of Food in *The Voyage Out* and *The Waves*' in *The Virginia Woolf Bulletin*, Issue 6, January 2001):

> After Julia's death, all meals were torture because Leslie used them as forums to display his grief. Julia's obsession was illness: she was a compulsive nurse. It must have occurred to all the Stephen children – especially to Virginia who adored her mother – that the best way to get attention was to be ill. And the most obvious sign of illness is loss of appetite.

As well as passing down a legacy that ensured that life would for many years still revolve around the ritualistic pull of the Victorian tea table, Julia and her claustrophobic household at 22 Hyde Park Gate imbued Virginia with lifelong eating distress. This meant that whenever she was stressed, overworked or depressed, the first sign of Virginia's inner turmoil would manifest itself physically in her refusal of food. Leslie Stephen was also to blame: meal times were occasions of great tension during the period of mourning for Julia because he would use every single meal as an outlet for his grief.

It could almost have been predicted that although Virginia's childhood writings contain few sinister descriptions of food, her adult work would often portray it as nightmarish, people's eating habits as disgusting or obscene, and overweight people as society rejects. *The Voyage Out* makes a bad dream out of an everyday scenario where two 'large' women plucking chickens are 'sitting on a bench with blood-smeared tin trays in front of them and yellow bodies across their knees'.[3] Birds rear their ugly heads again in *The Waves*, where they symbolize gluttony and destruction, piercing the shells of snails and feasting greedily off the slime within.

Virginia's diary makes occasional reference to the torture of having to watch dinner guests, on one occasion her sister-in-law, Karin Stephen, stuff their faces with suet pudding in front of her horrified gaze. Any female friend or relative who was seen to be putting on weight was regarded by Virginia as unfeminine. At various times she chastised Vita for gaining weight in middle age, was disgusted at the way Ethel Smyth 'chomped' her food, and even described Carrington, hardly the largest of women, as having a 'fat decided clever face'. Virginia Woolf's mother-in-law, Marie Woolf, was regularly condemned on paper by Virginia for one reason or another, but became the target of Virginia's full scorn purely for being 'fond of cakes'; this might well have struck Marie as being a little harsh, but Virginia's idealized concept of how a woman should look and behave was not modelled on the friends who loved her, but on the dead Julia and Stella, who were beautiful, slender and self-sacrificing. Photographs of them continued to take precedence at whichever house Virginia happened to be living or staying in; constant reminders of stern, chiselled and enviable classical beauty.

By not eating, Virginia could retain control over one tangible thing – her body. This, in turn, gave her the illusion that she was in control of her mind when other things, such as writing, socializing and her self-confidence, were crumbling. She felt that eating regular portions was akin to behaving as a terrible glutton, causing Virginia self-disgust and strong feelings of guilt, which in turn led to further refusals of food. It was a vicious circle, one that was impossible to break. Meal times were always difficult, even after her marriage to Leonard, although he carefully monitored Virginia's eating habits and was quick to initiate 'rest cures' wherever possible. But the rest cures involved lying in bed, being fed meat and milk. She would be unable to exercise and hence would put on too much weight. At one point, Virginia weighed over twelve stone. She knew that to maintain a settled routine of writing, she ideally should aim to maintain a weight of around nine stone, but most of the time she was below that target, and at the end of her life, severely thin, she appeared to have lost the will to even try.

Julia, then, both in life and death, was directly responsible for many damaging, negative characteristics inherited by her daughter, but was she responsible for any *positive* aspects of Virginia's womanhood? It seems that something of her tenacity and determination was passed down to Virginia, who was never afraid of hard work. Her capacity for friendship and humour must have come partly from Julia, who was much in demand as a confidante or adviser and who could be sharp and witty, and Virginia's love of writing letters was inherited as much from Julia, who wrote to all sorts of people on a daily basis, as from Leslie, who was, after all, the official 'man of letters' and a far more obvious source of inspiration. Virginia's fiction-writing ability was partly inherited from her mother, for Julia wrote amusing and colourful stories for children. Most useful of all, but often a considerable curse, was the passing down of Julia's Victorian matriarchal manner. Virginia admitted that this inherited way of behaving could be very useful, because she enjoyed knowing how to act socially and how to recreate the dignified, comforting rituals of afternoon tea and polite conversation, but this became a useful mantle for her to hide behind when necessary. It was what made the 'Angel in the House' such a difficult phantom to kill, for it represented Virginia's less attractive qualities of suppression, deceit, self-deprecation, guilt and superficiality.

These private demons that Virginia battled with made it impossible for her to behave confidently with the staff that she employed in her own houses. Although she had indeed inherited Julia's perfect tea-table manners, she was not good at playing the distant, haughty matriarch that Julia had been successful at portraying. Whilst this ability was passed down to Vanessa Bell, who managed to hire and fire staff without letting her emotions become apparent, Virginia suffered stress at the hands of Lottie and Nellie, her staff at Hogarth House in Richmond. She allowed them to resign when they felt like it, and then accepted them back when they regretted their hastiness. Going through agonies as she wrote and rewrote her novels, Virginia's state of mind was not always strong enough to make firm decisions concerning her staff, and lack of confidence in herself also made it difficult for maids to respect her as an employer. Even though she was Leonard Woolf's equal partner at the Hogarth Press for many years, Virginia preferred to leave the role of employer, and its responsibilities to her husband. Only one servant, Sophie Farrell, a stalwart of the original Stephen household, who went on to work for George Duckworth in her later years, continued to treat 'Miss Ginia' with any real respect, and her condolence letter to Vanessa after Virginia's death is one of the most moving of such letters that Vanessa received.

So Julia Stephen, the first significant woman in Virginia's life and the most powerful and influential 'Angel' that she was ever to know, provided the foundation upon which all of Virginia's future relationships were to be based. Whether these relationships were beneficial or otherwise, the fact remained that the traits Virginia inherited from Julia were never to leave her.

Whilst Julia did at least love her husband, Leslie Stephen, for their seventeen years of marriage and in that sense provided a positive early role model of heterosexual love for Virginia to witness, Woolf's shadowy half-sister Stella Duckworth's miserable death left Virginia with a deep mistrust of male-female relationships. Although when Stella was alive, Virginia had genuinely loved this surrogate mother figure with 'chivalrous devotion', she was forced to witness the effect of a healthy sexual appetite on her glowing half-sister when Stella returned, broken and dying, from her honeymoon. This brutally shocking transformation was profoundly disturbing to Virginia and played havoc with her development as a woman; it would seem that from the very moment of Stella's death onwards, Virginia viewed relationships between men and women with suspicion and some fear. She remained able to flirt, but the type of very physical flirtation that she used to her advantage with Leslie was never to manifest itself in quite such a confident way again. Although her later friendship with Violet Dickinson was often physical, taking the form of 'pettings', it was tinged with an unhealthy paranoia, an obsessive need for reassurance, and strong feelings of desperation that were quite unlike the natural, innocent flirtations of childhood.

By the time she embarked on her first 'serious' flirtation with a man, Clive Bell, Virginia had perfected the art of flirting at a distance: she relied on her pen, rather than her body, to achieve the desired effect. The crush that she had on Clive was an intellectual one; at least it was on her side (Clive, always alive to the attractions of the opposite sex, longed to kiss his beautiful sister-in-law). Virginia certainly enjoyed the thrill of luring him to her side with witty, intimate letters, but on ensnaring him thus, the sexual side of Virginia, which still recalled what had happened to Stella, would sink down to a safe, untouchable place, while the side of Virginia that loved flattery, reassurance and pleasurable analysis of her early efforts at fiction, rose up and begged further indulgence. Flirting, to Virginia, was a necessary skill to possess if she were to gain the sort of reassurance she needed; it was rarely intended as the precursor to sexual gratification and therefore she was often shocked by its inevitable consequence – a bitter and frustrated recipient who required more than this teasing, unconsummated flirtation. All in all, the death of Stella Duckworth left Virginia with an extremely negative view of heterosexuality.

After the deaths of Julia and Stella, two women continued to have great influence on the young Virginia Stephen. The first, who was always to be the recipient of Virginia's love, adoration and passion, was her sister Vanessa. Flung together after Julia and Stella's terrible deaths, the sisters confided only in each other, unable to express emotion in front of the grieving Leslie Stephen. Vanessa eventually instigated the controversial but necessary move from Leslie's cluttered, stuffy Victorian house at Hyde Park Gate to the bare, white-walled Edwardian rooms of Gordon Square, Bloomsbury. Virginia was rarely away from her sister's side until Vanessa accepted Clive Bell's offer of marriage in 1906, and even then the sisters wrote to each other with intimacy and affection, often on a daily basis, for the rest of their lives.

Incredibly, Virginia's period of obsession with her sister's husband, Clive, did nothing to lessen the love between herself and Vanessa. The adored elder sister, Vanessa, brought Virginia's loving nature to the foreground. Other than Leonard, Vanessa was the person whom Virginia loved and needed most. 'Nessa' was always on hand to reassure and to protect, and to sort out domestic problems and read the long, intimate letters that her sister would write to her. She also encouraged many of Virginia's most attractive qualities: playfulness, humour, loyalty, solidarity and, particularly in the early days, romantic passion. However, Vanessa also contributed greatly to Virginia's insecurity. Vanessa was always the more womanly, more maternal, consistently even-tempered beauty who, at one time, had three men vying for her attentions. Next to this voluptuous sister, Virginia often felt awkward: too tall, too thin, somehow not a 'real' woman.

Vanessa evoked both respect and jealousy in Virginia: the former for her strength of character (she refused, unlike Stella, to bow to Leslie's incessant demands and complaints); the latter because of the innate femininity and 'earth mother' demeanour that saw her settled at Charleston with three children and the love of two men, Clive Bell and Duncan Grant. After conceiving a daughter, Angelica, with Grant, Vanessa Bell was rarely to experience sexual passion again, but in the early days of her marriage to Clive, she had boasted often of her achievements to Virginia, causing Virginia to contrast herself unfavourably with her gorgeous sister, who could attract the attentions of clever, personable and creative men.

Although the competition between the sisters, as far as work was concerned, brought out Virginia's determination to succeed by gaining fame and material success as opposed to Vanessa's children and lovers, this arrangement began to go wrong as well, for Vanessa's paintings started to attract attention. For the first time, Virginia's propensity to jealousy became obvious in the many resentful retorts she spat out at her sister – *she* was supposed to be the only successful one, after all! Her jealousy was caused by insecurity and, despite their lifelong devotion, many small rifts grew up between the sisters. They were almost always resolved in the end, however, and if one wishes to see the loving, intimate side of Virginia Woolf, it is preserved for all to witness in the thousands of letters that she wrote to Vanessa. Despite sporadic bursts of jealousy and sisterly rivalry, the two women remained close for ever, and Virginia paid homage to her sister in several of her novels, most notably in the character of Katharine Hilbery in *Night and Day* (1919). On the day of Virginia's death in 1941, the notes left on her desk were addressed only to Leonard and Vanessa – the two people who, in the end, had meant the most to her.

Other than Vanessa, Virginia's only real female friend during the early years of the twentieth century was Violet Dickinson, an acquaintance of Stella's, who went on to offer Virginia emotional support through her early breakdowns and who was the object of the latter's adolescent desire for several years. The intimacy and playfulness that Virginia displayed towards her sister was also carried on into her friendship with Violet Dickinson. Significantly, it was Violet who initiated Virginia's first real career break as a book reviewer, and Violet who was the first strong role model, for she had not only travelled extensively, but also built a 'house of her own'. However, something about Violet, twinned with the pain of Julia and Stella's death, allowed Virginia's petulant, insecure side to overtake her vastly more attractive, down-to-earth one. Virginia was overly passionate in her dealings with Violet, demanding, childlike, pleading, jealous, and unreasonable in her requests for petting and reassurances. Her desires often became irrational, insubstantial and melodramatic. She became cruel, eventually dumping the devoted Violet when newer, younger friends came on to the scene.

Although Violet loved Virginia's letters and fully supported her writing career, she must have secretly been hurt and disappointed at the behaviour of this needy young woman. She remained loyal to her friend, even though Virginia rarely demonstrated any great loyalty towards Violet. However, despite the appearance of some of Virginia's less desirable qualities, the letters between herself and Violet do display much that is endearing or naïvely romantic.

No such romance was apparent when Virginia first came into contact with Ottoline Morrell. Ottoline, a woman on the fringes of the Bloomsbury Group, eventually became a long-standing, although never intimate, friend of Virginia Woolf. The false, gushing tone that Virginia used in her early correspondence with Ottoline shows Woolf in an unattractive light, for despite her unkind remarks about Ottoline's extravagance and her mockery of Ott's desire to live and flourish amongst writers and artists, it was also these very qualities that attracted Virginia and other Bloomsbury members to the Morrells' lavish country home, Garsington. There they would spend long weekends indulging in Ottoline's over-generous hospitality and unashamedly taking all that she had to offer.

Ottoline, one of the few women in Virginia's circle who was totally heterosexual, both fascinated and disgusted Virginia, who was reluctantly attracted to Ottoline's strangely flamboyant, seductive beauty. Despite finding Ottoline compelling to look at, Virginia constantly sneered at her lack of morals and inability to be a true artist. Effortlessly, perhaps even without realizing it, Virginia displayed one after another of her most unattractive characteristics: snobbery, envy, falseness, cruelty and fickleness. Never did Virginia seem less kind than when she was attacking poor Ottoline in her early letters.

The very things that attracted Virginia to Ottoline – her opulence, unusual looks, aristocratic background and beautiful homes – also repelled her, and unfortunately Virginia lost no time in documenting her repulsion to other friends. The painfully shy, loving, insecure Virginia Stephen by this time had faded away – and into her place had jumped a sharp, posturing, cigarette-smoking intellectual who made the most of Ottoline's hospitality whilst slating her in front of an admiring audience. The patient Ottoline had unleashed Woolf's superficiality, arrogance, gossip and unreliability, quite unintentionally.

Only much later on in this rather one-sided friendship did Virginia, with the hindsight brought about by age and the shared understanding of debilitating illness, relent in this behaviour and allow her finer qualities of kindness, patience and concern to shine through. Virginia only learned to appreciate her friend's loyalty, suffering and the endless help she gave to others just before Ottoline's death; even then, Woolf had little idea of just how much hurt she had caused her.

This duplicity of feeling towards Ottoline later caused Virginia to question *herself* too, and for this reason the relationship, which only really settled into a genuine fondness in the 1930s, is an interesting one to analyse.

Through Ottoline, Virginia became a friend of the contemporary woman writer, Katherine Mansfield. Katherine, along with Virginia's sister Vanessa, was different from the other women in Virginia's circle because she was not a traditionalist (despite their pioneering traits, most of the friends that Virginia had spent time with up until meeting Mansfield still retained their Victorian connection to the past). Katherine was the first true modernist that Virginia had known intimately, and she admired Katherine's work immensely (with one or two well-documented exceptions).

The Hogarth Press published Katherine's early story *Prelude* and the two writers met frequently at first, surprised at how similar their literary aims were. However, seriously ill and lonely, with an unreliable husband, Katherine became jealous of Virginia's stable, happy marriage and writing success, and Virginia slated Katherine's story 'Bliss', proclaiming it to be hard and cheap in style. In return for these less than positive reviews, Katherine wrote some coolly dismissive pieces of her own about Virginia's novels, deeming them slow and old-fashioned. In this way rifts grew up between them.

Katherine Mansfield, never averse to putting people down, was able to inspire pity and revulsion from Virginia. Their friendship, based not so much on reciprocal fondness as mutual ambition, encouraged

Virginia's protectiveness on occasion, but more often than not frustrated her. Katherine tended to maintain silent, prolonged absences in overseas countries, battling to save her health. Virginia's reluctant fascination with the bisexual, enigmatic and terminally ill Katherine is evident in her diaries and letters. Unusually for Virginia, she became jealous of Katherine not personally, but professionally. Katherine evoked in Virginia a competitiveness, a rivalry based on the desire for literary success.

By the time Katherine died in her early thirties, the two writers' relationship had become distant and disillusioned, leaving Virginia with a sense of great regret and yet a certain relief as well. She believed, mistakenly, that the competition would now diminish, but Katherine continued after her death to capture the hearts and minds of the public with several volumes of posthumously issued journals and stories, and she haunted Virginia's own thoughts and dreams for years to come, both as a literary rival and as a woman.

Mansfield's early death saddened Virginia greatly, but the subsequent reflections that Virginia wrote in her diary and used when thinking about Katherine's life occasionally seem to have been used as a writing exercise rather than a genuine display of sentiment towards this woman, whom she was now to confess that she had felt fascination and some sort of love for. Biographers have hinted at a sexual attraction between the two writers and have analysed to great extent the references to lesbianism in their short stories, but Katherine appeared not to have physically attracted Virginia during her lifetime – the latter's famous comment that Katherine smelt like a 'civet cat' seemingly giving weight to the fact. There is no doubt, however, that as a writer and modernist, Katherine Mansfield was the single woman contemporary able to present a serious threat to Virginia Woolf's literary reputation.

A woman acquainted with Ottoline and Katherine, the unusual Dora Carrington, tends to slip almost unnoticed through the hands of biographers, although there are several parallels to be drawn between herself and Virginia Woolf. Carrington was not considered to be a bona fide member of the Bloomsbury Group, but came to it by association with her soul mate and platonic partner, Lytton Strachey.

Loving, bisexual, often insecure and depressed or tortured by her art and her life, Carrington was at first viewed with suspicion by Virginia who, still close to Lytton, was jealous of any female who might threaten their special friendship. Eventually this mistrust became a genuine fondness, although Carrington, naturally youthful and cherubic in appearance, made Virginia feel old and dowdy in comparison. Carrington was the one woman who consistently brought out most of Woolf's positive qualities. Something about Carrington encouraged Virginia to react in a gentle, feminine way, at odds with her usual sharp or unforgiving analyses of people.

Virginia demonstrated true affection for Carrington, and although they were never the closest of friends, an accepting affinity grew up between them based on shared artistic goals, love of the Sussex countryside and unconditional devotion to Lytton Strachey. With Carrington, Virginia's teasing was not cruel, but laughingly inoffensive. It is only by studying Virginia's behaviour towards Carrington that we ever witness how she could behave purely as a sympathetic woman friend, rather than as a writer, critic, cynic or snob. After Lytton's death, rare, palpable warmth emanated from Virginia's heartfelt letters to Carrington; warmth that did not need to rely on wit or cleverness, thus rarely seen in letters to the various other women in her life (although it can be seen clearly in letters written to Leonard, Jacques Raverat, Roger Fry and Lytton).

The Woolfs were the last people to see Carrington before she shot herself, visiting her the night before to try and alleviate the depression that had followed on from Lytton Strachey's death. Carrington's suicide had a sobering, but positive effect on Virginia, who resolved not to end her own life, declaring that there was far too much left to enjoy in it. Woolf's decision, later on, to terminate her life precisely echoed Carrington's, and for that reason it is possible to assume that each woman recognized aspects of herself in the other, leaving it impossible and unnecessary for Virginia ever to put on a protective 'mask' in front of Carrington. There are many comparisons to be drawn between the life of Carrington, who constantly suffered agonies of doubt about her own artistic talent, and that of Virginia Woolf. Their attitudes to their chosen careers, their long-term platonic partnerships, their awkwardness with their own bodies and their attractions to and for other women, make them appear, in retrospect, uncannily similar. Perhaps the realization of these similarities was the overriding reason why their friendship never developed further; since although fond of each other, the two never became close.

A book looking at the women in Virginia Woolf's life would not be complete without a glimpse of the two characters who, from her middle age onwards, brought Woolf the most pleasure, but also the most pain, in her entire life. Vita Sackville-West was the first to stride manfully into Virginia's ordered, married existence. Sackville-West had the advantages of an aristocratic background, a strong, beautiful physique and a curriculum vitae of well-documented previous love affairs, including her highly sensational romance with Violet Trefusis. By the time Virginia met Vita Sackville-West, she had already experienced a love affair of sorts (Violet Dickinson), dabbled with the aristocracy (Ottoline Morrell), achieved success as a writer, got married, and dealt with many of the insecurities that had plagued her as a young woman. Vita then, unexpectedly sparked off a return to areas of Woolf's life that she thought were already well and truly explored. Here, once again, was the aristocracy in all its glory, laid out in front of Virginia's greedy eyes. Here was a woman capable not only of inspiring passion, but also of *giving* it, in copious quantities.

Vita resurrected many of the turbulent feelings that Virginia, settled in her marriage to Leonard, thought had died years earlier. Suddenly Virginia began to crave maternal affection again, demonstrating more jealousy and petulance when Vita spent too much time with other women, writing cruel words born from a fear of loss. Virginia, in a safe, loving, but platonic marriage with Leonard Woolf, had started to explore her physical desires for other women in fiction, but had not, until now, had any other valid outlet for them. Her relationship with Vita was sexual for a short while, but was mainly fuelled through an intimate, sometimes explosive and lengthy, correspondence. Vita also prompted Virginia's wit and her skill with words (after all, Virginia was considered by both women to be the superior author, although Vita's books sold vastly more copies).

Woolf had an attractive vulnerability, but also a superiority complex: she had lived longer than Vita, and therefore considered herself to be far wiser. However, the age gap also brought to the fore Virginia's uncertainties, making her feel 'dowdy' in comparison to the glowing, full-figured Vita. Whatever negative traits were exhumed by Vita, the many positive ones – the greatest of which was Virginia's capacity for true and lasting friendship – more than compensated.

Vita Sackville-West was obsessed with Virginia's mental fragility, her beauty and her prolific output of fiction, and she was utterly seduced by Virginia's portrayal of her as 'Orlando' (after which, seemingly purged at last of her desires, Virginia's physical cravings for Vita simmered down, to be replaced mainly by love and affection). Sadly, Vita could also be fickle, and soon the relationship started to cool as she began a new, intense affair with the Head of Talks at the BBC, Hilda Matheson, and then had more affairs with others, including the journalist Evelyn Irons. Her letters to Virginia became less frequent, causing the older woman to feel betrayed and that she had lost Vita's attention to newer, younger lovers, but their friendship, although never as deep again, did survive. *Orlando* had bonded the two women together for life. Although their initial ardour cooled after only two years, Vita remained a close friend, and Virginia craved her company right up until the end. After the loss of Virginia, Vita drew strength from her husband, Harold Nicolson, and paid moving tribute to Woolf with a specially written poem published in the *Observer*. Vita was always to live with the agonizing question of whether she, as a close friend, could have prevented Virginia's suicide.

The last woman to make a sizeable impact on Virginia's life was the composer and writer, Ethel Smyth. Ethel was responsible for revealing more (previously unseen) aspects of Virginia's character than any other woman had managed to. She coaxed Virginia's feminist beliefs, which had previously been suppressed, out into the open and onto the written page. With this sudden unleashing of long-repressed anger came a new honesty and frankness of Woolf's character that permitted almost any topic to be freely discussed in letters. Virginia demonstrated her biting wit and agility of mind more strongly in letters to Ethel than to anyone else. Ethel merely lit the touch paper, sat back and enjoyed the heat from the sparks. Virginia learned to argue, to debate with brilliance, to relate with candour and wit, and while she never managed to kill off the legacy of the 'Angel in the House' completely, she certainly managed to dent the angel's wings quite severely through her correspondence with Ethel. Her endless thirst for knowledge, always strong, became more intense as she witnessed Ethel's own artistic process of composition.

Ethel, unlike Vita, did not particularly enjoy Virginia's fiction, but she greatly admired her feminist polemics, *A Room of One's Own* and *Three Guineas*. She also respected *The Common Reader*, and on the strength of her curiosity about its author invited herself round to Tavistock Square. She burst into the house, firing non-stop questions. At the age of seventy-two, Ethel found herself in love with Virginia (who at first found the idea repulsive) and she bombarded her with letters and invitations. Slowly, during the ensuing eleven years, Virginia began to open up to this appreciative audience, confiding intimately to her about her work, her sexuality, her depression, her family background and her medical history. Although not an admirer of Ethel's musical compositions (despite having been a keen concert-goer as a young woman), Virginia admired immensely the actual method of her composing. The creative process that Virginia followed through in her fiction, and her tendency to improvise in bursts, were not dissimilar to the work of a musical composer, leading to some interesting parallels being drawn between the work of the two women. Ethel's own life and career influenced Virginia profoundly, providing the fortitude of character necessary for her to write *Three Guineas* and *The Years*.

Virginia's association with Ethel initially made her feel younger and more beautiful, clever, loved and admired than she had done for years. In many ways, acquaintance with Ethel must have provided Virginia with a pleasing ego-boost. Next to square-jawed, solid Ethel, Virginia was undeniably a beauty, able to recapture some of her old pleasure in her looks. Unfortunately, there were numerous stresses arising from this friendship: Ethel's fits of ardour, temper and boundless energy reduced Virginia to frustration and tears; she in turn could be scathing about Ethel's appearance and ungainly dress or eating habits. Her head ached with the strain of trying to find peace and quiet to write, away from Ethel's interruptions.

Ethel also brought to the fore a very real and painful fear of Virginia's – ageing. When they met, Ethel had already been in her seventies and Virginia found her at once revolting and intriguing. Because neither Julia nor Stella had reached healthy old age, Virginia had only limited experience of associating with the elderly (in fact, Stella had spoken of her own beauty as a 'thing of the past' at the tender age of twenty-six!). Julia's beauty had always remained visible beneath her severity, and she had not even reached her fiftieth birthday before she died. Thus Ethel brought out a side of Virginia that was disgusted by the ageing process, particularly because Virginia, shortly before her first meeting with Ethel, had just realized that she herself was no longer that young. On a visit in 1929 to an oculist, who had innocently commented 'Perhaps you're not as young as you were', Woolf recorded her shock and surprise:

This is the first time that has been said to me; and it seemed to me an astonishing statement. It means that one now seems to a stranger not a woman, but an elderly woman. Yet even so, though I felt wrinkled and aged for an hour, and put on a manner of great wisdom and toleration, buying a coat, even so, I forget it soon; and am a 'woman' again.[4]

It is significant that in this diary entry, as in other later ones, Virginia fails to connect being a woman with old age, seeming to believe that it is not possible to be both at the same time, that to be a 'woman' is far preferable. With this split in her personality, it was obvious to those who knew her well that Virginia's passage into old age would not be graceful or particularly easy. Ethel, for her own part, became difficult, forgetful and impatient with increasing age, and her friendship with Virginia finally became less intense, but in 1939, Virginia was still amusedly playing confidante to this incorrigible woman, who had yet again fallen in love, this time at the ripe old age of eighty-one!

Although it is impossible to separate fully Woolf the woman from Woolf the writer, writing being an integral part of her daily life, the final part of this book deals predominantly with the former, starting with the difficult details of Virginia's Victorian upbringing and then tracing her development, via some lesser-known photographs, from an unhappy teenager into a confident reviewer and writer whose beauty and intellect had a profound impact on those around her. A selection of previously unpublished letters of condolence, written after Virginia's death, to Vanessa Bell, divulge more information about Virginia's personality than most biographers could hope to, and go some way towards dispelling the myth of Virginia being permanently depressed. I take a walk around the three houses that most influenced Virginia's development as both a writer and a woman, where there is still something remaining of the atmosphere that she would have experienced at the time. A visitor to these 'literary shrines' might well believe that they have come away knowing a little more of Virginia's personality from soaking up the atmosphere at these houses. Finally, the book reveals how the surviving four of 'Virginia Woolf's women' came to terms with her death in 1941.

Through the eyes of 'Virginia Woolf's women', those women who knew her intimately, and from the effect, in turn, that they had on her life and fiction, I hope to draw an affectionate, unusual and honest picture of Virginia Woolf as a daughter, sister, writer, critic, friend – and woman.

1 The 'Angels in the House' – Maria, Julia and Stella

She was intensely sympathetic. She was immensely charming. She was utterly unselfish. She excelled in the difficult arts of family life. She sacrificed herself daily . . . in short she was so constituted that she never had a mind or a wish of her own, but preferred to sympathise always with the minds and wishes of others.[1]

From the moment of her birth on 25 January 1882, until the day she died, a steady stream of unusual, enigmatic and troubled women shaped and inspired the life and work of Virginia Woolf.

The power and influence of the three earliest of these women, her grandmother, mother and half-sister, should not be underestimated, for these 'Angels', with their self-sacrificing ways, haunted and tormented Virginia for many years after their deaths. They lived, ate, slept, entertained, worried, gave birth, became ill and died within the dark confines of a house that was painted black inside. They took up permanent residence in the dark recesses of Virginia's mind, watching over her, imbuing her with the deep-rooted Victorian values that she adhered to, sometimes willingly, at other times not, for the rest of her life. These three female stalwarts of the cluttered Victorian household at 22 Hyde Park Gate were responsible for the 59-year-long emotional war that Virginia fought and ultimately lost, although she finally managed, as she entered her forties, to find her own voice and defeat the ultimate enemy – the 'Angel' who had for years bestowed on her an inability to express herself freely with a pen. Her anger at these years of repression is finally laid bare on the pages still available to us, predominantly in *A Room of One's Own*, *The Years* and *Three Guineas*.

Adeline Virginia Stephen was only ten years old in 1892 when her grandmother, Maria 'Mia' Jackson, died after years of poor health. Even as an adult, Virginia could still recall the stifling, syrupy affection that Maria poured upon all her grandchildren as she 'held one so long in her arms'.[2] After the death in 1887 of her kindly, well-meaning husband, Dr Jackson, Maria spent most of her time suffering protractedly at the Stephen family home, 22 Hyde Park Gate, relying heavily on her daughter, Julia, and wallowing in hypochondria. She played the overprotective grandmother with a determination that bordered on the sinister (her letters, some nine hundred black-edged epistles of gloom, survive today, warning her family of the perils of eating sausages and not attending to the workings of their bowels).

Mia was one of the famous Pattle sisters, each renowned for their beauty (save for one, Julia Margaret Cameron, who compensated for her lack of visual appeal by becoming a famous photographer). Mia was certainly beautiful, but also puritanical and demanding. She married the gentle Dr Jackson of Calcutta and then allowed him to fade into insignificance beside her. She was an exhausting and stiflingly over-concerned wife. After her husband's death, Mia refocused her attentions on her daughter Julia, who had also lost a beloved husband, Herbert, and was now married a second time, to the biographer and writer Leslie Stephen. Leslie was understandably frustrated by his wife's devotion to her ailing mother, who seemed to spend most of her time living with them in Kensington, on holiday with them at St Ives or dragging Julia away to her house in Brighton. Maria's dependency fed greedily on Julia's tireless commitment, with the result that they were pulled inextricably closer together in a way that was to have an adverse effect on all of Julia's children. There were many emotional tensions and sentimental scenes played out at 22 Hyde Park Gate; these were the scenes that instigated in the young Virginia Stephen her earliest awareness of how a female family member ought to behave: with devotion, femininity, and utter disregard for her own health in preference to that of others.

During her lengthy periods of ill health, Maria wrote to Julia on a daily basis, even on days that they had spent together. The black-edged envelopes doggedly followed Julia around the country, dropping heavily onto the mat of whichever house she happened to be in, including Talland House, the family holiday home in St Ives, Cornwall. Maria joined the family for several of these annual sojourns and sat idly in the garden while her friend, the Victorian poet Coventry Patmore, read aloud his latest sentimental offerings.

It is hard not to dwell on the significance of Maria befriending and adoring this writer of 'The Angel in the House', with its message advocating the virtues of sympathy, charity, beauty and selflessness. Maria probably considered herself to possess all these virtues, but although she had indeed been a great beauty as a young woman, she appeared, in old age, far too obsessed with her own hypochondria to have any time to promote selflessness. What she lacked in the ways of charity and sympathy, however, Mia's virtuous daughter, Julia, more than compensated for during her short and ceaselessly tiring life.

'Cameron's women do not smile. Their poses embody sorrow, resignation, composure, solemnity, and love, determined love, love which will have a hard time of it' writes Sylvia Wolf in the introduction to her powerful selection of photographs, *Julia Margaret Cameron's Women* (1998). Cameron's niece, Julia Prinsep Stephen (née Jackson), fascinated her photographer aunt, and as Julia grew up, she was also much in demand from other artists and photographers, including Edward Burne-Jones (who used her as a model for *The Annunciation*).

Julia Stephen did indeed have a 'hard time of it' as far as love was concerned; in a series of photographs taken by Cameron between 1864 and 1874, the rapid progression of heartbreak and illness in her early adult life is eerily charted for posterity. The early shots of Julia aged sixteen and eighteen show a demure, innocent girl with her hair tied back humbly, gazing with modesty and humility into her aunt's all-seeing lens. In 1867, Cameron took a strikingly different set of photographs just prior to, and then after, Julia's marriage to her first husband, the handsome barrister Herbert Duckworth.

In these stark, pioneering, strangely timeless photographs, an unadorned Julia bursts, fiery and challenging, onto the pages. Here is Julia at the only time in her life when she was ready to defy the 'Angel in the House': an exciting world appears to lie ahead of her, where anything is possible, where women are strong, ambitious and in control. Her face radiates supreme confidence, reflecting the inner knowledge of her own beauty. Her hair streams loose and uncontrolled around her shoulders; her skin is rough-textured and porous, and yet her unadorned beauty here is breathtaking. This is the image that Virginia Woolf was to live in awe of all her life; these are the photographs that decorated the dark hallways at Hyde Park Gate, that were hung in mourning on holiday at Hindhead House and were later moved to the whitewashed walls of 46 Gordon Square in Bloomsbury. If there was ever a caption to be added now underneath this stunning series of photographs, it should surely be taken from her future daughter Virginia's story, 'The Moment: Summer's Night' (1947):

> Then comes the terror, the exultation; the power to rush out unnoticed, alone; to be consumed; to be swept away; to become a rider on the random wind; the tossing wind; the trampling and neighing wind; the horse with the blown-back mane; the tumbling, the foraging; he who gallops for ever, nowhither travelling, indifferent; to be part of the eyeless dark, to be rippling and streaming, to feel the glory run molten up the spine, down the limbs, making the eyes glow, burning, bright, and penetrate the buffeting waves of the wind.

The same series of photographs contains a sequence entitled 'Mrs Herbert Duckworth'. Here, Cameron introduces Julia in her guise as a newly married woman and wife of a successful barrister. Gone are the untamed locks and defiant expression; in their place are serenity, beautiful clothes and elegantly tied-back hair. But the same self-assuredness and poise shine through. Before the death of Herbert stripped her of her spirit, optimism and confidence, Julia Stephen appeared, in her aunt's photographs, to be ready and able to take on the world.

Tragically, in 1872 this picture-book dream was to be shattered. Herbert Duckworth died an unexpected and undignified death as he stretched up to pick a fig and instead burst an abscess. Julia was left a widow, pregnant and with two tiny children already. Although Cameron's next photograph of her niece is entitled 'A Beautiful Vision', it should perhaps have been called 'A Mournful Vision' instead. The ghostly sitter is white-faced, dressed in the widow's black mourning garments with a white cap and simple collar. The most striking and disturbing difference between this photograph of Cameron's niece and the earlier set is in Julia's eyes. Her pupils are dilated, her face stiff and withdrawn, her whole expression shrieks not of confidence, but of the futility of her life. Where once was reflected love and hope, now shows only a weary resignation to fate. Never again, after this photograph, did any portraits of Julia reflect much other than severity and ill health at worst, impassivity and acceptance at best. Although she learned to love her second husband and new family, the power and confidence of those early pictures was never again to be captured on film. The death of Herbert literally drained away her colour, her faith, her confidence and her place in life.

One of the last pictures that Cameron was to take of Julia, in 1874, is titled 'She Walks in Beauty'. It is hard to see the beauty in Julia's features: she is wearing a fancy gold chain and striking a defiant pose, but her face is a blurred white oval under the severe black hat, her hands appear skeletal as they poke from black-frilled sleeves, her features are hard, drawn and she looks remote. At this time in her life, Julia was lying, prostrate with grief, full-length along the top of Herbert Duckworth's grave. Her three children, George, Gerald and Stella, were to grow up in the shadow of a distant and melancholy mother. All three of them suffered as a result, and all three had their childhood cruelly curtailed short as they struggled to support and comfort the heartbroken Julia. Stella, as the only girl, learned from the age of five to be as devoted and selfless to her mother as Julia had always been with Maria. A pattern of behaviour was being established in 1874, a pattern that was to pass down the female line of the family and manifest itself, often with harrowing results, in its most famous member – Virginia Woolf.

After Herbert's death, Julia Duckworth continued to do only two things – to spend time with her needy mother, and to devote herself to good causes, visiting the sick and miserable. This was a self-imposed duty that she was to maintain for the rest of her life; it now formed some kind of effective barrier against the pain she suffered inside. For eight years she mourned Herbert relentlessly, telling her anxious relatives that she only wished to die. She moved to 13 Hyde Park Gate (now No. 22), where her next-door neighbour was Leslie Stephen, also in anguished mourning for his first wife, Minny Thackeray, who had left him with a sickly, backward daughter, called Laura. Julia was familiar with Leslie's writing and had been friends with him for some time, providing invaluable support throughout Minny's illness and death. This was a role that suited well her own gloomy temperament and newly resolved devotion to soothe the troubles of others.

Although both Julia and Leslie were grieving and, therefore, in a state of considerable sorrow, Leslie, unlike Julia, had not resigned himself to a lifetime of futility. He carried inside him a glimmer of

hope, and it resurfaced at the beginning of 1877 with the shocking realization that he was in love with Julia. It was not set to be the jolliest of
romances, however, as Leslie knew from the start. 'Julia was that
strange solemn music to which my whole nature seemed to be set',[3] he
reflected after her death. He confided his feelings to his new love, but
she merely patted his shoulder and told him she would prefer to
conserve their friendship. A year of this friendship followed, during
which time their letters became more intimate, but Julia still expressed
unwillingness to commit to a new, shared life. Early in 1878, however,
as the couple sat by the fire at Julia's house, she suddenly looked up and
agreed to become his wife. The marriage took place at Kensington
Church in the High Street on 26 March 1878, and Leslie, with his little
daughter Laura, moved into No. 13 to join Julia and her three children.

Eventually Julia, loved and worshipped by her new husband, came
to regain something of the confidence and humour that she thought
she would never possess again. Although she neglected to take much
heed of her own happiness, Julia learned to live through Leslie, her
mother and her children, as well as by acting as a friend, confidante
and matchmaker to the many young couples who visited Hyde Park
Gate. The three Duckworth children were gradually forced to accommodate four new half-brothers and sisters in the already crowded
household. The first of these, Vanessa, was born on 30 May 1879
(sharing a birth date with Stella Duckworth). Julian Thoby followed
in 1880, Adeline Virginia in 1882, and Julia's special favourite, Adrian
Leslie, in 1883. During this year, Smith Elder & Co. published Julia's
essays on how to nurse the sick and dying. The pieces illustrate Julia
at her most practical, as she advises banishing boring visitors from the
bedside of her patients and debates, with considerable wit (albeit with
the excessively pernickety attentions of the Victorian matriarch), on
the evils of crumbs in the bed sheets.

Leslie and Julia began their 17-year-long marriage at 22 Hyde Park
Gate. The road had originally been a piece of wasteland, upon which
resided one or two donkeys, until a schoolmaster, Joshua Flesher
Hanson, bought it in 1833. Slowly a row of mansions was erected,
some with Corinthian columns and Doric pillars, and they were occupied in the Stephens' time by dukes, merchants, lawyers and famous
names such as Charles Dickens and, later, Winston Churchill. The
house was built in 1843 and before Leslie and Julia took it, it had
belonged to a retired East India merchant named James Cowell. The

surrounding parts of Kensington, in particular Melbury Road and Holland Park Road, were full of artists, many of them living in houses built to their own specifications. The Prinsep family, from which Julia was descended, leased Little Holland House and shared it with George Watts. He had come to stay for a week and ended up staying for thirty years.

In Kensington High Street, Julia and her family would have been able to visit John Barker's, a massive emporium rather like today's Harrods, with a huge food hall, a drapery, bookshop, stationer, iron-mongery and teashop. Barker's rival was Pontings, a 'fancy goods and silk business' that was opened in 1873 and grew into a large department store selling glass and china on six floors, with one hundred live-in assistants. Other shops long since gone included the Aerated Bread Company (ABC), a teashop often mentioned in Virgina Stephen's diaries, Dr Jaeger's Sanitary Woollen System, Daniel Neal's School Uniform Shop and Cramer's Music Shop where Stella, the most musical of the family, would have purchased sheet music. In 1897 the busy High Street was festooned with flags and buntings on the occasion of Queen Victoria's Diamond Jubilee.

Number 22 Hyde Park Gate still stands but it is now divided into flats. It is a tall, narrow, odd-shaped building (the top two floors and a large back dining-room extension were sketched quickly on the back of an envelope by Julia and then built to accommodate her growing family). With a tiny patch of garden at the back and no front garden to speak of, this house provided the Stephen children with a claustro-phobic existence. At one point it contained eight children, three adults and several servants. There was little privacy either inside or outside the house; everybody down Hyde Park Gate knew the business of everybody living there, and the High Street was noisy and over-crowded with horses, hansom cabs and horse-drawn buses.

The highlight of the children's year was the summer holiday to St Ives, Cornwall, where Leslie had taken the lease on Talland House from the Great Western Railway since 1882. Here, freed a little from the tight restraints of Victorian society and encouraged by the climate to swim, walk and catch moths, the children relaxed and witnessed Julia at her best as she sat on the front step and watched them play cricket, or enchanted her guests on the spacious lawn.

Talland House, in a secluded setting on the north Cornish coast, overlooking Godrevy Lighthouse and the little town of St Ives, still stands today, a magical and evocative house where the Stephen family would have enjoyed the privacy of a large, sheltered garden (now much diminished in size and partly taken over by a car park). Early letters sent to Julia from Talland House find Leslie worrying (in his first letter of 4 June 1882) about the faulty boiler, which he is afraid will explode and cripple the Lobb family (who were being interviewed by Leslie as possible gardeners and cooks). He also reports that there were six beds on the first floor: in a nursery, main bedroom, dressing-room, smaller bedroom and two backrooms. He mentions that the path down to the beach is without steps, for the 'babies' to get down, and talks of the greenhouses. These were once magnificent, ornate glass and iron structures, full of peaches, nectarines and grapes, but sadly only the back walls now remain.

During the 1880s, the little town of St Ives was noisy, smelly and wholly governed by the fishing industry. Entire families worked on the yellow sands, gutting and packing pilchards, and all of the old houses (many of which still survive today) had cramped living quarters over ground floors full of hanging, drying fish, with cats to catch the mice that ate the fishing nets. There was poor sanitation, inadequate gas lighting in the town, and a very high crime rate, but, removed from the poverty of the town, in an enviable setting high up on the cliff, Julia Stephen and her family enjoyed thirteen magical summers at St Ives.

Occasionally Leslie visited Talland House alone, leaving Julia in London with his 'ragamice', as he affectionately referred to the children. His love for them pours out of every letter, especially towards Virginia, his self-confessed favourite: 'Kiss my ragamice and Ginia. There will be no more of that breed'.[4] As a small child, Virginia idolized her father, who had already predicted that by the time she turned ten years old she would become a writer, but she remained in awe of her mother. Julia's time was spread insubstantially between eight children and her work for the poor, and unless one of the children was sick, it was difficult for any of them to spend more than a snatched moment alone with her.

In 1892 Maria Jackson finally died after years of ill health. The blow to Julia was severe, for she had been in daily contact with her mother for forty-six years. The extant photographs from this period show her with sunken, hollow cheeks, greying hair and unforgiving eyes. Her health began to deteriorate as the effects of overwork, grief, motherhood and coping with Leslie's demands all began to take their toll, and in 1894, the St Ives idyll had begun to come to an end. A huge hotel, The Porthminster, was erected just to the right of Talland House, and Julia dramatically declared her view of the bay to be ruined. The heartbroken Virginia reluctantly helped to draw a 'lease for sale' sign, but no buyer was found during that year. Then, in May 1895, the pattern of winters in Kensington and summer holidays in St Ives, set since 1882, finally drew to a terrible close. After a bout of rheumatic fever that started innocently enough with a sore throat, Julia Stephen 'sank like an exhausted swimmer'[5] and died on 5 May at the age of fortynine, plunging the family into a prolonged bout of mourning, described by Virginia when she wrote *A Sketch of the Past*, as an 'oriental gloom'.

It took Virginia many years to come to terms both with the life and death of her mother. She did not begin to achieve this fully until she penned her elegiac *To The Lighthouse* (1927), drawing in detail on reminiscences of the Stephen family holidays at Talland House (although the book is ostensibly set in the Hebrides). Movingly, unflinchingly and in a way that touched her brother Adrian and sister Vanessa to the core, she paid tribute to her parents in the characters of Mr and Mrs Ramsay, succinctly capturing Leslie's gruffness and Julia's sadness with uncanny accuracy. Despite losing her mother at the age of thirteen, Virginia's perception and understanding of Julia's grief after losing Herbert Duckworth is poignantly demonstrated in the character of Mrs Ramsay, shedding new light on the little we know of Julia today. 'Never did anybody look so sad. Bitter and black, halfway down, in the darkness, in the shaft which ran from the sunlight to the depths, perhaps a tear formed' wrote Virginia, remembering her mother's melancholy nature. She mused further on this vision of woe:

What was there behind it? Her beauty, her splendour? Had he blown his brains out, they asked, had he died the week before they were married – some other, some earlier lover, of whom rumours reached one?[6]

Virginia's tribute to Julia in the character of Mrs Ramsay also allows us a tiny glimpse of the 'old Julia', the one who had known brief happiness. Although Mrs Ramsay possesses great sorrow and resignation, she also 'claps a deerstalker's hat on her head'[7] and runs over the grass in galoshes to snatch up a mischievous child. These little flashes of humour are tiny chinks of light in an otherwise dark and oppressive portrayal of Julia/Mrs Ramsay's malignant sadness. Virginia later recalled, as she wrote her only attempts at autobiography, *A Sketch of the Past/Reminiscences*, that Julia was 'very quick; very direct; practical; and amusing'. Julia appeared to have two distinctly conflicting sides, as did Mrs Ramsay – an old-fashioned, haunting beauty contrasted with a sharp, impatient severity. The loss of Julia was catastrophic to Virginia: 'she was the whole thing; Talland House was full of her'[8] recollected her daughter, many years later. In the same way, the death of Mrs Ramsay in *To the Lighthouse* symbolizes the end of the house, which crumbles and decays with neglect, while the ghost of Mrs Ramsay haunts the artist Lily Briscoe in the same way that Julia, until her exorcism in *To the Lighthouse*, haunted Virginia Woolf.

> They were the sun and moon to each other; my mother the positive and definite, Stella the reflecting and satellite.[9]

After Julia's sudden death, the burden of caring for the family and nursing Virginia through her first, early breakdown, fell upon the shoulders of Julia's eldest daughter, Stella Duckworth. Stella, born on 30 May 1869, spent all but the first and last two years of her life in the shadow and service of her grieving, melancholy mother. Writing in *A Sketch of the Past* (1939), Virginia recalled that her half-sister's 'first memories were of a very sad widowed mother who "went about doing good" . . . visiting the slums, and the cancer hospital in the Brompton Road'. The passage also refers to Stella as having 'lived in the shade of that widowhood' and that she perhaps 'took then the play that was so marked – that attitude of devotion, almost canine in its touching adoration; that passive, suffering affection; and also that complete unquestioning dependence'.[10]

Amongst the nine hundred archived letters, on their black-edged, cream paper, that Maria Jackson sent to her daughter Julia, are a small handful addressed to 'Bunch' (short for 'Honeybunch', Maria's nickname for Stella). They contain telling indicators of the sort of pressure that Stella, aged only four at the time of receiving the following letter, was being put under – she was expected to be the perfect grandchild:

> My darling Old Bunch, I like your story very much – I hope you will write another . . . when you write again, tell me how the music gets on.[11]

Although she was only a tiny child in 1873, Stella was already being forced into the role she was to hold until Julia's death in 1895, namely that of 'second best'. 'Stella is a jewel only inferior to you my angel for who could be like you?' wrote Maria to Julia. However, Maria did possess a very real, if suffocating, affection for her first granddaughter. A poem, entitled 'For Stella on her 5th Birthday' waxes lyrical about the little girl, albeit in the popular and over-sentimental Victorian language of the time. It contains a predictable tinge of unnecessary melodrama; the penultimate verse is particularly gloom struck, if flattering:

> Five summers only has thou known
> A rose bud, thou, without a thorn
> I may not see the rose when blown
> My night draws near – with thee, t'is morn[12]

At the age of ten, Stella had a new baby half-sister, Vanessa Stephen (from her mother's second marriage) whom she was expected to help care for. Thoby followed Vanessa in quick succession, and by the time 1881 had arrived, Stella was not only a surrogate mother, but also seemingly a nurse. She wrote to reassure her grandmother when Julia was suffering as a result of a difficult childbirth and exhaustion:

> Please make yourself quite easy now dear Granny about her. I am very careful when I give her medicine – I have been afraid to [do] very much washing in case of chilling her – with the exception of hands face and feet she washes herself elsewhere.[13]

Stella, at the time of writing that letter, was only twelve years old. There is some evidence that her own health was poor at this time, no doubt due to having to follow a punishing, grown-up regime of caring for others when she should have been enjoying her childhood. In her 1984 biography of Virginia Woolf, Lyndall Gordon notes that Stella had suffered from rheumatic fever as a child. In Maria's letters to Julia, there are some references to Stella having difficulty walking, but she fails to mention the cause:

> Dr Murray has just gone. He thinks that there is decided improvement in Stella, that she walks better and that her countenance looks so much stronger.[14]

41

In her controversial study of Virginia Woolf's work and the alleged sexual abuse that the Stephen girls suffered at the hands of their half-brothers, Louise De Salvo boldly – and mistakenly – declares that 'Julia, in fact, did not love Stella'.[15] It is certainly true, however, that Julia's abrupt treatment of the young Stella was of some concern to Leslie Stephen, who recollected that his wife was 'rather stern to Stella'. On bravely broaching the subject, he was told that she 'did not love the boys better than Stella: but that Stella seemed to her more a part of herself'.[16] Julia's retort presumably meant that Stella served as a permanent visual reminder of the late and loved Herbert, and consequently reminded Julia at every turn of the grief, suffering and loss that she had endured.

Julia was strict on herself, putting others' needs ahead of her own, and this same attitude of self-deprivation was therefore expected from Stella, the little daughter who was her mirror-image. Virginia Woolf recalled that her mother 'was severe' to Stella and that 'all her devotion was given to George'.[17] It was perhaps easier to love the boys, who did not remind Julia of herself so much, but Julia *did* love Stella and it is interesting to note that, in contrast to De Salvo's claim that the family nickname for Stella, 'The Old Cow', was because she was a 'mindless, slow-witted supplier of the family's needs for nurture',[18] Virginia herself referred to the tag as 'my mother's laughing nickname',[19] suggesting it was an affectionate nickname inspired by Stella's resemblance to a large, beautiful white flower – cow parsley. Affectionate or not, it remains the case that, at least in the surviving photographs of Stella and Julia together, there is little in the way of affection being shown between mother and daughter; Julia is usually to be seen staring stiffly past Stella's shoulder, while the latter gazes sadly, with ill-disguised devotion, at her beloved mother.

Stella's diary for 1893, kept in a dark green leather-bound book and often indecipherable, illustrates clearly the difference between her life in Kensington and her holidays at St Ives. In London, from February until August, the pages are full of references to Southwark, where Stella was helping Octavia Hill build cottages for the poor.[20] On 23 March, Stella mentions her nursing exam and attendance at a nursing lecture. The diary is littered with references to helping the Stephen children with various tasks, supervising their music lessons, taking them into town for clothes, or having teas at the ABC teashop. Already Stella was proving to be more of a mother to Virginia and her siblings than Julia.

The diary has the occasional moment of humour amidst the soulless descriptions of Victorian daily domestic life. Stella, at the age of twenty-four, was able to enjoy (although there is not much evidence to suggest that she actually *did*) a great number of concerts and plays, including an outing to see Ibsen's *A Doll's House* on 11 March. This performance provoked a rare spurt of vigour from Stella and is dismissed in the diary as being 'raving mad'.[21] The most musical of all the Duckworth/Stephen children, Stella also attended orchestra practice and played the piano, although all her attempts to convey the joy of music to Virginia and Vanessa failed dismally.

From 5 August, Stella's 1893 diary continues from Talland House in St Ives, where she shows an unusually strong emotion with her opening comment about the garden being 'rather too full of recollections'.[22] It is unclear as to what or whom Stella was referring, but she was not short of suitors during 1893, all eager to spend time with this gentle and beautiful woman. Jack Hills, whom Stella was eventually to marry, was already a firm friend of the family and took the children moth catching in St Ives. Walter Headlam had also been pursuing Stella, and on being rejected, transferred his attentions to Julia – 'Mother came home from dinner looking tired and unhappy. *Drat* Mr Headlam! What has happened?'[23] muses an angry Stella in her entry for 21 September 1893. Dick Norton, staying as a house guest during this holiday, also professed love for Stella, but as she noted acerbically in the diary, 'I'm afraid he likes me better than I like him and that's a great deal'.[24] It is possible that Stella's unhappy recollections of scenes in the garden at Talland House were connected with the unwanted and frightening advances made on her by yet another man – J.K. Stephen, Julia's favourite nephew, who was 'violently pursuing'[25] Stella and continued his pursuit until 1892, when he died in an asylum.

The majority of Stella's St Ives diary concerns the very typical pastimes of a Victorian family who had leisure and servants enough to fill their days to the maximum with a variety of entertainments and hobbies. Little mention is made of 'Ginia' in this diary, but as Stella was twenty-four and Virginia only eleven, the age gap was large enough to prohibit any particular intimacy growing up between the two. Virginia is first mentioned in the diary on 16 August, where she is reported to have gone fishing with Thoby and Adrian, and again the following week, when Stella took her down to the town to buy muslin. There is no further mention of this little sister until 19

September, where there is an ominous precursor of the ensuing years. Stella was already stepping into her role as Virginia's primary caregiver, a role she would maintain over the next four years as the nervous, highly agitated teenager recovered from an early nervous breakdown:

> Ginia took bad in the night. I went to her and have consequently been horribly sleepy and cross all day.[26]

At this point in her life, Stella was forming a closer bond with Vanessa, who at thirteen was already spending much of her time painting; the diary sometimes describes a morning spent sketching together in the rose garden at Talland House, whilst Julia sat on the front door step and read. In addition to her painting, Stella possessed a wide range of skills and hobbies, and she was surprisingly good at them, given that she must have had little time most of the year in which to indulge them. There are daily mentions of photography – Stella was a keen amateur photographer, as the album now housed in the Berg Collection at the New York Public Library testifies. Many portraits of the Stephen family on holiday (including one of a very young, chubby, robust Virginia on the cricket pitch at St Ives) survive today due to Stella's prolific output. Stella also played billiards, tennis, croquet and the piano – when visitors such as Margaret Lushington arrived, she would accompany them as they sang the popular parlour songs of the day.

Julia's early death in 1895 threatened to strip Stella of her tenuous hold on life, a life that had been lived in the adoring shadow of her loved, revered mother. Virginia, already a sensitive and highly strung 13-year-old, was plunged into black waters for the first time, a breakdown that was not documented at the time and about which very little is known other than that she did not start to recover fully until 1897. For Stella, Julia's death marked the end of any time snatched for herself. She became, with immediate effect, a 26-six-year-old surrogate mother to seven shocked and grieving children, and was moved uncomfortably but without complaint into the role of surrogate wife for Leslie, whose mourning was loud, protracted and frightening. He sucked anyone who came near into his morbid outpourings of grief. The house was dark and claustrophobic; the family, clad in suffocating black during the spring weather, must have offered a mournful spectacle as they straggled around Kensington Gardens in silence and then returned home to the black-draped windows and flower-scented corridors of 22 Hyde Park Gate.

Virginia Woolf recollected that for some time after her mother's death she was, of course, unhappy but often felt more as though she were drifting along in some 'sultry' or 'opaque' life. Her memories of the effect of Julia's death on Stella are recounted with clarity and pathos. They are vivid, and often refer to the colour white, to illustrate the terrible paleness that was heightened in Stella and which never really left her for the rest of her life: 'Stella grew whiter and whiter in her unbroken black dress';[27] 'Stella herself looked like the white flower of some teeming hot-house ... never did anyone look so pale'.[28] Virginia remembers Stella's 'snowy numbness',[29] from which no one could awaken her for nearly two years, and notes her sudden and total loss of interest in her own fate as she tended to the needs of her family, in particular those of Virginia and Leslie. Virginia recalled what appears to have been Leslie's unhealthy dependence on Stella matter-of-factly in 1939: 'emotionally then he fell upon Stella. It was the way of the time'.[30]

Virginia suffered from excruciating guilt when she looked back at her behaviour towards her patient half-sister during the difficult years of 1895–1896:

> I have many regrets; not then, but now I have them; chiefly with regard to Stella. For I must have added another burden. Given her anxiety. And bored and worried her; and could never make it up.[31]

Virginia goes on to bemoan the 'hours of irritation – and care ... taken out of her life – that was so short'.

Stella immediately took over the running of the busy household at Hyde Park Gate and also all of her mother's philanthropic duties, in addition to her own. Leslie was too submerged in grief to spare time for Virginia, Vanessa, Thoby and Adrian, so the children looked to Stella for all their physical and emotional needs. During this time she bonded well with Virginia, who remembered the 'chivalrous devotion'[32] that she and her siblings felt towards Stella.

Aside from remarking on daily events, Stella's 1896 diary served another purpose. In a code that marked each name with an 'x', Stella kept a record of her own, Virginia's and Vanessa's menstrual cycles, all three usually coming within a day or two of each other. It is interesting to see that, despite Stella's bottled-up grief and Virginia's bouts of nervy, irritable illness, their cycles remained remarkably regular. During Virginia's breakdown in 1913, Leonard Woolf noted that his wife did not menstruate for the entire duration of ninety-eight days.

In April 1896, Stella's diary reveals that she had visited a Dr Fairbank three times in one week; once for Adrian and twice for herself, but she fails, perhaps deliberately, to note down why. In October, the diary states that Ginia was taken to the trusted family doctor, Seton, who had been Julia's doctor. Dr Seton recommended that Virginia, who was suffering from a high pulse, should take fewer lessons and be 'careful not to excite herself'. Leslie, adds Stella, was also in a 'great state', which must have done little to reassure the young invalid. A week later, Virginia was taken yet again to Dr Seton, who this time insisted that she 'must give up lessons entirely till January, and must be out four hours a day'.[33] This worrying piece of medical advice marked the beginning of a long battle between Virginia and Stella. In addition, there was another event towards the end of 1896 that not only dramatically affected Stella, but also had a significant impact on the young Virginia, changing and shaping her views of love, trust, relationships and marriage. In August 1896, during a holiday to Hindhead House, Haslemere, Stella became engaged to John Waller Hills.[34]

At the time of his courtship with Stella, John Hills (known as 'Jack') was remembered by Virginia as 'a lean threadbare young man who seemed to force his way by sheer determination and solid integrity'.[35] Chillingly, she describes his pursuit of, and eventual engagement to, Stella in the terms of a 'system', which he had 'no doubt arranged on paper . . . and was simply following it out in detail'.

Virginia's honest recollections of Jack present a complex picture, not always flattering and often sobering. She deemed him to be a shrewd businessman in love, who considered his future wife's health and wishes very important, but saw her lacking in intellectual depth and yet was relieved by this, as it did not threaten his 'irrational desires'. Whether Jack's desires stretched to include other women is not clear, but Woolf recalls a conversation with Jack during which he told her that 'sexual relations had nothing to do with honour. Having women was a mere trifle in a man's life'.[36] Curiously, despite this less than respectful comment, the 15-year-old Virginia continued to respect and admire him. The change in Stella, who had been pale and drawn and was now glowing with colour and happiness, provided Virginia with her 'first vision of love between man and woman', a vision that, although it was to be cut cruelly short, initially filled the house at Hyde Park Gate with mystery and romance. The Stephen sisters spied excitedly on Stella and Jack, witnessing their declarations of love and snatched embraces. Although Woolf recalls the months of Stella's engagement as a happy time for the couple, she also throws doubt upon the strength of Stella's feelings for Jack, asking herself years later whether Stella might have 'found something in her left cold and meditative, reflecting when all should have been consenting?' Perhaps Woolf was subconsciously remembering her own engagement of 1912 to Leonard in this sentence, for she had admitted to him in a letter that 'there are moments – when you kissed me the other day was one – when I feel no more than a rock'.[37]

Leslie Stephen's emotions on hearing of Stella and Jack's engagement were, understandably, mixed: he didn't want to lose Stella and, at first, viewed her marriage as a great inconvenience and act of selfishness on her part. Stella finally had one of her rare surges of tempestuous anger and stormed up to Leslie's study where, according to Virginia, she complained 'how the family system tortures and exacerbates – especially the Vicn [Victorian] where one can't be open; when one is ignorant of motives and always conceals them under complete lies'.[38]

Leslie began to insult Jack in front of the children and even took an aversion to his name, complaining that it sounded similar to the crack of a whip. Eventually, in a letter to his friend Charles Norton, sent just after the engagement had been announced, he expressed his feelings with less venom and enough emotion almost to encourage pity:

> Stella is so much to me, that I have something of a struggle in seeing this young gentleman appropriate her . . . Stella is a quiet and gentle young woman with very strong affections which do not easily show themselves; but which I have learned to appreciate better in the last 15 months.[39]

After her initial excitement at Stella's engagement, Virginia's enthusiasm for the subject began to wane during the early months of 1897. A disastrous holiday took place to Bognor, in the company of Leslie,

Vanessa and the engaged couple. Virginia was expected to chaperone Jack and Stella, as they took freezing cold walks on the bleak sands.

Finally, on Saturday 10 April 1897, Jack Hills and Stella Duckworth were married at St Mary Abbots, Kensington. Oddly, given how keen the family were on amateur photography, no photographs survive from this event. Perhaps none were taken because most of the family, in particular Leslie and Virginia, were far from happy with events. 'I will not put down even here the thoughts that have agitated me' wrote Leslie in his *Mausoleum Book* on the day of the wedding itself. Virginia allows us a little more detail in her diary, but confesses 'goodness knows how we got through it all – certainly it was half a dream, or a nightmare'. In the absence of photographic evidence, we are left with only this vivid picture of Stella in her bridal outfit: Virginia's description of her 'walking in her sleep – her eyes fixed straight in front of her – very white and beautiful'. It was probably the only time Stella had been out of black clothes since Julia died two years previously, but her wedding, supposed to be a time of happiness and optimism, seemed funereal in atmosphere.

The following day, prolonging the grim mood, the Stephen family went on the long trek to Highgate Cemetery and placed the wedding flowers on Julia's grave. Stella and Jack had departed the evening before – 'Mr and Mrs Hills!' as Virginia noted with rather forced happiness in her diary. She had said goodbye with relief to Stella, little knowing that she would never see her half-sister smiling and well again. By 28 April, Stella was home early from honeymoon and in bed at her new house, 24 Hyde Park Gate. On the following day, a visit from Dr Seton resulted in the diagnosis of 'peritonitis', which Virginia found 'rather frightening'. By 4 May, she notes with apparent relief that Stella was putting on weight and looked a lot better, but adds, in a way that hints at her fragile state of mind, that 'this is most satisfactory – but I am unreasonable enough to be irritated'.[40] By 9 May, when Stella had improved sufficiently to be allowed up, the 15-year-old Virginia displayed a confusing mixture of emotions in this extraordinary sentence:

Now that old cow is most ridiculously well & cheerful – hopping about out of bed etc. Thank goodness, nevertheless.[41]

The 'nevertheless' appears to have been added in as a last-minute concession to good manners and clearly illustrates the curious blend of love and resentment that Woolf felt for Stella, particularly since the engagement. It is also probable that Virginia had enjoyed the sudden freedom from being virtually chained to Stella's side as she went about her daily business, hence her irritation at what appeared to be a speedy recovery; but underneath the lightweight comments about Stella and her illness, it is easy to detect an enormous, churning mass of fear in Virginia, who was still wholly reliant on Stella for the maternal protection that was whisked away from her by Julia's death.

On 18 May 1897, Stella wrote an affectionate letter to Thoby, mentioning that her second nurse had been sent away. She appeared to be out of danger, and attention was now switched to Virginia, who was becoming ill and nervous, worrying Stella greatly. On 12 July she forbade Virginia from going out, due to all her 'aches'. The following day, 'Ginia' developed a fever and was carried into Stella's house three doors down, so that she could keep an eye on her. Dr Seton visited and put Virginia to bed, while Stella, in her usual selfless way, sat up all night next to her. On 14 July, Stella sat with her until 11.30 p.m., soothing away the 'fidgets'.

The last day that Virginia saw her half-sister alive was 15 July. Stella came into her bedroom in a dressing-gown and appeared to be 'quite well'. 'She left me', continues the diary entry for this day, 'and I never saw her again'. On 17 July Stella refused to see the doctor, but authorized him to take Virginia back to No. 22. As George carried Ginia down the corridor, wrapped in Stella's fur cape, Stella called out 'goodbye'. By 7 p.m. the next evening, a Dr Broadbent and his colleague, Williams, had performed an emergency operation on Stella, informing the family that 'everything was successful'. But at 3 a.m. the following morning, on 19 July, George and Vanessa crept into Virginia's bedroom and broke the terrible news – Stella was dead. 'That is all we have thought of since; and it is impossible to write of' concludes the diary entry for that awful day.

Stella's death certificate recorded a vague diagnosis of 'operation shock' and 'suppositive acute peritonitis', but in a letter to Vanessa Bell as late as 1941, Violet Dickinson, Stella's friend, confided that one of Stella's nurses proclaimed her to be 'malformed' and that 'marriage had finished her off'. Whatever the cause of Stella's tragic death, the gentle surrogate mother figure, whom the children had come to rely on, had been snatched away only two years after Julia's death. From 19 July 1897, the nightmare from which Virginia never fully extracted herself for the rest of her life began in earnest.

The immediate shock and horror of Stella's sudden death is no more apparent than in the pages of Virginia's 1897 diary, where the next day's page is left completely blank and the following entry starkly reports that Stella had been buried in Highgate next to Julia, and that none of the children had attended. This is perhaps not as odd as it seems, for the entire family were agnostics. On Thursday 22 July, Virginia was in serious shock – the diary entry reads only that she 'forgot what happened'.[42] The house filled up with the same set of grieving relatives, still barely over Julia's death, and a mad Duckworth cousin who insisted on praying in the room where Stella had died at No. 24. The Stephen family decided to get away from all this by taking their annual summer holiday, this year at Painswick in the Cotswolds at a house lent to them by Fred Maitland, but it was a nightmarish summer. While they were there, the first anniversary of Stella and Jack's engagement occurred, a row broke out between George and Leslie, and an anguished Jack poured his heart out to Virginia in the summerhouse as she stared dismally at a leafless tree outside, an image that was to haunt her for the rest of her life.

Although the holiday was spent in mourning, it had at least provided a break from the atmosphere at Hyde Park Gate. Now, faced with going back to this house with the absence of both Julia *and* Stella, Virginia was terribly distraught, recording on the day of their departure that she was 'very strange and unhappy'. Oddly, she reserves words of stronger passion not for Stella's death, but for her pen. 'With terrible agony & excitement chose a nib for my pen' she notes on 24 September, but 'it was too fine – oh the despair of that moment'. A miserable trip to Jack Hill's family home at Corby took place, where Virginia was haunted by the spectre of her dead half-sister: 'here she hangs like a pale rose; against that queer still brick wall' she recalled in an early draft of *A Sketch of the Past*.

'Vanessa's name was of course suggested by Stella's' noted Leslie Stephen in his *Mausoleum Book*. He is referring to the two nicknames of Jonathan Swift's lovers, Esther Johnson and Hester Vanhomrigh. So, already possessing a literary name, it seemed fitting that Stella would go on to provide the inspiration for some of Virginia Woolf's fictional heroines. While Virginia was still a small child, Stella had already featured in her mother's short stories. Although ostensibly written for Virginia, Vanessa, Thoby and Adrian, Julia Stephen's

Stories for Children often feature the 'good' child who seems, subconsciously or otherwise, to have been modelled on Stella. Clara, the heroine in 'Tommy and His Neighbours', is just the sort of child that Stella appears to have been – quiet, well-behaved, shy and always at her lessons. 'The Monkey on the Moor', which features a 'wicked little girl' called 'Ginia', revolves around Annie, the little girl who befriends everyone, invites them to tea in the nursery and has eyes that are 'blue' and 'kind'. In 'Cat's Meat', Lady Middleton, a caricature of how Julia saw herself at the time, returns from one of her endless missions to help the poor and is poured a cup of tea by Maggie, who 'although only seven was a helpful little creature'. The pouring of tea at 22 Hyde Park Gate had remained Stella's duty up until her death; afterwards, Jack Hills gloomily remarked that only Stella and Julia had known how to handle the heavy silver pot.

'Even now it seems incredible' remarked Virginia Woolf in *Reminiscences*, referring, over ten years after the event, to Stella's untimely death. 'We cannot easily make sense of an apparently pointless and destructive event like Rachel's death' says Jane Wheare in her introduction to the new Penguin edition of *The Voyage Out*. Although certain characteristics of the heroine, Rachel Vinrace, in this first of Virginia's novels, can be traced to Woolf herself, glimpses of Stella can be seen in parts. The 'voyage' of Woolf's title is often construed as referring to her move from Kensington to Bloomsbury. It could also be applied to the voyage of self-discovery that Stella was just embarking on at the time of her death – a journey that had taken her away from the cloying gloom of 22 Hyde Park Gate to a house of her own with a new husband. *The Voyage Out* can therefore be seen as a homage to the gentleness and sympathetic nature of women such as Stella, whose intelligence was often to be overridden and ignored by the men in their lives. Was Woolf thinking of Jack Hills when, in the guise of Terence Hewet's long, cliff-top reply to Rachel (who has confessed that she feels intimidated by St John Hirst's intellect), she allowed vent to her feelings about men and their role within the family? Jack Hills had been a solicitor:

Consider what a bully the ordinary man is . . . the ordinary hard working, rather ambitious solicitor or man of business with a family to bring up and a certain position to maintain'.[43]

It is significant that in *The Voyage Out*, Rachel has a gift for playing the piano – the one talent that had been allowed to develop in the absence of conventional school and university education. Virginia Woolf did not play the piano, after a series of disastrous lessons, but Stella had an aptitude for the instrument, although she had never benefited from any formal education.

The confusion over Rachel's illness and death in *The Voyage Out* cannot help but bring to mind the terrible confusion and tension of Stella's final days. Rachel's first doctor, Rodriguez, maintains that she is getting better when in fact her family can see her failing fast. After a new doctor is brought in, Rachel appears to be recovering, as indeed Stella did during the last five days of her life. She then dies and Terence, at her side, utters the words 'no two people have ever been so happy as we have', words that perhaps Jack Hills uttered to Stella as she died (he was present at her death, as the certificate verifies), and words that were later echoed by Virginia Woolf in her suicide note to Leonard. Even Rachel's hour of death, 3 a.m., precisely mirrors that of Stella's.

After Rachel's death, Evelyn's 'what did it matter then? What was the meaning of it all?' echoes the young Virginia's diary entries just after Stella's death – 'it is hopeless and strange'. Rachel – gentle, talented, about to enter into marriage – is taken away from those who love her in the cruellest of ways, leaving chaos, grief and confusion behind her. In *The Voyage Out*, Virginia Woolf is able to let us glimpse the bewilderment and misery that she felt on losing Stella, which she had not been able to express in 1897.

Night and Day, Woolf's next novel, also contains memories of Stella and her difficult relationship with her stepfather, Leslie Stephen. Although the inspiration for Katharine Hilbery is clearly Vanessa Bell, to whom the book is dedicated, and Katharine is a strong character much like Vanessa (in an early draft of the novel, Woolf makes Katharine an aspiring painter), there is, in the chapter where Katharine announces her engagement, a sudden and vivid recollection of Leslie Stephen's reaction to Stella's engagement. It recalls his self-pitying outbursts of grief and annoyance:

Had he loved to see her swept away by this torrent, to have her taken from him by this uncontrollable force, to stand by, helpless, ignored? Oh, how he loved her! How he loved her![44]

The Stephen children's reactions to Leslie's temper are recaptured within this novel as well, Woolf seeming to give vent to her own pent-up annoyance in the following passage where Mr Hilbery

> strode out of the room, leaving in the minds of the women a sense, half of awe, half of amusement, at the extravagant, inconsiderate, uncivilized male, outraged somehow and gone bellowing to his lair with a roar which still sometimes reverberates in the most polished of drawing rooms.[45]

To the Lighthouse (1927) also explores some of the difficult emotions that arose in the aftermath of Stella's death. It is at once lyrical and visual, complementing the images from Stella's photograph album of the time, telling the story of the Stephen/Ramsay family at their beloved holiday home. Written thirty years after Stella's death, and almost twenty years after she first explored her half-sister's death in *Reminiscences*, the book pays homage to Stella's beauty and gentle nature in the character of Prue Ramsay, but even so many years later, there is still a sense that Woolf is not fully ready to explore the horror of Stella's death. 'Prue the Fair', as Mr Bankes refers to her at the opening of the book, is a submissive and feminine young woman who worries extensively about keeping the rest of the family happy, taking full responsibility for Mr Ramsay's rage when he, for example, finds an earwig in his milk. She has only just, like Stella, begun to explore the possibilities of happiness in her own life. In a touching tribute to the relationship between Stella and Julia, Prue is shown to idolize her mother, Mrs Ramsay. Watching her come downstairs one evening, Prue admits to herself that this relationship is 'the thing itself'; 'she felt as if there were only one person like that in the world; her mother'.[46] Prue was expected to marry and have children, but her eventual marriage is described within three abrupt sets of parentheses, as though describing this slightly tedious event would take away the impetus from the more important descriptions of spring evolving into summer. Woolf chooses to make the event more vivid for the reader with this use of stark, brief text. She repeats the formula for her next mention of Prue:

> [Prue Ramsay died that summer in some illness connected with childbirth, which was indeed a tragedy, people said. They said nobody deserved happiness more.][47]

By bracketing the text once more, Woolf forces two immediate reactions from her reader: firstly, shock, due to the suddenness of the announcement; secondly, bemusement – why is such an enormous bereavement described in three brief sentences and then not mentioned again? Inevitably, the answer seems to be found in Virginia's reaction to Stella's death in 1897, and the brevity of her subsequent diary entries. The references to childbirth are something of a revelation – Woolf makes no reference at all to Stella's pregnancy in her 1897 diary, neither does she speculate on it in the earlier reminiscences contained in *Moments of Being*; but here, in *To the Lighthouse*, thirty years after the bereavement itself, Woolf makes her first allusion to the controversy that surrounded the cause of Stella's death.

As if to make amends for keeping Stella at arm's length in *To the Lighthouse* and to compensate for Prue's unhappy fate, Woolf's next 'family' novel, *The Years* (1937), fully resurrects Stella in the character of Eleanor Pargiter. Eleanor, whilst possessing the sweet-naturedness of Prue Ramsay, also displays determination and dedication to good causes coupled with the qualities of spirit and individuality, qualities that Stella was just starting to develop after leaving 22 Hyde Park Gate.

Eleanor Pargiter is 'the soother, the maker-up of quarrels, the buffer between her and the intensities and strifes of family life'[48] in the same way that Stella, replacing Julia, had been the unselfish soother of Leslie and Virginia's illnesses and bad tempers. Eleanor is given to philanthropic acts, for example planning to build cottages for the poor, just as Stella was doing in Southwark for Octavia Hill. Once again, Leslie's jealous possessiveness of Stella is mirrored in Colonel Pargiter's reaction to Eleanor's independence: 'a spasm of jealousy passed through him. She's got her own affairs to think about'.[49] After Rose Pargiter's death, the Colonel comes to rely on Eleanor in the same way that Leslie came to rely first on Stella and then on Vanessa. Eleanor, however, never marries, but stays resolutely single – it is as if Woolf, perhaps still partly blaming Stella's death on Jack Hills, has decided to keep Eleanor away from any man who might pose a threat to her health and independence, giving her instead a long, peaceful, *single* life. This book, the last of Woolf's to feature any characters inspired by Stella, ends with a realization of happiness for Eleanor, and also with the sense that Virginia, in 1937, has now finally laid Stella to rest:

The sun had risen, and the sky above the houses wore an air of extraordinary beauty, simplicity and peace.[50]

Although both Julia Duckworth Stephen and Stella Duckworth Hills may have found their well-earned peace and posterity in the pages of Virginia Woolf's novels, Virginia herself, after their deaths, was left with a negative and damaging view of heterosexual love. Although later in her career she came to view at least one female member of her family, her great-aunt Julia Margaret Cameron, as a positive role model who had managed to balance a career with a happy marriage, Mrs Cameron was dead by the time Virginia had been born. Instead, by the time she turned thirteen, Virginia had seen her beautiful mother die in the large marital bed at 22 Hyde Park Gate, worn to the bone by grief, over-work and the demands of her overbearing husband. By the age of fifteen, Virginia had witnessed the transformation of Stella into a flushed, ecstatic vision of love – 'oh and I remember the rapture of that love. I got it full and strong and very beautiful'[51] – and then watched helplessly as her half-sister returned from honeymoon appearing suddenly broken, exhausted and dying, seemingly destroyed by the only man that she had ever loved.

To an impressionable, nervous teenager like Virginia, the loss of two such central figures to their own dogged beliefs in selflessness at all costs was instrumental in planting the seeds of her perennial depression. These, in time, grew into a painful struggle between the pull of her creative genius and the behaviour expected from an 'Angel in the House'.

The ghosts of Maria, Julia and Stella were to haunt Virginia Woolf for the duration of her life. They continued to gaze out mournfully from photographs and paintings. Their musty black dresses continued to hang in the huge oak wardrobes at Hyde Park Gate. They were rarely discussed, except in sudden bursts of anguish; their widowers and children awkwardly avoided speaking the dead women's names, consequently the grief was never fully exorcized and these 'Angels' retained, in death, much of the presence and enigma that had so powerfully surrounded them in life.

Although Virginia was capable of much laughter and enjoyment in later life, when her face was caught in repose often the mournful, severe expression of Julia Stephen would become more prominent. There was to be a cluster of other women who, in a variety of ways, would influence Virginia Woolf profoundly, but it was Julia's ghost, above all others, who continued to preside, much as she had done at the Victorian tea table, in the memories of everyone who had known her. A family friend, William Rothenstein, eulogized Julia Stephen and her enigmatic daughters in this vivid cameo of Hyde Park Gate family life:

> George was cheerful and talkative, but his sister Stella, and Virginia and Vanessa his step-sisters [sic], in plain black dresses with white lace collars and wrist bands, looking as though they had walked straight out off a canvas by Watts or Burne-Jones, rarely spoke. Beautiful as they were, they were not more beautiful than their mother.[52]

2 Vanessa

The calm of the moment was as an instinctive shield to cover her wounded senses; but soon they would collect themselves and fall to work upon all these difficult matters so lavishly heaped upon them – and with what result?[1]

In April 1941, when Virginia Woolf made the decision to leave her home at Monk's House in Rodmell and took the brave, lonely walk to her death in the River Ouse, she left suicide notes for only two people. One was addressed to her husband, Leonard Woolf, the great companion and support of her life; the other was to the woman who had shared the complexities of her life from babyhood until the very final day, a stretch of time spanning fifty-nine years. Writing the final words to her sister, Vanessa Bell, Virginia concluded that 'if I could I would tell you what you and the children have meant to me. I think you know'.[2]

The Stephen sisters experienced a very different childhood from Stella's. Although still bound by the cast-iron rules of Victorian society to appear at the tea table and entertain the ceaseless round of visitors to 22 Hyde Park Gate, the children also had the delights of Kensington Gardens at the end of their road, with the Round Pond and the Serpentine for sailing their toy boats on. As young children, Virginia and Vanessa loved to lie under the trees in the park, reading copies of *Tit-Bits* magazine and eating chocolate. These years, before the bereavements and breakdowns began, were magical, childish and healthy, with summers spent at Talland House and winters tucked up in Kensington in the nursery with a blazing fire going, although even when she was very little, Virginia was still insecure enough to fear Vanessa falling asleep before she did, and would put a stop to this by addressing her loudly. She already felt inferior to this clever, sensible elder sister, remembering in an early draft of *A Sketch of the Past* 'how imperfect' she had felt compared to Vanessa, 'how vain and egotistical, irritable'.[3]

By the time they reached their teens, with no formal school to attend and only a few hours of lessons at home, the Stephen girls had plenty of time on their hands for shopping, reading, visiting friends and playing in Kensington Gardens. On these occasions they were usually chaperoned by Stella or taken by Leslie – Julia was often out visiting the poor.

Virginia, remembered by Vanessa Bell as a prodigious child who charmed the grown-ups into laughter and whose appearance was that of 'a sweet pea of a special flame colour',[4] studied Latin, French and History at home under Julia's guidance, and suffered the boredom of piano lessons as well as the torture of Leslie's mathematics tuition. Vanessa was luckier – from 1896 she studied drawing at Arthur Cope's School of Art three times a week. Virginia would stay at home alone, studying her Greek, writing her diary, borrowing books from Leslie's extensive library of literary classics, or experimenting with her writing style. When Vanessa was not at her art class, the sisters often spent mornings companionably closeted away in a little glass room off the back of the drawing-room, almost entirely made up of windows and perfect for quiet writing and painting.

This period of calm was not to last. After Stella's death, the pattern of weekdays changed immediately and for the worst. Vanessa was expected to take her dead half-sister's place as the female head of the household, organizing the servants each morning and reporting details of every penny spent back to Leslie (who liked to proclaim that his family were on the brink of being sent to the Workhouse; in reality they were quite well off). This Vanessa reluctantly did, but without the compliant submissiveness that had proved so damaging to Stella. Virginia recalled that her sister 'stood before him like a stone',[5] mute, glaring and angry, realizing now the effect that her father's harshness had had on the two women whose footsteps she had filled – and who now lay dead.

In the wake of Stella's death, it also fell to Vanessa to provide support to another anguished mourner – Jack Hills. He grieved openly and often, whilst Vanessa sat in patient sympathy by his side. At first she complained to Virginia about Jack's treatment of Stella; looking for someone to blame for her death, they found plenty of reasons to do so, but suddenly and catastrophically for Virginia, the complaints stopped and Woolf's thoughts began to fall on deaf ears as she realized that Vanessa was showing all the signs of falling in love with Jack. He appeared to be in love with her, too – after all, he was highly sexed and lonely, and Vanessa possessed a strong physical resemblance to his dead wife. The relationship was quickly destroyed by the Duckworth brothers before it got any further (in those days it was illegal to marry the widower of your deceased sister), but it left a tension between Virginia and Vanessa that took some time to heal and did not help Virginia's fragile state of mind.

In the meantime, a new threat to their ordered lives arose: George Duckworth, who had an independent income, a job as private secretary to Austin Chamberlain, and a string of invitations to balls and parties, decided that his reputation would be improved further still if he were to attend such events with a beautiful, motherless half-sister on his arm. In 1897, he started to introduce Vanessa, aged eighteen years old, into society, but without much success, for, as Virginia had known for years, 'what was inside Vanessa did not altogether correspond with what was outside'.[6] Vanessa had certainly inherited the legendary Pattle beauty from Julia and Stella, but it had manifested itself in a less ethereal, more statuesque way. She *looked* a vision of loveliness in her white dress and blue enamel brooch, yet underneath she resented the forced pomp of these occasions with some vigour, longing only for her paints and easel. Virginia, too, was attracting admiring glances wherever she went, a fact that she acknowledged with easy vanity:

> Vanessa might have been a famous beauty. I, though far more intermittent, irregular and ill-kempt than she was, had more of the average of good looks.[7]

After a year or so of dragging Vanessa to these events, George gave up on her and started to try and persuade Virginia to attend in her place, putting incredible pressure on the nervous, unwilling teenager by telling her that unless she accompanied him he would be forced to hire a 'whore' for the evening. Virginia attended several events with little more success than her sister had – remembering that Vanessa had been frustratingly silent at the dinner table, she endeavoured to earn

George's praise by waxing lyrical on a good many subjects, mostly unprompted. The society ladies tittered and George was furious. He scolded her all the way home, bemoaning his bad luck at having such a badly brought-up girl for a sister. To make matters worse, he had started to creep into her bedroom late at night, flinging himself upon the bed and proclaiming love. This he did to Vanessa as well, but whether his treatment of the Stephen girls could be described as abuse is a controversial matter, which still encourages considerable debate even today. It is certainly true that in later years when the girls wrote to George, they still used terms of great affection, and they even went on holiday with both Duckworth brothers; unlikely behaviour from the victims of any serious sexual abuse. There is no doubt, though, that at the time, this intimidating and suffocating conduct caused distress to the highly private Stephen girls, both of them reserved in their affections and taught to repress emotion in front of their father, and mourning the mother and half-sister who might, had they lived, have afforded them some protection.

In 1902, the daily routine at Hyde Park Gate changed once more when Leslie was diagnosed with cancer of the intestine. Vanessa, who had withdrawn almost totally from her demanding, overbearing father, was unaffected save for a profound sense of relief that her own suffering might soon be over. She had always been closer to Julia, never understanding Leslie's gruff affection for his children. In turn, Leslie could see too much of Julia's beauty in Vanessa's appearance, which caused him great pain. Vanessa withdrew from her father's sickbed, spending as much time as she could painting at the Slade School, where Pre-Raphaelitism had been by now forgotten; William Rothenstein recalled that during this time, Vanessa 'looked as though she might have walked among the fair women of Burne-Jones's *Golden Stair*; but she spoke with the voice of Gauguin'.

It was left to Virginia to become her father's only close companion during the two years of his illness until he died. Although the family hired nurses to see to Leslie's medical needs, Virginia spent a large part of each day sitting with him, recording his daily decline in letters to her friend Violet Dickinson. Vanessa was absent most of the time, studying at art college or visiting friends, attending only when her presence was absolutely necessary. Thoby and Adrian were away at university; George and Gerald were busy with their work in the City.

After a difficult and painful last few weeks, Leslie finally died on 22

February 1904. Vanessa was overcome with a sense of relief and release, and threw her energies into organizing the dramatic family move from Hyde Park Gate to less respectable Bloomsbury. A few days after Leslie's funeral, the family holidayed in Pembrokeshire and then Paris, where Vanessa first encountered Clive Bell at the studio of Rodin. 'Ginia', her father's favourite, initially seemed to be coping well with his death, but then she suffered a complete breakdown, which lasted from May to September. She was taken care of by Violet Dickinson and a series of nurses at Violet's home in Welwyn while Vanessa arranged furniture at 46 Gordon Square, the new house in Bloomsbury. As she slowly recovered, Virginia returned to her family and lived amicably with Vanessa, Adrian and Thoby (George and Gerald had decided to live separately) for two further years. Without the repressive atmosphere at Hyde Park Gate hanging over them any longer, the sisters revelled in the comparative freedom of their new life; friends came round and stayed late, meals were not punctual, and Virginia had her own room at the top of the house, where she wrote and read without interruption. But the happiness, as so often, was not to last; after a family holiday to Greece in September 1906, both Vanessa and Thoby returned home seriously ill. Vanessa slowly recovered, but Thoby did not, and died of typhoid. The death of this sturdy, handsome elder brother was to be only half the double-blow to Virginia's fragile state of mind because two days later Clive Bell proposed to Vanessa for a second time – and was accepted.

Virginia's duplicity of nature, fuelled by fear and insecurity, started to show at about this time. Although she professed to be pleased about her sister's engagement, and wrote to Madge Vaughan that Vanessa appeared 'wonderfully happy, and it is beautiful to see her',[8] privately she felt betrayed enough to confide her true feelings in a letter to Violet Dickinson, cruelly comparing Clive to her beloved dead family:

> When I think of father and Thoby and then see that funny little creature twitching his pink skin and jerking out his little spasm of laughter I wonder what odd freak there is in Nessa's eyesight.[9]

Gradually she began to accept Clive, realizing that he could be a stimulating correspondent and important 'sounding-board' for her own early fiction, in particular *The Voyage Out*, which was the first novel that she was beginning to work on. Vanessa continued to live at

46 Gordon Square after her marriage, whilst Virginia and Adrian set up home together round the corner at 29 Fitzroy Square. Leslie, Julia, Stella and Thoby had all died over the last eleven years; Vanessa had married: the original Stephen family unit was now reduced to the two youngest members living together awkwardly, with little in common. Their incompatibility as housemates resulted in physical fights, and the walls were splattered with butter stains as a result.

After the shock of not living with Vanessa for the first time in her life, Virginia began to adjust gradually to her new home and circumstances. After all, she saw almost as much of her sister as she did before, and on the rare days when she didn't, letters flowed backwards and forwards between the two instead. A variety of nicknames, left over from their childhood at Hyde Park Gate, crept back into Virginia's letters, most of them referring to animals: 'Ape', 'Honeybee', 'Beast' or 'Tawny'. In these letters, Virginia openly craved the maternal and sometimes erotic affection that she had come to rely on, instructing Clive to 'kiss my old Tawny, on all her private places – kiss her eyes, and her neck socket'.[10]

Virginia, envious of her sister's newfound married happiness, also began to court favour and affection from Clive. A flirtation between the two sprang up in Cornwall, when Vanessa was too wrapped up in her first baby, Julian, to pay much attention to anyone else. Clive, flattered, and feeling shut out by his wife, reciprocated with passion and longed to make the flirtation physical; Virginia, existing cerebrally and intellectually, was happier to draw the line at long, stimulating walks and clever letters. She hung anxiously and appreciatively on his words of criticism about her *The Voyage Out*, which she planned to ask Gerald Duckworth to publish.

Vanessa inevitably became aware of the growing closeness between her husband and her sister, but because she had, for so long, been trained not to display unnecessary emotion, she turned a blind eye to it and kept her letters to Virginia light-hearted and playful. Underneath her calm exterior lurked hurt and depression, brought about by the two people she loved and trusted the most. It must have seemed an unfair payback for all the years she had loved and cared for Virginia at Hyde Park Gate. In addition to this stressful situation, Clive had already been unfaithful from the very start of the marriage, and in 1914 took up with Mary Hutchinson, an affair that lasted until 1927. It is therefore unsurprising that Vanessa planned to base her entire life around motherhood and painting, the only two occupations where she remained relatively in control.

In 1912, at the age of thirty, Virginia married Leonard Woolf, her 'penniless Jew';[11] in reality, he was a hardworking writer and politician who had been friends with Adrian and Thoby Stephen at university. Vanessa thoroughly approved of Leonard as a match for her sister, doubtless feeling some relief at the thought of not being Virginia's primary caregiver any longer. Her feelings were justified almost immediately, for Virginia's health was deteriorating badly. She and Leonard had set up in rooms just off Fleet Street, where they attempted to get into a writing routine, but after a disastrous holiday at the Plough Inn in Holford, Virginia was brought back to Adrian's rooms at Brunswick Square, where she attempted, for the second time, to take her own life, this time by overdosing on the sleeping draught, Veronal. She was saved, but remained seriously ill, and the lodgings at Cliffords Inn were obviously not suitable any longer. Letters from the anguished, helpless Vanessa, at Asheham or Gordon Square, arrived on Leonard's mat:

> I have had your letter this morning telling me about the violence. I can't help hoping it was only due to the sleeping draught but of course it is very depressing. How I wish I could help.[12]

Both Vanessa and Leonard were concerned that the possibility of Virginia becoming pregnant could exacerbate her mental illness; Vanessa admitted that she had been 'coming to think that on the whole she [Virginia] could plunge into a new and unknown state of affairs when she starts a baby'.[13]

Virginia's nightmarish descent into madness continued, lasting on and off until 1915, when Leonard found, leased and prepared a new home, Hogarth House in Richmond, installing four nurses. During this time she was violent, manic, depressed and anorexic. She often didn't recognize Leonard, or physically attacked him. Finally, slowly, she began to recover. Leonard bought a printing press to give his wife an enjoyable hobby, which would allow her a break from writing for an hour or two each day. By 1916, Virginia was finally able to settle into the routine from which she was hardly to deviate again for the rest of her life: writing in the morning, revising or walking in the afternoon, reading in the evenings.

Vanessa had remained in constant touch throughout this difficult period, writing letters and visiting regularly. After all, in 1911, when Vanessa had suffered a miscarriage and severe depression herself, Virginia had provided the support and love that her elder sister had needed.

Soon after Virginia's recovery, Vanessa and her two boys, Julian and Quentin, moved with Clive and Duncan Grant to Charleston Farmhouse near Firle, which they decorated with extraordinary care and originality. Vanessa began to establish herself as a professional painter, exhibiting at the Omega and New Movement in Art shows during 1917. Virginia had published *The Voyage Out* and was in the process of writing *Night and Day*. Both sisters were strong and positive at this stage in their lives. They kept a watchful eye on each other's achievements, scared of one becoming more successful than the other, but they also commenced a joint project: Vanessa was to illustrate Virginia's *Kew Gardens* for the Hogarth Press. Virginia was delighted when she saw her sister's woodcuts, although she continued to compare herself unfavourably with Vanessa:

> I think the book will be a great success – owing to you; and my vision comes out much as I had it, so I suppose, in spite of everything, God made our brains upon the same lines, only leaving out 2 or 3 pieces in mine.[14]

In July 1919, Virginia and Leonard purchased Monk's House, Rodmell, a country retreat that was to remain their weekend and holiday home together until Virginia's death. From here, Virginia would walk or cycle across the South Downs to Charleston in time for tea with the Bell family. The two sisters had settled into their respective lives; Vanessa had stoically accepted that the new love of her life, Duncan Grant, had reverted back to homosexuality after fathering her daughter, Angelica. Vanessa was becoming an expert at hiding her disappointment, so instead she took pleasure in painting companionably by Duncan's side, a practice that they continued for another forty years.

On the surface at least, Vanessa and Virginia appeared to have much in common. As a result of the rigid routines that had been imposed on them at Hyde Park Gate, both of them cared little for convention, formality or the elaborate Edwardian dress of the time. Indeed

Virginia had a dread of changing rooms in dress shops, and Vanessa preferred to wear painter's overalls. Both women were committed to their chosen form of art, although Virginia was becoming more successful than her sister, who had after all to share her energies between painting and motherhood. The two women were still extremely beautiful in their late thirties and they continued to take some comfort from having inherited Julia Stephen's polite, Victorian tea table manner (Vanessa masked her true emotions behind it, whereas Virginia appreciated the dignity that it allowed, but resented the way it restricted her writing). Both women enjoyed and appreciated the solitude and beauty of the English countryside, drawing upon it for inspiration. They each lived with a much-loved, sympathetic partner – Vanessa with Duncan, Virginia with Leonard – and Virginia was an adored aunt to the Bell children. They shared many unique and lifelong friendships, including those with Clive Bell, Maynard Keynes, Lytton Strachey, Roger Fry, Desmond McCarthy and Dora Carrington.

Despite their unbreakable bond of closeness, there were also some profound differences between the sisters and their attitudes to life, and these caused many tensions and resentments to occur. Whereas Vanessa's natural instinct was to look to the future and protect and cherish her own children, Virginia did not have strong maternal urges and, adhering to the past, still counted *herself* as one of Vanessa's children, writing in 1918 just after the birth of Angelica:

Think what an interest all her ways will be – much more than a boy's – though I admit there's a good deal to be said for the firstborn (by which I mean, of course, darling B.)[15]

'B', of course, was 'Billy Goat' – Virginia's childhood nickname.

Vanessa was robust, earthy and Madonna-like in her appearance. Around her, chaos reigned supreme at Charleston, but she remained the resolute, matriarchal anchor in the centre, soothing, calming and organizing. She was resolutely practical, having inherited this trait from Julia, and took naturally to ordering servants around (although she was not above doing her own cooking, and often would make scones in the kitchen). She was ruthless when it came to employing the right sort of help at Charleston, hiring and firing a number of 'helps' in quick succession, finally settling upon Grace Higgens, a cook who helped look after the children and who eventually stayed for forty years. It was a sign of Vanessa's calmness and capability in her home environment that Grace could never find a disloyal word to say about her or any of her 'Bloomsbury' friends. Virginia, in contrast, was never to master the employer/servant relationship properly. Her two hired helps, Nellie and Lottie, drove her to distraction, and vice versa, over a period of eighteen years. They constantly caused conflict, resigned and then came crawling back; Virginia was not assertive enough to refuse them and so the pair would move back in, only for the trouble to start up all over again.

Vanessa was often to be found sitting at her easel in the attic studio at Charleston, or in the garden room, sewing or sleeping while the men entered into animated discussion. She was serene and measured, earthy yet controlled, likened by Virginia to a bowl of golden water that bubbled up to the brim but never overflowed. In contrast, Virginia was edgy, nervous and often hyperactive. All her life she was prone to fits of excitement or temper, both of which set alarm bells ringing in Leonard, for they often indicated the beginning of a bout of debilitating illness. She was ungainly when she walked; tall and thin, awkward, ill at ease in her own body, unsure of her femininity, insecure and reluctant to look in the mirror. Even so, her many friends and admirers were transfixed by her face as it changed and grew expressive in conversation. Her looks were more unconventional than Vanessa's; delicate, transitory, ethereal; changing, in her forties and fifties, into a very fragile, haunted beauty. Although in her youth she had not resembled Julia as much as Stella or Vanessa did, something of Julia Stephen's weary severity crept into Virginia's face as she grew older.

Virginia was unhappy with her body image and weight for most of her life, finding it difficult to eat and going for long periods without doing so. Vanessa, on the other hand, although a frugal eater who disliked foreign food, started each day with a breakfast of toast and salt, dined off roast meats in the evening and was generally well nourished both by the produce from the Charleston farm and by her capable cook, Grace, who transformed it into delicious meals.

A certain amount of rivalry also arose over the respective merits of each sister's country house. Naturally, Virginia thought Monk's House to be far more tasteful than Charleston, but Vanessa disliked the quietness and austerity of Monk's, preferring the cheerful, rough-and-tumble informality of her chaotic farmhouse.

The sisters threw themselves into their work in the way that they themselves had predicted back in the nursery at Hyde Park Gate. For both women, work was a compulsion rather than purely a pleasure. Vanessa painted away the hidden frustrations of her personal life, although even her paintings did not always reveal much of her inner emotions, prompting Virginia once to write that her sister's pictures were 'silent as the grave'. Virginia focused her mind away from illness and depression into fiction, although on some occasions she saw the benefit of being ill for short periods, and used these times to mull over new ideas.

She was always to say, somewhat unfairly, that *she* deserved the career success as Vanessa had got the family life, and she kept a nervous eye on Vanessa's growing reputation as a painter, deeming it unfair that her sister should have both. It is certainly true that if Vanessa had not had the three children to look after, she might have achieved considerably more fame as a painter. Yet she had domestic help with the children, enough money to live comfortably, and a few hours per day to concentrate on her art, which, on the infrequent occasions that she exhibited, sold well and was admired by other artists. Vanessa was innovative, inspiring several designs for Roger Fry's Omega Workshops and showing her paintings at both his Post-Impressionist Exhibitions. In return, he reviewed her work favourably for *Vogue* magazine in 1926, declaring that she must take her place with the leading British painters of the day. Virginia remained envious of Vanessa's family and the hectic, affectionate atmosphere at Charleston, although her pain was alleviated by realizing that she was becoming financially successful through her writing (*To the Lighthouse* financed several improvements to Monk's House).

The sisters found the expression of emotions to anyone other than each other, difficult. Vanessa's calm exterior hid a passionate nature, and as a wife she was demanding and needy, marrying Clive in the confident hope of sustaining a full, satisfying sexual union. Although the marriage produced two children and enabled Vanessa to boast to Virginia about her sexual expertise (in comparison to Virginia's apparent frigidity), the physical side was short-lived, resulting in her damaging affairs with Roger Fry and Duncan Grant. Again, after the initial passion had worn off between Vanessa and Duncan, that relationship settled into the familiar pattern of Vanessa providing comfort and acting as confidante to Duncan, who brought a string of male lovers back to Charleston for her to look after. The effect on this passionate but emotionally repressed woman must have been devastating, but once again Vanessa kept her true feelings tucked away, concentrating instead upon her artistic talent and the demands of motherhood. Although Vanessa and Duncan were to remain together for more than forty years after Angelica's birth, Vanessa rarely had sexual relations again during that period.

Virginia's sexuality was far more complex, but unlike Vanessa, she had the constant and total support of a husband who was rarely absent from her side. Although after her honeymoon it seems as if the marriage became platonic very quickly (even during the honeymoon Virginia had written to her friend Ka Cox, enquiring in a puzzled way as to why people made such a fuss about copulation), there was instead a bottomless supply of affection, loyalty and intimacy to be drawn upon. Leonard was forced to do exactly what Vanessa Bell had done – he buried his physical desires deep down inside and substituted other pleasures instead: writing, publishing, gardening and pets. Virginia was not to be pressured or worried in any way, so a companionable routine of walks, talks and writing became the preferred existence for them both. Their relationship was based on trust and hard work, and they remained close enough to bemoan any absences from one another greatly, using pet names such as 'Mandril' and 'Mongoose' to demonstrate intimacy.

Virginia adored Leonard, writing that 'of course the way to make me want Mong[oose] is to be away from him: it is all rather pointless and secondrate away from him'.[16] Virginia, unlike the resolutely heterosexual Vanessa, was to become tempted by both men *and* women, but her passions were based on what she remembered of Stella and Jack's courtship before their marriage: flirtation, without the inclusion of the body. She formed close and ardent friendships with women all through her life, from Violet Dickinson in the 1890s to Ethel Smyth in the 1930s, but although the flames of desire certainly burned within Virginia's novels, they rarely did so in her life, with the exception of her relationship with Vita Sackville-West. Her marriage took priority, steady, rock-solid and always the source of much pleasure. Even after twenty-five years, as she walked hand-in-hand with Leonard around a London square, Virginia marvelled at how happy they still were.

Whilst Vanessa shone quietly and privately at her art, Virginia not only excelled at writing, but also at conversation; of the two sisters, she became the more extrovert. She 'held court' at any number of intimate, literary gatherings at Monk's House or Charleston, indulging in long witty monologues that had her admiring audiences in hoots of laughter. She often talked in the style that she wrote in, using long, unfurling, endless sentences that spiralled up and around the heads of her guests before exploding into spectacular flights of fantasy. Vanessa could not have appeared more different in company, feeling no need to compete with Virginia for the limelight. Her daughter Angelica recalls that:

> She presided, wise yet diffident, affectionate and a little remote, full of unquenchable spirit. Her feelings were strong, and words seemed to her inadequate. She was content to leave them to her sister and to continue painting.[17]

In 1937, tragedy struck the ordered lives of the Bell and Woolf families. A shell killed Vanessa's eldest child, Julian, during the Spanish Civil War. He had been part of a British medical unit based in Spain, on the Palace of the Escorial, for the Republican offensive to cut the supply route of the Nationalists encircling Madrid. Mortally wounded, he died in the dressing station at the Escorial at the age of twenty-nine. His body was never brought back home to England.

For the first time in her life, Vanessa fell totally to pieces. The roles that had been played out between 1913 and 1915 were reversed once more; now Virginia became the caregiver, Vanessa the invalid. Vanessa was later to write to Vita Sackville-West saying that she would never have got through the dreadful months following Julian's death if it hadn't been for Virginia's love and support. Virginia dealt with her own grief in her customary way, by writing a memoir of Julian a few days after she had received the news. In it, she candidly analysed her relationship with her sister's eldest child, remembering that she had tried to persuade him not to go to Spain, comparing him with Clive, his father, and recalling fondly that they had both teased her rather caustically. It seems that Virginia, still repressed by her upbringing, had experienced difficulty in relaying this fondness to Julian himself:

> But our relationship was perfectly secure because it was founded on our passion – not too strong a word for either of us – for Nessa. And it was this passion that made us both reserved when we met this summer.[18]

Vanessa spent the first week of her grieving in bed at the studio in Fitzroy Street, unable to be moved back to Charleston. Eventually she was brought back to the farm, where her recovery from the shock was slow and traumatic. During this period, Virginia put her own work on hold and visited her sister several times a week, writing every day. The letters are those expected from a descendant of the 'Angel in the House', tender, compassionate and selfless. Virginia's pen sought to give Vanessa the comfort she needed by reverting back to the animal nicknames of childhood years; 'singe', 'dolphin' and other old familiars pepper the letters. In an ironic reversal, Virginia's letters are also full of concern over Vanessa's eating and sleeping habits. Mainly, though, they are poetic, amorous love letters, one even ending with a quote from *The Winter's Tale* ('How I adore you! How astonishingly beautiful you are! No one will ever take the winds of March with beauty as you do').

Julian's death brought the sisters closer than they had been for many years, stripping the relationship bare of any petty rivalries, allowing Virginia to lay open her feelings for the sister she adored and needed. Vanessa, though, could still not open up her heart directly to Virginia; she chose, instead, to express her gratitude in a letter to Vita Sackville-West, who in turn relayed it to Virginia. Very occasionally, however, Vanessa managed to swallow her pride and find the right words. At the beginning of 1938, she wrote, to her sister:

> You do know how much you help me. I can't show it and I feel so stupid and such a wet blanket often but I couldn't get on at all if it weren't for you.[19]

Towards the end of 1937, Virginia was not progressing well with her work. Caring and worrying about Vanessa had sapped her of strength and precious writing time, but she published *The Years* and forced herself to press on with *Three Guineas* and *Roger Fry*. Her health was becoming precarious; the final typing of *The Years* had brought on several bouts of flu-like illness and agonies of self-doubt. As Vanessa slowly began to recover over at Charleston, Virginia was beginning to deteriorate, finding it hard to eat or sleep, increasingly losing faith in her ability to write. She still enjoyed any visit from Vanessa, though, and Angelica Garnett recalls that:

There were many occasions when I went to see Virginia alone with Vanessa and I amused myself while they enjoyed what they called a good old gossip ... they understood each other perfectly and were probably at their best in each other's company. They were bound together by the past and perhaps also by the feeling that they were opposite in temperament and that what one lacked she could find only in the other.[20]

At this stage, towards the end of her life, Virginia's truly close friends were few; Vita, Ethel Smyth, Leonard and Vanessa were the only people whom she trusted well enough to confide openly in. Despite Angelica's observations about each sister finding the qualities she lacked in the other, Virginia was unable to find the will to live, even from her beloved Nessa. Vanessa became greatly concerned about Virginia in the last few weeks of her life, but her letters, particularly the final one, are bossy and not overly sympathetic; perhaps this was Vanessa's way of convincing herself that Virginia was *not* about to descend again into the grip of terrifying mental illness. That final letter may have unwittingly caused additional despair, with its emphasis on Virginia having to pull herself together to be able to cope with the war, and for her not to worry Leonard; but, despite the dictatorial content of the letter, Virginia still loved to receive it and wrote to tell her sister so – in one of the suicide notes that were left propped up on her writing desk.

Vanessa was not as devastated after Virginia's death as those close to her thought that she would be. Fearing a similar collapse to the one that had followed Julian's death, the family clustered around her anxiously in the days following the discovery of Virginia's body. Instead, Vanessa withdrew further into painting and lived the next twenty years of her life in relative isolation, relying only on the company of Duncan, her children and grandchildren, and the calming routine of putting paintbrush to canvas. She continued to maintain an affectionate relationship with her brother-in-law, Leonard Woolf, up until her death, corresponding with him on the subject of Virginia's letters (which he was considering publishing) with some apprehension:

In most of those I have read yet there are a good many remarks about all her friends that they wouldn't like ... a great deal about Clive that would enrage him.[21]

The letters were not, in the end, published in their entirety until many years later, when most of the friends that Virginia had referred to were dead.

Vanessa Bell became, in her old age, something of a reluctant authority on the 'Bloomsbury Group', receiving letters from students, writers and curious members of the public, some of which prompted weary and occasionally biting responses. Vanessa would patiently reply to each enquiry, but confided to Leonard that

There was never such a thing as the Bloomsbury Group. I don't want to be brutal to the woman but I simply cannot go on telling people about such things.[22]

Vanessa continued to retain a sense of humour as she entered her seventies, writing mischievously and with a hint of her old bossiness to Leonard after he had gone into hospital for an operation:

Don't be too severe with them [nurses] for you are completely at their mercy and I'm sure they'll think nothing of murdering you if you upset them too much.[23]

No doubt Vanessa and Leonard must have found it a relief to be able, finally, to joke about nurses after the early, terrible years of Virginia's illness.

Other than the company of friends, one of the great pleasures that old age brought to Vanessa was a clutch of grandchildren. Angelica had married David Garnett and produced four daughters; Quentin had married Anne Olivier Popham and had two daughters and a son. The children knew Vanessa as a doting grandmother, and Duncan and Clive as two amusing grandfathers who would allow them to experiment with paints and brushes in the airy studio.

The traditions of Angelica's childhood continued with parties, dressing-up and swimming still part of the magic of Charleston, but Vanessa was growing increasingly frail. She was still working hard, designing book jackets for posthumous editions of Virginia's work, and she made the occasional trip to France with Duncan. There was a more marked remoteness about her, which frustrated Angelica, who found her mother cool and distant. Vanessa's faithful servant, Grace Higgens, was to realize that, after forty years of working for 'Mrs

Bell', she knew little more about Vanessa than she had on the day she started service. Vanessa had withdrawn almost entirely from everyday life. The barriers she had been putting up since the loss of Julia and Stella at Hyde Park Gate were now so firmly bolted into place that she could not have knocked them down – even if she had wanted to.

Silent and uncomplaining to the last, Vanessa Bell died at Charleston at the age of eighty-one after a bout of bronchitis, almost twenty years to the day since Virginia had ended her life in the River Ouse. Vanessa's shadows haunt the studios at Charleston; her pictures hang on the walls and her painted furniture remains in the rooms. Her paintings sell for enormous amounts of money and have been widely exhibited, most notably at an important exhibition of Bloomsbury art at the Tate Gallery. Her talent for art and design has been passed down to the next generations, in particular to Angelica, a sculptor, artist and writer, and to Vanessa's granddaughter, designer Cressida Bell.

Virginia and Vanessa paid touching tribute to each other in their chosen media of art and literature; a far easier way for Vanessa, in particular, to do so. She always found it hard to express her feelings face-to-face or even in letters, but putting paintbrush to canvas, she was able to capture the essence of Virginia with greater ease. Three early, famous paintings of her sister can be seen today. The first, painted in 1911 and now in the National Portrait Gallery, was painted at Little Talland House. Virginia, at that stage in her life, was working on *The Voyage Out* and was aware that Leonard Woolf had fallen in love with her. The new style of contemporary painting that her sister favoured was having a profound impact on Virginia's own writing, although this was not to emerge until later in the decade. Despite taking pleasure in the first Post-Impressionist Exhibition in 1910, Virginia resented the amount of excited conversation about art that threatened to overshadow her own literary discussions:

> The furious excitement of these people all over the winter over their pieces of canvas-coloured green and blue, is odious.[24]

Vanessa's 1911 portrait of Virginia is the most vividly coloured of the three. Virginia is shown subsided into the corner of a bright orange armchair that is boldly outlined in black. Her knitting is a startling red, but in contrast to the props, Virginia's clothing is subdued, in muted greys and browns. Her demeanour is timid and withdrawn, and she has a forlorn air about her. Vanessa has deliberately left the face featureless, save for the nose and a vague impression of downcast eyes. The lack of features becomes a comment on the shyness and doubts that Virginia possessed at that time, for whilst Vanessa already had marriage and painting, Virginia was embarking uncertainly on a first novel with no guarantee of publication, let alone success. She had survived two serious breakdowns and was not far from beginning another. Although at first glance the picture suggests a moment of relaxed intimacy between sisters, a further study reveals it to be a disturbing portrait, revealing sadness and self-doubt in the sitter.

Another oil painting of Virginia, finished *c.* 1912, evokes a similar mood, but this time the face of the sitter is left *completely* blank, in complete contrast to the detail shown on her lace collar, her hat and the deckchair she sits on. Vanessa has added red pieces to Virginia's dull brown dress, and at first it is these that catch the eye. On further scrutiny, however, this painting proves to be as sad and disturbing as the previous one. The arms of the sitter are folded defensively, and if Vanessa had added features to Virginia's face, they would probably have been screwed-up with impatience and looking slightly confrontational; Virginia did not like intrusive probing of her character, or being the subject of paintings and photographs. That featureless face suggests annoyance, but also wistfulness. On seeing it at an exhibition in the 1960s, Leonard Woolf remarked that it captured more of the true spirit of Virginia than any other portrait had ever done.

The third Bell painting, completed in 1912 and now hanging at Monk's House, is the only one of the three to attempt some form of conventional likeness, although it perhaps goes too far to the other extreme, presenting a doll-like, rounded Virginia with full cheeks and doe-like eyes. In muted shades of green (matching the colour that Virginia favoured for the walls of Monk's House), Vanessa imbued her sister with a gentle prettiness and a soft, pensive expression. Virginia is shown seated at a table with an open book in front of her. Her clothes are feminine, her hair is fetchingly waved. It is a physically more flattering, yet less revealing, portrait of Virginia Woolf, lacking the emotional intensity and complex layers contained in the previous two.

Virginia, in turn, portrayed Vanessa recognizably in three books. *The Voyage Out,* her first novel, explored the struggle that Virginia had in the early days of her marriage. It also dissected the relations between men and women in a patriarchal society and captured the emotional intensity surrounding the early deaths of several people whom she loved. The 'voyages' that the book describes are inspired by the trips Virginia Stephen took to Paris and Italy in 1904 and 1906, the year of the fateful trip to Greece that resulted in Thoby's death. One of the book's characters, Helen Ambrose, is a calm, maternal figure, married and, in the early stages of the novel, espied embroidering, or reading G.E. Moore's *Principa Ethica* (a book that Vanessa would have once discussed excitedly with the rest of the Bloomsbury Group and which formed the basis of their morals and values). The other heroine of *The Voyage Out* is Rachel Vinrace, who is eager, impulsive and inquisitive. It is easy to draw true-life parallels between Helen/Vanessa and Rachel/Virginia, or to view the two female protagonists as a 'contrast of Greek and Biblical figures: Vanessa's statuesque splendour; Virginia eager, impulsive, searching'.[25]

By studying the love triangle at the heart of *The Voyage Out*, between Helen, Terence and Rachel, comparisons can be drawn to the 1908 real-life triangle between Vanessa, Clive and Virginia. The pleasure that Virginia got from Clive's company, and he from hers, particularly at the embryonic stage of the flirtation in Cornwall, is clearly visible on Woolf's page as the enjoyment that Terence and Rachel have during their long cliff-top walks. Terence, like Clive Bell, despises 'conventional marriage', preferring to envisage Rachel in his arms as they exchange the feelings that they believe are inexplicable to others. It is as though Woolf were trying to exorcize the complex happenings of the year 1908 by exploring them in fiction. This was not altogether successful, owing to her inability to divorce herself entirely from her characters' feelings, and for this reason Vanessa Bell disliked the book, finding it too painful to read.

Virginia Woolf's second novel, *Night and Day*, was dedicated to Vanessa with the words 'To Vanessa Bell, but, looking for a phrase, I found none to stand beside your name'. This time, the heroine, Katharine Hilbery, is an undisguised portrayal of Vanessa. Katharine is possessed of a deep romanticism, has an air of being elsewhere and is under enormous pressure from her family to be practical, whilst secretly she longs for a career. Whenever Katharine is feeling troubled by having to entertain an endless succession of dull visitors to the Victorian family home, she absorbs herself in mathematics – this clearly echoes Vanessa's longing to return to paints and turpentine when she was being forced by the Duckworth brothers to play the role of the perfect hostess. Katharine, like Vanessa, possesses a strange combination of the ethereal entwined with a tendency towards a 'solid' existence. Virginia wanted to capture and pay tribute to her sister's enigma in the character of Katharine, telling Vanessa that Katharine should be:

> Immensely mysterious and romantic, which of course you are, yes, but it's the combination that's so enthralling; to crack through the paving stone and be enveloped in the mist.[26]

Physical descriptions of Katharine are also inspired by Virginia's observations of Vanessa. Katharine has 'quick, impulsive movements' like her mother, Mrs Hilbery (and Julia Stephen had also been described as having these movements), she possesses 'decision' and 'composure', again two characteristics very marked in Vanessa. Katharine Hilbery has little aptitude for literature and is 'inclined to be silent', shying away from expressing opinions in front of others. She does, however, enjoy a happy ending, finding a partner, Ralph Denham, who understands her passion for mathematics. When Ralph finds Katharine to be a very different person in the flesh from the beautiful woman he fantasized about marrying, here again the couple appear to be based on Clive and Vanessa Bell.

Virginia Woolf's tribute to her childhood holidays in Cornwall, *To the Lighthouse*, also features characters who bear some similarity to Vanessa Bell. Although the main inspiration for Mrs Ramsay is Julia Stephen, there are elements of Vanessa, in this portrayal of a solid, real woman living in a shifting, uncertain world. Mrs Ramsay's matriarchal role in the household also brings to mind Vanessa at Charleston. However, there is more of Vanessa to be seen in the character of Lily Briscoe. Lily has severe doubts about her own painting, and is not always able to vocalize these doubts easily. She has not been educated well and has not travelled extensively, but she is self-possessed and emotional beneath a cool exterior. Like Vanessa, she has the tendency to draw vertical lines down the middle of her paintings (Vanessa employed this technique on her tiled fireplace design of Godrevy Lighthouse, still visible at Monk's House). Lily advocates abstract art, stating that it is acceptable, as it was to Vanessa, to paint figures without any definite facial features. Lily's overriding love and admiration for Mrs Ramsay is one of the main focal points of the novel; here, poignantly, Virginia has captured Vanessa's love and respect for their own beautiful mother, Julia Stephen.

The true love of her life, Duncan, struggled on at Charleston, putting pen to paper two months after she had died to try and make sense of it all. He pondered his many years of what he called 'deference' to Vanessa's opinions and feelings, concluding that he could still continue to guess what her opinions were likely to have been on most matters, but as her feelings no longer existed, he now had to consider himself to be well and truly on his own. He lived on at Charleston with many visitors, but essentially alone, until his death in 1978.

3   Violet

In the first Elizabethan age
When Shakespeare stood on Southwark's stage
A sprig of an unknown tree and place
Sired two sons from an Eton base
And founded a dynasty. Mid hopes and fears
Descendants winged westward across the years,
From William the priest, to the pilot Cay
Each travelled serenely a pilgrim way.[1]

In Virginia Stephen's diary for 2 April 1897, she makes her first, unremarkable mention of the older woman who, over the next forty-two years, was to become both an intimate friend and a supporter of Virginia's literary career. The occasion was the fitting of Stella's wedding dress at Mrs Young's in South Audley Street:

> Margaret Massingberd was there, and Violet Dickinson, and soon Cousin Mia galumphed into the room with a parcel for my darling Stella . . .

Violet Dickinson was a friend of the whole Stephen family, but was particularly close to Stella (who at the time of Virginia's first mention of Violet was only three months away from her death). Violet shared Stella's philanthropic outlook on life and was given to acts of kindness and charity, helping the poor and volunteering in London's mental hospitals.

'Dickinsons aren't easily defined . . . we put in our thumb and we pull out our plum from a miscellaneous company of yeomen, merchants, bankers, squires' admitted Violet in her history of the

Dickinson family. She was certainly well connected; her father was a landowner in Frome, and her maternal grandfather was the Bishop of Bath and Wells. Generations of Dickinsons had inhabited the family seat, Kingweston, in Somerset, and Violet, as a favourite cousin, spent much time there throughout her life. Born in 1865, she weighed nearly ten pounds at birth and by the age of fifteen was six feet tall, which she later eccentrically attributed to 'being planted on clay soil from infancy'.[2] She was a tomboy, recording in her memoirs that some neighbours had tried to present her with 'a large bulky doll of singularly unattractive appearance'.

Violet had no need to work for a living, residing comfortably with her brother, Ozzie, in a house at Manchester Square and a cottage, Burnham Wood, near Welwyn, which she had designed and built herself. Never marrying, she cheerfully advocated spinsterhood and retained total independence throughout her long life. She visited mentally defective criminals and also those who were suffering from mental illness at the London Hospital; experiences which doubtless aided her understanding and support of Virginia Stephen's nervous breakdown during 1904. Although Violet's charity work put her in the same selfless category as Julia Stephen and Stella Duckworth, there was one essential difference: Violet was full of happiness, brusque common sense, jollity and optimism, all of which were qualities much needed and admired by the young Virginia.

She was an ardent traveller, setting off around the world in the company of Lord and Lady Cecil or the daughters of the Marquis of Bath, Beatrice and Katie Thynne (with whom Violet always spent Christmas at the family seat, Longleat). Violet was just as at home yachting in Norway, sightseeing in Spain or spending time at Kingweston with her cousins. Here, she insisted that wireless sets be installed in every room, including the servants' quarters, as well as the library and schoolroom. Violet's impeccable connections, her modesty, chastity and respectability were to become the subjects of much good-natured teasing between herself and Virginia during the first year of their friendship; in their early correspondence there are many joking references to Violet's imaginary husband and improbably large number of illegitimate children.

Virginia's passionate and all-consuming longing for Violet Dickinson developed rapidly during the summer of 1902, shortly after Leslie had received his diagnosis of cancer. Since 1897 until then, her emotional pen had been mainly reserved for her cousins, Madge and Emma Vaughan – Madge had been Virginia's very first 'crush' as a teenager (although Madge was some seventeen years older) and Emma became a treasured confidante and playmate, as well as a willing recipient of Virginia's juvenile fiction and drawings.

The first recorded letter from Virginia to Violet, sent in the early months of 1902, is a short and polite note to 'Miss Dickinson', offering to lend her a book on Scottish lighthouses. Virginia was only twenty years old, Violet seventeen years her senior, and in these first, hesitant letters, it is possible to pick up on Virginia's heightened awareness of that age difference. Violet, after all, was a well-travelled woman of the world, with many distinguished acquaintances; Virginia had yet to travel widely and was still living in the insular world of 22 Hyde Park Gate with the Duckworth brothers and Leslie, who was unwell and demanding. Throughout April 1902, Virginia's letters to Violet retain their slightly stiff, distant style, signed under her initials and with a content mainly consisting of formal bulletins about Leslie's health. As the summer progressed, the formal reserve began to slacken and many anxious requests for Violet's company took its place. Virginia was starting to realize that the attention and understanding that she was lacking at home could become readily available from Violet's kind heart. Missing Julia and Stella, and now deprived of Leslie's gruff affection and literary conversation, Virginia was desperate to find these comforts in a new source.

During the summer holidays of August 1902, Violet had joined Vanessa, Virginia and Leslie at their holiday home in Fritham, the New Forest. For the first time Virginia recorded her impressions of Violet on paper, in a fragment entitled 'Violet Dickinson at Fritham'. The piece starts with a somewhat vague and confusing story about hounds chasing through the forest under the command of 'Aunt Maria' (Violet), who is six-feet-two and has 'long travel-stained limbs'. It ends with a concise and frank summary of her new friend's character, in language that clearly conveys her admiration and respect. The tone is wholly innocent, but boasts a privileged knowledge of Violet's personality with its tone of superiority in the final line. It is not a mature piece of writing, compared with the twenty-eight short journal pieces that Virginia also began work on during 1903, but as a revealing portrayal of Violet's appearance and character, and an affectionate tribute to a blossoming friendship, it is worth including.

To a casual observer she would appear, I think, a very high-spirited, rather crazy, harem-scarem sort of person – whose part in life was (to be) slightly ridiculous, warmhearted and calculated to make the success of any kind of party. She has a very wide circle of acquaintances, mostly of the lorded and titled variety in whose country houses she is forever staying – and with whom she seems to be invariably popular. She is 37 and without any pretence to good looks – which humorously she knows quite well herself and lets you know too – even going out of her way to allude laughingly to her gray hairs, and screws her face in to the most comical grimaces. But an observer who would stop here, putting her down as one of those clever-ish, adaptable ladies of middle age who are welcome everywhere and not indispensable anywhere – such an observer would be superficial indeed.[3]

By September 1902, Violet had become 'my woman' to Virginia, who started most letters with a variant on that phrase and began to sign herself off as, amongst other things, 'your lover' and 'your loving goat'. She also began to refer to herself as 'Sparroy', a name made up from the curious mixture of 'sparrow' and 'monkey', suggesting a small animal that is at once cheeky and playful, yet also requires feeding and nurturing. In other letters she is a 'kangaroo' or a 'wallaby nosing around with her soft, wet snout for a letter'. Many references are made to creeping into Violet's 'pouch'. Usually it is Virginia who expresses her cravings to be petted and nurtured by Violet, but occasionally she reverses the roles and offers to fold Violet in her 'feathery arms, so that you may feel the Heart in her ribs'.

The weaker Leslie became, the stronger Virginia's emotions towards Violet grew, but it was not just Virginia who relied on Violet's cheerful disposition to see them through this difficult time; 'Violet is the family friend we all cling to when we're drowning'[4] she admitted in a letter to the woman herself. Most of Virginia's letters during late 1902 and early 1903 are a mixture of blunt updates on her father's health, longings to see Violet, snippets of information about books and literary exercises, and endless allusions to animals needing, wanting and demanding comfort from each other. Sometimes it is easy to detect the old 'separation anxiety' in Virginia, the same anxiousness that had plagued her as a child when she peered anxiously from the window at 22 Hyde Park Gate, watching for Julia to return. Violet was taking Julia's place as the 'mother figure' of the Stephen family, and Virginia felt her absences keenly.

In April 1903, Violet moved into the cottage she had built for herself in Hertfordshire, Burnham Wood. She had approached the task of finding the land and building the cottage with her usual vigour and forthrightness:

> Sometimes she tapped a tree and nodded her head and wrote in the perennial notebook which swings by her side ... sometimes she dropped on her knee and smelt the ground.[5]

The cottage was a great success – Virginia referred to an early visit as a 'refreshment' – and visitors flocked to stay with Violet, finding a perverse delight in digging her vegetable patch as a deviation from their stressful London lives, although Violet had ensured that the house was attractively and comfortably furnished for her guests. One such guest was Ella Crum, who with her husband, Walter, was a life-long friend of Violet's and the butt of many of Virginia's jokes. Ella over-sentimentally recorded her impressions of the haven that was Burnham Wood in the visitors' book:

> In Burnham Wood through all the summer day
> Stirred by soft airs, the pink-lipped foxgloves sway
> From seas of fern spring oak trees, straight and fine
> With clumps of Rhododendron, red as wine
> And hosts of woodland flowers in sweet array,
> Life loiters here; all beauty, leisure, play
> With it I loiter, both farewell to say
> To all the careless hours that have been since
> In Burnham Wood.[6]

Towards the end of 1903, Leslie's hold on life was weakening, Vanessa was already house hunting in Bloomsbury for the new family home, and Virginia was writing on an almost daily basis to Violet Dickinson. Violet was full of concern and love for the motherless Stephen girls, especially after reading Virginia's gloomy reports of Leslie's sickness, weakness and raging temperatures. On 22 February Leslie finally died, with the result that Virginia entered a two-month period of denial. Outwardly she seemed calm, writing maturely and cordially to her friends about her father's life. In letters to Violet she mainly bemoaned her lack of kindness to the lonely Leslie after Julia's death; occasionally there are references to 'queer little expeditions' that she was forced to take with George Duckworth, who was still exerting his power over her.

Writing and reading about Leslie only served to distance Virginia from her bottled-up grief. In the meantime, a long holiday was quickly planned, to Pembrokeshire in Wales, then Venice and Florence (where Violet joined them) and on to Paris. The Welsh part of the holiday was tolerable, and parts of the Pembrokeshire countryside reminded Virginia of her beloved St Ives. George Duckworth had to return to London, and after he'd gone the atmosphere in the holiday house improved greatly and Virginia enjoyed being alone with Nessa and Thoby. The scenery at Manorbier inspired Virginia to write, and she devoured books of Greek tragedy as well, writing to Violet that she found the country 'a good place to work in'. Years later, Virginia was to recall Manorbier as being an important landmark in her burgeoning career – for it was here where she realized what the theme of her first novel, *The Voyage Out*, would be.

The Stephen family returned home for a few days in March 1904 and then left for Venice in the company of Gerald Duckworth. On arrival they found themselves with no accommodation, but managed to obtain three small, dirty rooms before eventually moving into the Grand Hotel, where they resented the extravagance. Virginia wrote excitedly of Venice to Violet, imploring her to come and witness the beauty of it for herself, but by 25 April the thrill of being abroad was starting to fade. Virginia begged her cousin, Emma Vaughan, to send her news of England and stated that 'to live in a degenerate tho' beautiful country is depressing'.[7]

The weeks were temporarily lightened by the arrival of Violet, but after she had departed, Virginia began to display signs of the temper that had been prominent during the period of Stella's illness and death; 'how cross I have been, how dull, how tempersome'.[8] This time, with both parents now dead and the imminent sale of 22 Hyde Park Gate looming, her hold on stability and reality began to lessen, and by the time the family had returned to Paris in early May 1904, Virginia had lost her grip on sanity, too, and was descending, for the second time, into a lengthy and severe mental breakdown.

During April 1903, Virginia had joked with Violet about the new cottage at Welwyn, warning her not to allow the house to become 'tainted with Death and sorrows, such as always cling to you and make you a kind of walking hospital'. She added prophetically that 'Poor Sparroy will ask for a bed there soon'.[9] During the summer of 1904, according to Violet's guest book, the entire Stephen/Duckworth family came down to Burnham Wood with the intention of leaving Virginia in the care of Violet and three nurses. Virginia began to deteriorate into a stranger, a person whom Violet had not seen before. She intensely mistrusted Vanessa, who was often in attendance; she hated her nurses, supposing them to be evil, becoming violent with them; she heard voices, imagining that the birds were singing in Greek outside her window; she could not eat; she was convinced that King Edward VII lurked in the azalea bushes; and she attempted, for the first time, to commit suicide by jumping out of a window, which luckily was too close to the ground to enable her to achieve her wish.

Although Virginia was unable to read or write during this period and thus left no records, some idea of the horror that Violet Dickinson must have witnessed and of Virginia's mental instability at this time, can be gained from reading the 1892 Victorian short story by Charlotte Perkins Gilman, *The Yellow Wallpaper*. The symptoms and the 'rest cures' that Gilman's heroine endures illustrate a descent into paranoia and mental illness very similar to Virginia's situation.

As well as a horrific account of madness, the story is a telling indicator of the social and economic relationships between men and women at the time: the husband in the story controls, as did Violet and later Leonard with Virginia, an ailing woman, setting down strict rules in order that she might recover. The nameless heroine in *The Yellow Wallpaper* has been brought to a secluded countryside estate in summer, away from the stresses of city life. Her husband, John, is 'practical in the extreme', just as Violet Dickinson was. The invalid is a writer, forbidden to work until she is well again and in the meantime expected to take tonics, air and exercise, all remedies that were to be suggested over and over again to Virginia, from the 1890s up until her death in 1941.

In *The Yellow Wallpaper*, the nightmarish descriptions of the foul smells that the invalid believes are pervading the house, and her visions of a woman crawling around underneath the wallpaper and trying to climb through the pattern, clearly echo the terrifying delusions and hallucinations that Virginia Stephen suffered in 1904 during the long, hot summer of her illness. The heroine's sister-in-law, Jennie, at first described as a kind, helpful carer, is suddenly referred to as 'sly' and forevermore mistrusted, just as Virginia mistrusted Vanessa and Violet. During the daytime, the sick woman in *The Yellow Wallpaper* has visions of the phantom woman trapped behind the wallpaper getting into the garden, where she can be seen 'creeping all round' it and hiding 'under the blackberry vines'. By the end of the story 'there are so many of these creeping women' that she cannot bear to look out. There are obvious parallels between Gilman's creeping woman, and Virginia's visions of King Edward VII lurking in the bushes. Throughout the story the woman believes herself to be sane, and her husband and carers to be plotting evilly against her. What Violet Dickinson had to see whilst nursing Virginia, and how she managed to cope, is not recorded – but John, the husband character from *The Yellow Wallpaper*, faints with horror as he encounters his wife crawling round the bedroom, the wallpaper ripped to shreds and, more horrifically, the bedstead 'gnawed'.

Virginia's madness lasted the entire summer, during which time she stayed inside Violet's house and was too unwell to write even the shortest letter. It was not until September, thin and shaken, that she joined the rest of the family in Nottinghamshire, where, for the first time in five months, she put pen to paper, writing once more to Violet to explain that she felt herself to be a 'recovered bird' and that she was trying to eat more food in order to regain her physical and mental health. Her joy in living began to seep back and letters to Violet during September are full of plans to begin writing serious articles.

While Vanessa began to furnish and decorate the new family home at 46 Gordon Square, Virginia was sent to stay with her Aunt Caroline Emelia Stephen in Cambridge. Here she was resignedly, but frustratedly, cooped up with her Quaker aunt, who was given to loud monologues. Virginia resented the enforced absence from her family. Violet, as always, provided as much care as was possible from a distance, sending huge food parcels of biscuits and chocolate to Cambridge. Before moving on to stay with the Vaughans at Giggleswick in Yorkshire, Virginia was at last allowed home to London for a few days in November. One of the first things she saw on the desk in her new room at 46 Gordon Square was a china inkpot from Violet, characteristically huge and 'deep enough to write a dozen articles'.[10]

The inkpot, an innocent gift, came to have greater significance. By the time Virginia had settled into Gordon Square at the beginning of 1905, she was aware that she had incurred considerable debts. The bills for doctors, medication and the constant attention of nurses, had drained away a significant part of the family inheritance from Leslie. She felt ready, and willing, to work hard and make her mark in the world of journalism. Although she could easily have achieved acceptance as a writer because she was the daughter of Leslie Stephen, Virginia chose not to trade off his name. Instead, she let her love for her 'beloved woman', Violet, open the door to a professional writing life.

Violet, well connected and a firm believer in Virginia's literary talent, introduced her to Margaret Littleton, the editor of the women's supplement of the *Guardian*. Unrelated to the newspaper of the same name that we know today, this was an Anglo-Catholic clerical paper. Perhaps it was an unlikely place for an agnostic's daughter to commence her career, but Leslie was dead, and Virginia knew that the article she wrote for the *Guardian* might reward her with a cheque. The article, on the Brontës and Haworth Parsonage, was published on 21 December 1904. Violet's other connections, Kitty Maxse (whose husband published the *National Review*) and Bruce Richmond, editor of the *Times Literary Supplement*, also proved invaluable to Virginia. By the end of 1905 she had published over thirty pieces and was established as a critic, reviewer and essayist. She had also started compiling ideas for her first novel.

As ever, Violet had proved a loyal and steadfast friend to Virginia by playing such a crucial part in the development of her career. She did not approve of the Stephen family's move to Bloomsbury, making no secret of the fact that she thought Julia Stephen would have heartily contested it, but she continued her unfailing support of Virginia, whose letters now began to boast happily of the details of various acceptances and submissions that she was making to newspapers and periodicals. In addition, the letters contained an inordinate amount of cheerful teasing as Virginia jokingly accused Violet of being a 'dangerous' woman who was 'not at all the right kind of influence over young girls'.[11]

Unsurprisingly, Virginia was now reluctant to visit Violet at Burnham Wood – her first visit since the awful summer of 1904 – but she did, in order to bid goodbye to Violet who was off on a world tour with Nelly Cecil for the next four months. In the meantime, as if to compensate for Violet's absence, Virginia revisited her beloved St Ives for the first time in eleven years, a trip she greatly enjoyed. She missed

Violet painfully, complaining that nobody in her family took very much interest in her 'scribblings', as she sat in her room in the lodgings at Carbis Bay.

On her return to London, Virginia noted that M.H. Spielman's *The Life and Work of Kate Greenaway* had been published, and it included many flattering references to Violet, who had been a close friend to the children's author since the early 1890s. Reading the introductory paragraph, which described the blossoming friendship between Violet and Kate (who was twenty years older than Violet), may well have caused Virginia some pangs of jealousy:

> From that time forward the two ladies, the old and the young, were much in each other's company at 'private views' and other ceremonies, and the fact that her friend was tall and slim beyond the average and Kate was noticeably short and stout, not only drew attention to their companionship but served as a constant text for the exercise of Kate's humorous invention. Their correspondence by letter was incessant and Miss Greenaway's pencil was generally requisitioned to give an added note of piquancy and fancy to her written communications.[12]

Kate had died in 1901, before Violet and Virginia's friendship had begun, and in any case, the biography goes on to explain how Kate was in 'constant fear' of losing her friends, a dread that Virginia herself would have closely identified with. However, it unsettled Virginia to realize that Violet had participated in another intimate correspondence for seven years, a correspondence which included many spirited literary discussions and the inclusion of clever, personal drawings and sketches. Following the publication of this book in 1905, Virginia's letters to Violet became more emotional. They hint at feelings of insecurity and fear as Virginia wondered 'what fragment of your body will be thrown to me among the howling crowd of your friends?'[13]

In December 1905, Violet returned home from her world trip. She felt refreshed and healthy, and had tales of new experiences and friendships. By the beginning of 1906, plans were being made for Vanessa, Virginia, Adrian and Thoby to go to Greece, with Violet in attendance as a self-styled 'foster mother'. George Duckworth impressed some last-minute cautions upon his half-sisters, but they set forth with great optimism on 8 September.

The women travelled to Greece together and met up with Thoby and

Adrian at Olympia. The whole family visited Corinth, where Vanessa became increasingly unwell. Suddenly the family holiday, awaited with such excitement, had to be called to a halt. Vanessa, lying in bed in her hotel room, had suspected appendicitis, but she also seemed to be suffering from depression. The family ran up large bills for medicine, and also for bottles of champagne, which appeared to be the only thing that revived Vanessa. The strain on poor Violet Dickinson must again have been almost intolerable: Virginia sat writing miserably in the sickroom, and Thoby and Adrian quarrelled downstairs.

The group eventually set off home via Constantinople, minus Thoby, who had returned to London a fortnight earlier. They arrived back at Bloomsbury on 1 November, after a slow, arduous journey, only to find Thoby seriously ill in bed. He had initially been diagnosed with malaria, but this was changed to a diagnosis of typhoid – and it was soon discovered that Violet was extremely ill with the same fever. Vanessa's predicament was less clear – eventually Dr Savage pronounced her to be tired, weak and with a case of appendicitis, although no operation was ever performed. She recovered quickly, but Thoby worsened.

Violet, at her house in Manchester Street, struggled with typhoid, whilst Virginia believed her to be less ill than she actually was ('I am so sorry about the influenza' she wrote on 9 November), but a week later, Virginia promised to provide hot water bottles and smooth pillows for Violet if necessary. On 17 November, her daily bulletin to Violet about Thoby's health ominously describes the operation that was about to be performed on him, and then ends on an extraordinarily light-hearted note, with a description of herself rolling on a mat like a wallaby, inviting Violet to 'look for fleas'.

On the morning of 20 November 1906, Thoby Stephen died of typhoid fever. He was aged twenty-six. The remarkable letter that Virginia sent to Violet on that very day holds no hint of this latest, terrible Stephen family bereavement. Instead it is a gossipy letter, describing relationships between friends and reassuring Violet that the invalids are all progressing well! Over the next four weeks, Virginia continued to send Violet progress reports on the dead Thoby, complete with stories of his preference for mutton chops and his good-humoured baiting of the nurses. She does inform Violet that Vanessa had finally accepted Clive Bell's proposal of marriage, two days after Thoby's death.

Virginia's double loss – of her sister to Clive and the death of her elder brother – is not reflected in her letters. It is only possible to guess at the turmoil beneath the jovial, optimistic tone of her daily epistles to Violet, for Virginia's talent for fiction was perhaps never more apparent than during the four weeks when she pretended that Thoby was still alive. On 29 November, a letter informs Violet that Thoby is 'still on his back – but manages to be about as full of life in that position as most people are on their hind legs'.[14] Stories of Thoby's flirtations with nurses and his endeavours to draw in bed with a pencil continued to drop onto Violet's doormat until 18 December when Violet, having just received the news from Virginia that Thoby was 'decidedly better', then read the news of his death in the *National Review*. Her reactions are (fortunately) not recorded, but a contrite Virginia wrote a letter of apology for all the lies, admitting that she had not had the courage to tell the truth and risk hampering Violet's own recovery.

Violet patiently continued to provide support and friendship to Virginia, sensitively perceiving that with Thoby's death and Vanessa's marriage to Clive, it would be needed more than ever. From 23–25 January 1907, Virginia returned to Burnham Wood where she celebrated her twenty-fifth birthday with Violet. At around this time, she may have been having ideas for *Friendship's Gallery*, a tribute to Violet, which was presented to her in August, typed in violet ink and bound in violet leather (the habit of writing in purple ink remained with Virginia for the rest of her life, a lasting reminder of Violet and her influence). *Friendship's Gallery* was intended for Violet's eyes only, as Virginia made clear in a letter at the beginning of August, or for those of Nelly Cecil, their mutual friend who also features prominently in the story. Virginia's fear of showing this piece elsewhere was based predominantly on her conclusion that it was immature, unfinished and not an example of her best writing. Therefore she was perturbed to find that, during October, Violet had read excerpts from this very personal piece to members of the awful Crum family. Violet was immediately chastised for this, and Virginia demanded that the gift be returned to her, but it is a sign of its great value to Violet that *Friendship's Gallery* remained in the Dickinson family until the death of Ozzie Dickinson in 1955.

The text of *Friendship's Gallery* can be seen as a forerunner to *Orlando*, Virginia's later homage to Vita Sackville-West. It pays tribute, in a similarly jaunty but less complex way, to a beloved woman friend who is from an aristocratic background. It possesses a similar bawdy humour to that which pervades *Orlando*. On the surface it is a spoof biography that shows witty appreciation of Violet and her circle of well-connected lady friends. The piece is divided into three sections – in the first, Violet is portrayed as 'a tall rod of a plant with queer little tassels always quivering'[15] and much is made of the comicality of her height, her love of books and her speedy dashes to the bedsides of those who are ill. The second section, 'The Magic Garden', describes the aristocratic ladies well known to both Virginia and Violet – Katie and Beatrice Thynne, Lady Bath, Nelly Cecil and Kitty Maxse. The third section takes the form of a fantastic story told to children to help them sleep, in which Violet features as a 'Giantess' who could 'heal cripples . . . tame wild beasts' and 'make small children appear out of bags'.[16]

On a deeper level it is possible to detect within *Friendship's Gallery* clear traces of the strong beliefs that were to determine and shape Virginia's writing career. Her admiring descriptions of Violet building her own cottage lead naturally to comparisons with the ideas that Virginia was to demonstrate years later in *A Room of One's Own*. Her clever but scornful renaming of a baby boy as 'Violent' reinforces the reader's growing perception of Virginia as a budding feminist who much preferred the company of women to men. Her dialogue, bringing to life Violet's witty and unconventional conversation in polite company, also hints at her feelings about the limitations imposed upon women by Victorian society. Therefore, *Friendship's Gallery* could also be said to precede the thinking behind *The Years*, *Three Guineas* and many of Woolf's essays, letters and articles. It also appears to be an exorcism of the difficult summer of 1904 spent recovering at Burnham Wood, as Virginia includes a description of the house and garden, as well as mentions Violet's unfailing practicality and kindness towards her.

In addition, *Friendship's Gallery* is a tribute, intentional or otherwise, to Stella Duckworth and Julia Stephen, and it appears to offer us an early version of Julia's fictional counterpart, Mrs Ramsay in *To The Lighthouse*, as well. As the heroine, Violet, strides 'across the grass to slap some mournful dowager on the back' or takes 'a sick man to the London hospital', here are the memories that later lead to Mrs Ramsay running across the grass in her deerstalker's hat; here are the ghostly presences of Julia and Stella, angelically tending to the poor and needy.

Although *Friendship's Gallery* is immature in places, and the writing style is inconsistent and often overly foolish, it is nevertheless an important indicator of Virginia Stephen's development as a writer. It also reminds us that, far from being the fragile, haunted-looking person who gazes out from old photographs, Virginia in 'real life' possessed an earthy, robust wit and enjoyed laughing and teasing. Violet brought these attractive qualities to the fore, and for that reason her part in Virginia's life should not be underestimated.

Virginia's gift of *Friendship's Gallery* marked a change, the first in five years, in her relationship with Violet Dickinson. In April 1908, during a holiday at St Ives, Virginia began a new flirtation with Clive Bell and gradually began to replace Violet with this charming, witty male admirer. Clive was a stimulating correspondent with a great interest in Virginia's early writing, and she even trusted him enough to show him incomplete drafts of *The Voyage Out*. Her great need and passion for Violet, which had been intense since 1902, finally began to diminish, although their correspondence continued to demonstrate great affection and nostalgia.

Violet disapproved even more of Virginia's proposed move into a shared house at Brunswick Square than she had the first move to Gordon Square; Virginia intended to set up home with three single men (Leonard Woolf, Duncan Grant and Maynard Keynes), a move that would have seemed scandalous in 1908. Characteristically, Violet pushed her own worries aside and continued to offer a listening ear to Virginia, particularly when, during 1910, Virginia suffered a short, milder resurgence of her 1904 breakdown. Gradually, though, Violet's own letters became less frequent, prompting a worried Virginia to enquire as to why Violet never seemed to answer her letters any more. It seems she still expected to receive Violet's full attention, whilst neglecting to return it in quite the same way.

Virginia's short period of illness in 1910 did not develop into the full horror of her previous bout, although she was required to spend six weeks in a nursing home. She had good reasons to try and maintain her health – the first novel was progressing well, and she was due to marry Leonard Woolf, which she wrote to tell Violet about in 1912. Her letter is full of anxious requests for Violet to approve this match (which she did). After the wedding, Violet, eager as ever to help, sent Virginia the well-intentioned gift of a cradle, but Virginia's precarious state of health during 1912 led Leonard, in conjunction with her doctors, to decide that having a baby would be a serious threat to her health.

In late July 1913, having delivered the typescript of *The Voyage Out* to Gerald Duckworth, Virginia's mental health began to spiral down-wards again, and she was sent back to the nursing home for a fortnight. But it was not until she left there to return home to London that illness struck again with full force: on 9 September, after a disastrous holiday in Somerset, Virginia took an overdose of veronal and was sent to recover at George Duckworth's spacious estate, Dalingridge Place. Violet's concern can be interpreted from reading the letter sent to 'My dear Miss Dickinson' from Jean Thomas, the proprietor of the private nursing home where Virginia had previously recuperated:

> Virginia and Leonard are at Mr George Duckworth's with two nurses and all seems to be going as quietly as can be expected at present. It was a huge dose of veronal medicine she took at Brunswick Square and she was only saved by a stomach pump being used at once. It is the novel which has broken her up. She finished it and got the proofs back for correction and suddenly couldn't sleep and thought everyone would jeer at her . . . it was all heart-rending . . . they will blame Sir George [Savage] probably but they have never really done what he advised except get married. And the marriage brought more good than anything else till the collapse came from the book and as the doctors say, it might have come to such a delicate, brilliant creature after such an effort however much care and wisdom had been shown. But one just aches and aches because of it all and it is so sad that you too must suffer for her – this friend of yours.[17]

Virginia spent most of 1914 recuperating, then at the beginning of 1915, she turned thirty-three. Suddenly, with less warning, another attack of illness came on in mid-February, culminating in a more severe and violent breakdown on 4 March. With Virginia in a local nursing home from 25 March onwards, Leonard organized the move to Hogarth House in Richmond. Virginia was installed there with four nurses to look after her. Again, an illustration of how badly she had been affected, and of how concerned Violet must have been, can be found in Jean Thomas's 1915 letter to Violet:

> It has been a very sad time with Virginia. She has been about as low as possible, and has had three nurses constantly in attendance, also Leonard's undivided attention and devotion and a great part of the time a very clever, wise doctor, Mr Fergusson working under Mr W. Craig.

She has not been here – indeed I have not seen her since her mind gave way, it seemed best to leave the nurses to be worked by Leonard and Dr Fergusson . . . Virginia went into a local nursing home with her 3 nurses while Leonard moved from their rooms into Hogarth House. Then when all was straight a week ago, Virginia was moved into their own house. She was excited by the move but is quieter now and really getting better, they think. But her mind seems to be played out and simple as it apparently has never been before.[18]

By 1916, Virginia had recovered and was never to suffer such a severe breakdown again, until the beginnings of a serious attack led her to end her life in 1941. Her friendship with Violet faded over the years until their contact was very sporadic, but Violet never failed to write letters of appreciation on the publication of each of Virginia's novels. In 1924, Dickinson called *Jacob's Room* 'exquisite', and in 1927, after *To The Lighthouse* had been published, she wrote predicting that Virginia would deservedly be swamped in 'adulation', 'praise' and 'appreciation'. Violet's comments did not mean as much as they once had to Virginia. In 1933, on seeing Violet Dickinson and Nelly Cecil walking towards her unexpectedly, Virginia went so far as to *hide* from the two old ladies, one of whom she had once loved so passionately.

There were still some occasional teasing references to the past in their correspondence. In 1937, Virginia wrote to Violet enquiring 'am I right in saying that to be 6 ft tall in the age of Q[ueen] Victoria was equivalent to having an illegitimate child?',[19] and in 1938, she complained jokingly that 'only the village idiot' ever wrote to her about her books. As a gift, Violet typed out all of Virginia's letters to herself and sent them, neatly bound, for her to keep. Virginia was touched, but very embarrassed to see so many examples of her early writing spread out anew before her now highly critical eye.

Violet admired Virginia's biography of Roger Fry in 1940 and wrote to tell her so. Scrawling back from Monk's House, with an air raid going on overhead, Virginia replied to explain that she had not managed to get Roger's 'charm' into the work, which she much regretted. This letter is the last extant from Virginia to Violet. After reminiscing fondly about their time at Fritham in 1902, she ends her letter with the invitation 'and so one day let us meet'.[20] That day, sadly, was never to be realized.

*

Virginia's friendship with Violet could be categorized as a 'romantic' one, which in the Victorian era would have consisted of a passionate and intense companionship, involving an enormous interlinking in each other's lives and often daily contact, as well as the sharing of intimate confidences and private desires. These relationships were commonplace and considered healthy in the late nineteenth and twentieth centuries, but if the language that flows through Virginia's letters to Violet is analysed today, it takes on a different meaning, often proclaimed to be unashamedly lesbian in tone.

Books such as *Virginia Woolf, Lesbian Readings* (Barrett and Cramer, New York University Press, 1977) see this relationship as a 'warm-up' for the later one between Virginia and Vita Sackville-West. The many animal references to wallabies and kangaroos in Virginia's letters to Violet are taken not merely as terms of a deep love or a nurturing, mother/child protection, but as the language of total ecstasy. In *Surpassing the Love of Men*, Lillian Faderman has argued that 'ecstasy' within a romantic friendship at the turn of the twentieth century was not necessarily achieved through sexual activity:

> These romantic friendships were love relationships in every sense except perhaps the genital ... thus they might kiss, fondle each other, sleep together, utter expressions of overwhelming love and promises of eternal faithfulness, and yet see their passions as nothing more than effusions of the spirit.[21]

Faderman goes on to discuss Victorian women's commonplace 'deep-rooted antipathy' towards heterosexuality, feelings caused by the risks of childbirth and the knowledge that to love a man 'meant pain and burdens and potential death'. Virginia undoubtedly had experienced this emotion, in the wake of what happened to her exhausted mother and submissive, pregnant half-sister. With other *women*, though, a woman could inhabit 'the same sphere and she could be entirely trusting and unrestrained'.[22]

Moreover, women such as Virginia, who were ambitious and sought to make a name for themselves in a particular field, would have searched for a 'kindred spirit to appreciate their achievements and sympathise with them for the coldness with which the world greeted their efforts . . . such a relationship was thus charged with a warmth, a fervor, a passion that went beyond simple friendship'.[23] Women who lived 'by their brains' needed a 'profound friendship' that extended through 'every phase and aspect of life, intellectual, social, pecuniary'.[24] As the first true critic of Virginia's early work, Violet certainly fulfilled the role of 'kindred spirit'.

Whether or not the two women experimented in what would today be termed a 'sexual' way is hard to prove, although there can be little misinterpretation of the sentence 'it is astonishing what depths – what volcano depths – your finger has stirred in Sparroy', written by Virginia to Violet in July 1903. It is probable that, on occasion, the two women shared a bed – in the early years of their friendship, Virginia makes written allusions to having a double bed ready in anticipation of Violet's visit to join her on holiday. Virginia's reminiscences in letters to Violet shortly before her death recall 'all kind of scenes' up in the bedroom at 22 Hyde Park Gate. It is clear that Virginia much preferred the company of Violet to that of any man in her life – in an early letter in which she demands a 'hot' reply from Violet, Virginia outlines her idea for a play, all about a man and a woman who grow up almost but never quite meeting each other in the flesh.[25] The dramatic divide between the Virginia who loved and revered women, and the Virginia who had seen the damaging effects of heterosexual love on those she had loved and lost, is clearly illustrated in the outline of this unwritten play.

Regardless of the question marks that still hang over the exact nature of their early relationship, there can be no denying that Violet was the first true emotional and physical love of Virginia's early adult life. Whether Virginia knew that she was 'in love' at the time is hazy – Quentin Bell states that it is 'clear to the modern reader, though it was not at all clear to Virginia, that she was in love and that her love was returned'.[26]

Virginia's death in 1941 brought to an end a long, loyal and important friendship between two women. By the time Virginia's body had been found, Violet was feeling 'utterly thankful' that Virginia was finally out of misery and away from illness. Her letters to Vanessa continued to offer support and advice, never failing to mention some anecdote or other concerning Virginia, often with admiration and always with love and pride.

In 1945, three years before her death, Violet retreated into virtual isolation at Burnham Wood. With a broken hip and struggling to see the best in a 'melancholy world', she reminisced to Vanessa about the Hyde Park Gate of the 1880s and 1890s, remembering Julia's beauty, Stella's saintly nature, the shy and awkward young Virginia who wouldn't look her in the eye, and the gloomy atmosphere of the house, which Violet had been forever trying to brighten up. The ghosts of the past returned to haunt her – she was still pondering, in 1942, the exact cause of Stella's death in 1897, and on getting rid of an old bureau, she came across a bundle of letters from Vanessa, which brought back vivid memories of Virginia's illness in her care during the dreadful summer of 1904.

Violet continued to write with great warmth and gratitude to Leonard and Vanessa, and informed the latter of her almost childlike pleasure as she waited to receive her copy of Virginia's *Death of the Moth* (published posthumously in 1941). She continued to visit her own family home at Kingweston in Somerset, where her second cousin Joy remembers her as 'a charming elderly lady, tremendously interested in one branch of the family which she was researching . . . she was forever plying my mother with all sorts of questions in the back of the car'. Joy goes on to recall that 'my brother and I were impressed by the long black jumper & skirt, possibly the sort of garb favoured by the intellectuals and the Bloomsbury set'.[27] Violet's long and detailed history of the Dickinson family still exists today, in the possession of her relatives at the Dower House in Kingweston.

In her last surviving letter to Vanessa Bell, Violet remarked that it was a great nuisance becoming deaf, but with typical selflessness, her last line exhorted that 'the one comfort is never to pity oneself'.[28] Throughout Virginia's life, Violet had provided endless interest, support and care, remaining loyal and concerned whilst managing to retain her great independence and self-respect. She had given Virginia her first taste of enduring, heartfelt love and helped her to launch her writing career. She had shaped the young Virginia Stephen's way of thinking and was a highly influential role model: a woman who had built a 'room of her own' and lived the life of her choosing.

In 1948, Violet Dickinson, Virginia's truly loyal friend, whose great pleasure in life had been to look after the Stephen girls, died, with dignity, just as she had lived. She was eighty-three.

Julia Margaret Cameron, 1870. Combining marriage with a successful career as a pioneering photographer, she was an early role model for her great-niece, Virginia

Julia Duckworth Stephen and Vanessa Stephen, 1883. The effect of Julia's first bereavement, combined with the exhaustion from bringing up eight children and working with the poor, clearly shows here. She was in fact only thirty-seven when this photograph was taken

Julia Duckworth Stephen and Adeline Virginia Stephen, 1884. Adeline was known from birth as 'Virginia', 'Ginny' or 'Ginia' to her family

Virginia and Thoby Stephen at Hindhead House, Haslemere, August 1896. Thoby, the adored elder brother, died of typhoid in 1906. Here, both children are wearing black armbands in mourning for Julia who had died the previous year

Stella Duckworth and Jack Hills at Hindhead House, Haslemere, August 1896. The couple had become engaged during this holiday. On the ground at their feet lie two gold wedding rings, clearly visible when the photograph is enlarged

Virginia Stephen, aged fourteen, on the roof of Hindhead House, Haslemere, August 1896. As a teenager, Virginia rarely looked directly into the camera lens. The house and balcony, once owned by Professor John Tyndall, still survive today, but new houses take up the grounds in a modern cul-de-sac

With her sister, Vanessa Stephen, in Boulogne, France, November 1896. This holiday was a treat from the Duckworth brothers and the girls were chaperoned by their Aunt Minna

At The Old Rectory, Painswick, Gloucestershire, August 1897. The shock of Stella's sudden death, only three weeks previously, is visible in Virginia's face. The two walking sticks beneath her feet suggest that she was rather frail herself

Virginia at Warboys Rectory, Huntingdonshire, 1899. Virginia kept a journal, markedly more mature in style, during this holiday. Returning from this holiday must have been a mixed blessing. George and Gerald Duckworth were exerting pressure on Virginia and Vanessa; they expected the motherless sisters to accompany them to an endless round of parties and dinners

At the Manor House, Ringwood, summer 1898. Virginia did not keep much of a diary for this year, but was recovering from the aftermath of Julia and Stella's death. Here, on holiday with the family, she reads a daily newspaper

Group at Netherhampton House, Salisbury, August 1903. Virginia is shown as a fully-fledged member of Edwardian society. She sits on the ground with a book. Vanessa stands to the right, and Thoby stretches his arms behind his head. This was the last holiday that included Leslie Stephen – he died of cancer in 1904

Violet Dickinson at Burnham Wood, 1904. Violet cared for Virginia in this house during her long illness that same year. As an independent, single woman who had 'built a house of her own', Violet may have sown the seeds that were to grow into *A Room of One's Own* many years later

Ottoline Morrell, 1904. Often misunderstood and mocked by various members of the Bloomsbury Group, Ottoline and Virginia only grew close towards the end of Ottoline's life

Virginia Stephen and Julian Bell at Blean, near Canterbury, 1910. Although Virginia is clearly enjoying her nephew, this photograph was in fact taken during a period when she had suffered a less serious relapse of her 1904 breakdown

Vanessa Bell, 1914, by Ray Strachey. It is likely that this was taken at Wittering where Mary Hutchinson had a holiday home, Eleanor House. Vanessa liked this part of the world, and also rented a holiday home at Bosham during 1915. Her love for Duncan Grant was growing, and her affair with Roger Fry was coming to an end, during this period

Katherine Mansfield, 1920. Virginia was always both repelled and fascinated by Katherine. Successful and talented, yet terminally ill and miserable, Katherine proved to be Woolf's only literary rival. They shared much in common professionally – enough for Woolf to be envious of Katherine's writing achievements

Vita Sackville-West with Nigel and Ben at Sissinghurst Castle, 1924. Vita came to be one of the most important people in Virginia's life. After their brief affair had come to an end, Vita remained a good friend and support, and Virginia restored Vita's beloved Knole to her by writing *Orlando*

Carrington and Lytton Strachey at Ham Spray, 1928. The devoted Carrington was only to have a couple of more years' happiness with Lytton after this photograph was taken. His cancer led to her devastating suicide in 1932

Ethel Smyth, 1901. Whilst many photographs depict Ethel as the square-jawed, masculine old woman that she grew into, this one shows the fiery spirit of a militant suffragette. Virginia admired Ethel's ability to write and compose with individuality and flair; Ethel admired Virginia's feminist beliefs and inspired much of the material that Woolf used in *The Years* and *Three Guineas*

Virginia Woolf, 1925. This was the year when Virginia's affair with Vita was at its most intense and passionate

4   Ottoline and Katherine

Lady Ottoline Morrell, not always discriminating about people, recognised the uniqueness of Virginia Woolf.[1]

Towards the latter part of 1908, Virginia's friendship with Violet Dickinson was cooling considerably. Now living at Fitzroy Square with her brother Adrian, Virginia's confidence was beginning to grow, both personally and professionally. Her need for Violet was diminishing, but her desire to be admired was as intense as ever. Who better, then, to enter her life at this time than Lady Ottoline Morrell, aristocrat and aspiring literary hostess, with a penchant for entertaining and a glamorous home in Bedford Square, within five minutes of Virginia's own house?

Ottoline Violet Anne Cavendish Bentinck was infamous as a society hostess. Those who have only seen her portrait as painted by Simon Bussy in 1920, showing the grotesquely jutting chin, long nose and small, piercing eyes under a blanket of coppery hair, will have gone away with the impression that Ottoline was some kind of witch; it might have been difficult to believe that the beautiful Stephen sisters could have wanted to spend much time with this odd-looking woman. The portrait is an unkind caricature – Ottoline was, in fact, much sought after in her youth, possessing an unusual beauty and considered a 'good catch', admired by many distinguished suitors for her honesty and raucous sense of humour.

Ottoline was born at East Court, Hampshire on 16 June 1873, the daughter of General Arthur Bentinck, heir to the Fifth Duke of Portland, and August Bentinck, his 39-year-old Irish wife. Ottoline was close to her father, whose health was already failing when she was born; even at the age of four, on hearing of his death, the little girl had suddenly become aware of the fragility and futility of life, and as an adult, Ottoline remembered exactly how she had felt at that moment: 'I should also one day die and go out into the unknown'.[2]

Ottoline's half-brother, Arthur, became the heir to the Duke of Portland, and in December 1879, he, Ottoline, their brothers and their mother (newly titled Lady Bolsover) were driven in style to stately Welbeck Abbey in Nottinghamshire. From that day onwards, Ottoline was obliged to grow up in a huge, cold and lonely home. Fortunately, the new Duke's inheritance included Bolsover Castle, a half-hour drive from Welbeck, and here, in a smaller and more intimate atmosphere, Ottoline developed a passion for interior design and furnishing. Many years later she used what she saw at Bolsover in her country home, Garsington, in Oxford. This happy time was also to be cut short: Arthur married and Ottoline's mother had to leave Bolsover to the young Duke and Duchess. She took Ottoline with her, and they moved into a charming house, St Anne's Hill, in Chertsey, but the relationship between mother and daughter began to go sour. Lady Bolsover became an obsessive invalid, terrified of being left alone, and her daughter, now aged sixteen, was expected to spend every night sleeping in the same room.

Alone and afraid, Ottoline threw herself into religion for comfort, giving up food, pretty clothes and any book that wasn't Christian in content. Her own health plummeted; the Duke and Duchess of Welbeck were appalled by her tired appearance and took her around London for a long season of parties and society events. This failed to have any positive effect, and eventually Ottoline and her mother went to recuperate in Italy. However, they both fell ill and Ottoline was sent to stay with her Aunt Louise in Florence. Here, Ottoline's lifelong love affair with Italian architecture began, but it was rudely interrupted when she was forced to return to London with her ailing mother.

At nineteen years old, Ottoline sat helplessly and watched her mother die over the following two months. With both parents now dead, she was taken back to the family home at Welbeck Abbey and immediately began a desperate search for a surrogate father figure, starting with the Archbishop of York and moving on to a disastrous love affair with Axel Munthe, a rich doctor in his forties. Eventually, and by now showing signs of her great and unusual beauty, Ottoline gave herself a strict talking-to and took herself off to Oxford, where she became an out-student at Somerville College, studying history and political economy.

One day, cycling to college dressed all in white with her red hair blazing, she caught the eye of Philip Morrell, a solicitor. They struck up a vague friendship, but Ottoline was still determined to find her father figure, and this solicitor, however charming and friendly, seemed too young. Philip pursued Ottoline for a further two years and proposed twice, but her hesitant letters to him (strongly resembling Virginia Woolf's own to Leonard after she had accepted *his* proposal) reveal that she had grave doubts about the physical side of their relationship. She worried, on paper, that platonic love would not be enough to keep Philip happy, and admitted that she did want to share a life with him – but one based on affection and trust rather than passion. Unexpectedly, the roles were reversed immediately after their honeymoon; Philip suddenly admitted that he found it hard to be sexually attracted to *her*. This was a shock to Ottoline, but it did not affect the immense loyalty that they both had to the marriage, which stood the test of time and was strong enough to survive their considerably involved love affairs with other people.

In August 1905, Ottoline discovered, without much joy, that she was pregnant. She was somewhat cheered by the task of finding a new house, eventually settling upon 44 Bedford Square, Bloomsbury (a few streets away from 46 Gordon Square, where Vanessa and Virginia Stephen were hosting their 'Thursday Evenings'). Ottoline was not yet, at this stage of her life, interested in the arts or in being surrounded by literary people, but instead with designing a large and pretty house in London for herself, Philip and the expected first child. On 18 May 1906, Ottoline in fact became the mother of twins, but after two days, the little boy died of a brain haemorrhage. Ottoline was operated on in a nursing home shortly afterwards, and returned home to cope with her one remaining baby, daughter Julian. Mother and child did not bond well, and the little girl endured an upbringing mainly at the hands of various nurses and governesses while her mother and later her father embarked upon love affairs that took up most of their time.

In December 1908, Virginia Stephen mentioned to Violet that Lady Ottoline Morrell was coming for tea at Fitzroy Square. Little other mention is made of Ottoline until January 1909, when Virginia wrote to Ottoline in a style markedly different from that of her easy, familiar letters to Violet. Her one-paragraph letter to Ottoline gushes with false pleasure, begging Ottoline to become her new friend and citing 'shyness' as her reason for not going into further, flattering detail. Teasingly, egotistically, Virginia then taunted Violet Dickinson with the news that Ottoline was becoming very fond of her and that it was extremely pleasant to receive Ottoline's adoration, which she compared to sitting under a huge lily, absorbing pollen like a seduced bee. Vanessa Bell always believed Ottoline to be bisexual, and Morrell did indeed seem entranced by Virginia:

> This strange, lovely, furtive creature never seemed to me to be made of common flesh and blood. She comes and goes, she folds her cloak around her and vanishes, having shot into her victim's heart a quiverful of teasing arrows.[3]

Ottoline, thirty-six years old in 1909, began to entertain Virginia and her friends at Bedford Square or, occasionally, Peppard Cottage, the Morrells' weekend retreat in the country. The Bloomsbury Group presented a challenge to this eccentric woman, and she to them with her colourful clothes, strange singsong voice and strong religious faith. The group fell upon her with glee, most of them proclaiming her to be dual-natured for professing religious devotion whilst simultaneously admitting to her indiscreet love affairs. However Virginia, present at many of these evenings, was far guiltier of duplicity of nature than Ottoline; she kept up a bizarre, flattering courtship in her letters to Ott, until the latter mistakenly believed herself to have acquired a true friend. Meanwhile, in other letters to Vanessa, Lytton and her cousin Madge Vaughan, Virginia slated Ottoline, whom she declared had the 'head of a Medusa' but was 'simple and innocent' in spite of this unfortunate physical handicap.

Not all of the 'Bloomsberries' were so critical of Ottoline: Roger Fry, who had accepted a large sum of money from her towards help for his mentally ill wife, was grateful to and began to fall in love with Ott, although she hardly seemed to notice. Lytton Strachey also, fell under her spell, and he lived for a while at Peppard Cottage, jealously sharing Ottoline's time with her new lover, Henry Lamb. Duncan Grant, the only member of the group unable to be malicious, saw past Ottoline's unusual appearance to the good-natured soul beneath and became her dear and trusted friend for over thirty years. But something within Virginia made it impossible for her, during the first twenty years of knowing Ottoline, to be either at ease or entirely natural in her company. Although Virginia was always keen to make friends with members of the aristocracy, something about Ottoline's physical appearance disturbed her. This curious mixture of attraction and revulsion resulted in a rollercoaster of emotions, displayed in letters in such a way as to show their author in an unattractive light. Ottoline, despite her grand background and constant stream of willing takers for her generous hospitality, was lonely for genuine friendship and offered it to Virginia, only to be left with this memory of a hurtful rejection:

> She seemed to feel certain of her own eminence. It is true, but it is rather crushing, for I feel she is very contemptuous of other people. When I stretched out a hand to feel another woman, I found only a very lovely, clear intellect.[4]

With the physical side of her marriage to Philip in decay, and the fluctuating emotions of the Bloomsbury Group to contend with, Ottoline looked elsewhere for comfort and attention. She did not have to look far – in September 1909, Logan Pearsall-Smith, a keen liberal who was involved in the forthcoming general election, brought his brother-in-law, Bertrand Russell, to meet the Morrells. Bertie Russell was already trapped in a marriage to a woman, Alys, whom he no longer much desired; his predicament was therefore similar to Ottoline's. Although not physically attractive, Russell, small, dark and with a twinkle in his eye, charmed Ottoline with his 'great wit and humour'.[5] These two unique characters were to meet again shortly afterwards, at a dinner party, where Bertie suddenly turned to Ottoline and told her all about his troubled marriage. The timing was not right, however, since Ottoline was by now involved with the complex, highly emotional artist, Henry Lamb.

Lamb was everything, at least physically, that Russell was not. He was an Adonis, with curly blond hair, a slim figure and a unique way of dressing in old-fashioned silk or velvet garments. He sported a gold earring and had a playful sense of humour. When he was in a good mood he proved an enchanting and alluring companion for Ottoline, but when he was depressed and bad-tempered, it took all of her natural patience and love to see them both through these difficult periods. Ottoline, always fascinated by artistic people, fell deeply in love with Lamb to the point where her feelings bordered on obsession. He, in turn, became moody and churlish if she did not give him all of her time and attention. Ottoline moved him into Peppard Cottage, along with her devoted Lytton, who was also under the Lamb spell. There was no privacy, and hordes of guests streamed down by train every weekend, expecting to be entertained. Ottoline's enjoyment of her country cottage began to decrease, and she eventually asked Roger Fry to help her find another, larger home.

A visitor who *was* welcome, despite the fact that she still mocked Ottoline behind her back in letters, was Virginia Stephen, and she stayed for a weekend in December 1910. This time, Ottoline recorded in her diary that she had enjoyed Virginia's company more than on previous occasions, perhaps this was because Virginia, who had endured another spell in a nursing home earlier in the year, was humbler and less abrasive than usual during this period of recuperation. The two women had much in-depth conversation of the sort that Ottoline enjoyed most:

> She feels artists are 'rather brutes', that literature and poetry are much finer. I thought Virginia wonderful, and much more natural and full-blooded and human than when I saw her last. Her lovely intellectual imagination is like a bird – a swallow flying over life with sword-like wings.[6]

But, tellingly, Ottoline cannot resist bemoaning 'how hard it is to accept people as they are, not as one wants them to be'.

She continued to try and accept Henry Lamb for who *he* was until March 1911, when after an innocent note from Bertrand Russell informing Ottoline that he intended to call in on her at Bedford Square, Ottoline found herself catapulted into the most important and passionate affair of her life. Philip was away, and Ethel Sands and Ralph Hawtrey, the only other guests, had left early. Ottoline and Bertie sat up all of that night pouring out their hearts to one another, avoiding physical contact but finding enough in common for Bertie to voice immediately the wish that neither of them were married to other people.

Their affair, which lasted for the next five years, was beset with problems and imbalances from the start. Ottoline still allowed Philip to make love to her on the rare occasions he wanted to do so; he was being indiscreet with a number of young girls anyway (among them, members of the Morrells' own household). Bertie, on his frequent trips abroad, met and slept with other women, but some invisible attachment to Ottoline was to bring him back time after time. It was always Ottoline who threatened to end the relationship, and so they would get stuck in patterns of enforced silences and absences, which would be broken by a miserable Bertrand begging to see her, professing undying love. Their letters flew back and forth and knew no restraint. Bertie eventually left Alys, his wife, after a bitter and nasty feud, but Ottoline would not even contemplate leaving Philip. Her marriage meant too much to her, and Philip had started suffering from periods of mental instability, which meant that he had a greater need for his wife's love and support.

There were changes afoot in Ottoline's other friendships during the period 1911–1912. Roger Fry, until now her devoted and appreciated friend, angrily and unfairly accused her of spreading rumours abroad concerning his love for her. Shocked and confused, Ottoline found herself cut off by the majority of the Bloomsbury Group, although Virginia wrote to her in June 1912 to report details of her forthcoming marriage to Leonard Woolf, and Lytton continued to visit her using her as a crutch for his emotional problems and self-doubts. The rift with Roger was not healed until 1928 and it saddened Ottoline greatly to have lost his trust and friendship. In addition to these distressing events, Ottoline's daughter Julian developed tuberculosis and had to attend a clinic in Switzerland, and Philip was starting to suffer from more disturbing episodes of 'nervous illness', the term that doctors used in those days to refer to any sort of mental imbalance.

A picture of Ottoline painted during 1913 by her dear friend Duncan Grant makes a striking contrast compared with Simon Bussy's wicked caricature of her. Although Grant cannot resist playing up the plumage in her hat, the sharpness of her jutting chin, and her brightly coloured hat, he manages to convey subduedness in the darkness of Ottoline's dress; something in her demeanour portrays great melancholy, and her eyes have a worried expression. It is a sympathetic and mature portrait by a man who was always quick to leap to Ottoline's defence. Ottoline was beset with doubts about her own worth at around the time of Grant's portrait; she wrote to Virginia expressing admiration for the younger woman's beauty and genius, admitting that she felt, in comparison, 'utterly tedious' and 'old, antiquated and heavy'.[7]

In 1914, Ottoline was introduced to the shy young artist Dora Carrington, and to the writer D.H. Lawrence, who had just published a book of short stories. Lawrence, in turn, introduced Ottoline to the writer Katherine Mansfield. These new friendships soon found the perfect venue to develop, for in 1915, Ottoline and Philip took Garsington Manor in Oxford, as their country home. Ottoline was attracted by the garden's formal Italianate design, and only one month after moving in, the Morrells had already gone a significant way towards creating the magnificent gardens that still remain today. Here, in a long series of weekend visits, the Bloomsbury Group mixed (or tried not to) with other writers, artists, politicians and intellectuals.

Ottoline transformed the rooms inside Garsington into a rich panoply of colour and comfort. The Red Room had gold-edged panelling, the entrance hall was full of soft Persian rugs, and the guest bedrooms were tastefully furnished with books, desks and marble washstands. During the First World War, Garsington became a refuge for a variety of visitors, all of whom expected Ottoline somehow to exceed her meagre food allowance in order to keep them well fed and warm. Between the years 1915 and 1928, those who passed through Garsington's beautiful front entrance included Aldous Huxley, Clive Bell, Leonard and Virginia Woolf, Katherine Mansfield, Dorothy Brett, Dora Carrington, Lytton Strachey, D.H. Lawrence, G. Lowes Dickinson, T.S. Eliot, Thomas Hardy, E.M. Forster, Siegfried Sassoon, W.B. Yeats and many others. Among the list of distinguished politicians, dignitaries, royalty, aristocrats and economists can be found the names of H.H. Asquith, Maynard Keynes, Bertrand Russell, the Duke of York (later George VI), Vita Sackville-West and Harold Nicolson.

In April 1917, Ottoline again tentatively held out the hand of friendship towards Virginia, whom she had not seen since the Woolfs' marriage in 1912. The breakdown of relations with Roger Fry had caused a rift and cessation of correspondence, but Virginia seemed genuinely pleased to hear from Ottoline, and accepted an invitation to tea at Bedford Square. On this occasion, an admiring Ottoline recounted the following impression of her friend:

> She entered with such energy and vitality and seemed to me far the most imaginative and masterly intellect that I had met for many years.[8]

As usual, the illusion was shattered soon afterwards, when Virginia paid her first visit to Garsington, where she 'sat on a throne and took it for granted that we should worship'.[9] Ottoline much preferred the company of Lytton, whom she decided was more 'rational' and 'real' than Virginia.

Despite Ottoline's reservations, Virginia seemed to enjoy her first and subsequent visits to Garsington, if her effusive letters of thanks are to be believed. Much of the best evidence for this is preserved not in letters, but in the photographs that Ottoline took of Virginia in conversation with Lytton Strachey, Philip, and G. Lowes Dickinson. They are among the most interesting and revealing photographs ever taken of Virginia 'in flight'; Ottoline has perfectly captured the writer in animated conversation, hands clasped together, eyes thrown heavenward, or caught her gossiping with great enjoyment whilst the trademark cigarette dangles from her lip. In one photograph, Virginia is seen in thoughtful profile, head bent over a book, spectacles perched on her aquiline nose. In these pictures, she is shown at the peak of her personal and professional life. Around her 'throne', famous literary figures sit at her feet in rapt attention and devotion, watching as she spirals into one of her imaginary, witty, flights of fancy. There is no doubt that Virginia enjoyed her visits to Garsington greatly and felt 'in her element' amongst the other guests. Sadly, there is also much evidence to suggest that Ottoline was not only irritated, but also disappointed and bewildered by Virginia's obvious arrogance upon these occasions.

Although their reunion in 1917 had got off to a shaky start, Virginia and Ottoline finally began to grow closer. Virginia was now thirty-five, had recently recovered from her longest period of breakdown yet (1913–1915), and was entering a productive, happy period of her life. Ottoline needed and appreciated the renewed friendship with Virginia, because Philip was becoming increasingly unwell (a plight that Virginia, no stranger to mental illness, showed much sympathy for). Also, Ott's affair with Bertrand Russell had finally come to an end. Russell never underestimated the positive effect that the affair with Ottoline had had on him; in his autobiography he noted that 'she cured me of the belief that I was seething with appalling wickedness' and admitted that she had made him 'less self-centred and self-righteous'. Although Ottoline occupies a scant four pages of his memoirs and is, in one part, said to have had a face resembling a horse, Russell does pay tribute to the 'deep sympathy between us which never ceased as long as she lived'.[10] His descriptions of Ottoline's appearance would have hurt her, though, had she lived long enough to read the autobiography. However, even Russell's insensitivity would have paled in comparison to the semi-fictional portraits of Ottoline that were about to be painted by two young men whom she had counted among her most intimate friends.

Ottoline met D.H. Lawrence and his wife Frieda as a couple for the first time in January 1915. Although she did not like Frieda, thinking her coarse and ill-mannered, she grew fond of Lawrence and, as was her way, tried to help him with his writing by supporting him emotionally and financially. She stuck by him when his novel, *The Rainbow*, was banned for its lewd content. She allowed him to bring his unsuitable friends to Garsington, many of whom repelled her and insisted on playing childish dressing-up games on the lawn.

Lawrence was untrustworthy from the start, sucking up to Ottoline and then viciously ripping her character to shreds behind her back to Dorothy Brett and Katherine Mansfield. Virginia, too, had been guilty of this behaviour for many years, but she never intended her digs at Ottoline to be for general consumption, confining them instead to her letters and private diaries. Lawrence took the unpleasantness to unacceptable limits; shortly before Christmas 1916, Ottoline gained access to the manuscript of his new novel, *Women in Love*. On reading it, she was extremely shocked and hurt at the crass portrayal of herself that was thinly disguised in the character of Hermione Roddice:

> She was impressive, in her lovely pale-yellow and brownish-rose, yet macabre, something repulsive. Her long pale face, that she carried lifted up, somewhat in the Rossetti fashion, seemed almost drugged, as if a strange mass of thought coiled in the darkness within her, and she was never allowed to escape.[11]

Hermione is described as 'bullying' and as having a singsong voice. Her interest in books is ridiculed, as are her clothes, which are described as being 'dirty dresses' like those worn by an 'old hag'. The fictional house featured in *Women in Love* is clearly based on Garsington. Ottoline was furious and at the same time desperately worried that there might be some truth in this unkind portrait. She at first tried to lay the blame at Frieda Lawrence's door, but there was no evidence to suggest that Frieda had collaborated as closely with her husband on this book as she supposedly had on *Sons and Lovers*. Lawrence was, somewhat naïvely, surprised at Ottoline's adverse reaction to his book. He had continued to eat her food and accept her gifts while he had been penning these hurtful descriptions. Eventually Philip Morrell went to Lawrence's agent and threatened to bring legal action against any publisher who brought out the book, and Lawrence was unable to have it published in England until May 1921. The intimacy which in retrospect had proved to be one-sided, between Ottoline and D.H. Lawrence ended abruptly until an attempt at reconciliation was made some twelve years later.

Ottoline was often to attract satirists, and at the end of 1921, just after *Women in Love* had finally been published, another trusted friend, Aldous Huxley, revealed an unflattering portrait of her as Priscilla Wimbush in his new book, *Crome Yellow*. Priscilla had a

large square middle-aged face, with a massive projecting nose and little greenish eyes, the whole surmounted by a lofty and elaborate coiffure of a curiously improbable shade of orange.[12]

What incensed Ottoline was not so much these unflattering descriptions of her own appearance – she was getting rather used to them – but the fact that Huxley had incorporated many caricatures of her friends into his book as well. Huxley, like Lawrence, had enjoyed Ottoline's hospitality for many years and even had his own room at Garsington. To find rude and unfunny descriptions of her friends Brett, Carrington, Bertie Russell and Mark Gertler, caused Ottoline to inform Huxley that his book reminded her of 'poor photography', nothing more and nothing less.

By the beginning of 1922, Ottoline was starting to sift out her true friends from the rest of them. She loved, and was loved by, Virginia, Duncan Grant, and Desmond and Molly McCarthy (her many preserved letters to 'Dearest Molly' are touching and genuine in their loyalty and affection). In nearly every one of her letters to these trusted friends, Ottoline begs for a visit or a letter. Virginia and Leonard did make an effort to visit Ott more regularly, and after one particularly memorable weekend at Garsington, Ottoline's note of thanks to Virginia reads like a love letter; humble, self-effacing and, despite the advantages of her aristocratic connections and her imperious manner, demonstrating the insecurity that possessed Ottoline throughout her life:

> I carry with me a most lovely remembrance of that evening – you and the window with the tree behind you and the garden and everything. I felt myself intensely stupid and Leonard – although I love him – frightens me very much and makes me acutely self-conscious.[13]

Alas, again her treasured friend was to let her down; Virginia's *own* interpretation of this evening (in a letter to Roger Fry) was that Ottoline had been 'garish' and that the moonlight, which had provided such an attractive backdrop to Virginia's own beauty as she posed by the window, had shown up Ottoline's face powder rather unflatteringly.

Antipathy had also sprung up between Ottoline and Vanessa Bell, although much effort was made by Virginia and Duncan to dissipate it. Despite this, Virginia continued to write to Ottoline regularly, matter-of-factly remarking in a letter to Barbara Bagenal (24 June 1923) that Ottoline had stripped her of all 'joie de vivre', leaving an unwelcome echo of her drawl and the overpowering scent of dried roses and face powder in her wake. Nonetheless, the two women were still growing closer; Ottoline was impressed by *To the Lighthouse* when it came out in 1927, and wrote Woolf an admiring letter, and Virginia, vividly described by Ottoline at this time as 'a lovely phantom', began to realize that Ottoline suffered appalling headaches and periods of incumbency similar to her own. She wrote back, offering genuine words of comfort and sympathy.

Ottoline's headaches grew worse as she regretfully decided to sell Garsington and live at 10 Gower Street in London; the house was becoming expensive to maintain and the visitors were draining both her energy and the Morrells' finances. In February 1928, all of a sudden she developed a vicious cancer of the jaw, which meant a long stay in hospital and an operation to have her lower teeth extracted and part of her jawbone removed. A postcard to Molly McCarthy written from the Fitzroy Square hospital makes gloomy reading: '*awful, awful* pain – and still it goes on. It has been a nightmare, the pain indescribable'.[14] But far worse than the pain was the indignity of having to live with a seriously disfigured chin, which she did her best to disguise by swathing veils and scarves beneath it, tying them with typical Ottoline flamboyance. The private emotional cost to her must have been immense.

The Bloomsberries, alarmed to find out that Ottoline was not, as they at first thought, merely *playing* the melodramatic hypochondriac, rallied around to try and make amends. Duncan Grant, who had always genuinely cared for her, sent a much-treasured letter of sympathy; Roger Fry shamefacedly tried to make peace after all the years of antipathy; Virginia, always sympathetic towards others' illnesses, wrote a letter that touched Ottoline, who up until this point had still admired Virginia mainly for her intellect rather than her perception. This letter proved to be a great turning point in their friendship and whilst Virginia found it hard to give up poking fun at Ottoline in her letters to friends, she finally began to admire Ottoline's strength and loyalty over and above all her other characteristics. She encouraged Ottoline to start writing her memoirs, and promised to read them and make constructive comments. The two women had already grieved together over the death of Katherine Mansfield in 1923; they now shared an intense and deep grief at the death of Ottoline's 'most loveable' Lytton Strachey in 1932, and the terrible suicide of his partner, Carrington, shortly afterwards. Together with Vanessa Bell, they mourned the huge loss, two years later, of Roger Fry.

Ottoline suffered a stroke in 1937 that paralysed and threatened to kill her. Philip answered Virginia's anxious letter of enquiry not with the truth, but with a false reassurance that Ottoline was in good health – in fact she was dying – and a remarkably tactless request that Virginia should start an affair with him! Virginia refused to give him any more encouragement and there was silence until Ottoline's death on 21 April 1938.

Philip asked Virginia to write an obituary, which she reluctantly did. A service of remembrance was held on 26 April at St Martin-in-the-Fields, London, with an order of service combining a traditional selection of hymns and readings. A biblical quotation, at once inappropriate and yet seeming also to capture something of Ottoline's own preferred phraseology, was printed on the cover:

> I should utterly have fainted but that I believe verily to see the goodness of the Lord in the land of the living.

In dramatic contrast to this service was the 'farewell message' that Philip found amongst Ottoline's papers. Written nearly three years previously, she had left a request that he circulate it amongst her friends if she should die. Hence, Virginia found the following extraordinary document lying on her doormat in December 1938:

> Don't mourn for me, dear friends. When you are quiet and alone remember me kindly, and when you are in a lovely country – in England or Italy or Greece – give an affectionate thought to me who drank in the beauty and the poetry of the lands that you are gazing at.

Furthermore, said Ottoline in her eccentric farewell:

> I should like to call to my side and wave good-bye to the many friends I had in the shops.

She concluded by saying that she did not want her friends to

> send any wreaths for my dead body, but gladden my soul by giving something for a night shelter or a coffee stall for the poor and destitute – those who have no shelter.[15]

Virginia wrote to Margaret Llewelyn Davies shortly after Ottoline's funeral and admitted that she had grown 'very fond' of Ottoline, who in her eyes had become 'shabby and humble and humorous'. But even her much earlier impressions of the woman she had known since 1908, although not always flattering, were often perceptive. Ottoline herself would probably have agreed with Virginia's portrayal of her odd combination of aristocracy and insecurity, immortalized in the character of Mrs Flushing in *The Voyage Out*:

> She had a strongly marked face, her eyes looked straight at you, and though naturally she was imperious in her manner she was nervous at the same time.[16]

In 1916, Lytton Strachey, while staying with Ottoline at Garsington, met the writer Katherine Mansfield. Katherine expressed great enthusiasm for Virginia's *The Voyage Out* and desired to meet the author. This information was duly relayed back to Hogarth House; the Woolfs were looking for new, talented writers to contribute stories to the Hogarth Press, and were keen to commission Katherine.

The first meeting of Virginia Woolf and Katherine Mansfield took place during February 1917 and was seemingly not a success, at least according to Virginia, who related to Vanessa that her visitor had appeared 'hard' and not very pleasant company. The two women met again in June, when Virginia, despite her initial misgivings, invited Katherine to dinner at Hogarth House and listened to her talking about her life and work with growing interest. Katherine submitted *Prelude*, her story about a family moving to the country, told in short sketches through the eyes of one family member after another; it is a long story, related with clarity and humour. The Woolfs were impressed and invited Katherine to stay at Asheham for a long weekend, and there, Virginia and Katherine walked over the South Downs and developed an interest in each other's writing. *Prelude*, on publication, was a great success and sold out very quickly. This pale, striking, dark-haired author was to have a profound impact on Virginia Woolf personally and, more significantly, professionally, over the next six years.

Prelude can be read as an autobiographical sketch of Katherine Mansfield's childhood in New Zealand. It is drawn partly from memory, partly from imagination, and Katherine's mother must have filled in further details because Katherine herself was only five years old at the time of the move. *Prelude* describes, through the eyes of the children and their dissatisfied parents, Mansfield's move from Tinakori Road, in the city, to a country house, Karori. The mother in the story is clearly based on Annie Beauchamp, Katherine's mother, a frustrated, repressed woman who constantly bemoaned her lost opportunities, blaming them partly on Harold, her wealthy husband. Annie, as photographs testify, was very beautiful, but cold and formidable. She was neither a relaxed nor a natural mother, but prided herself instead on good organization of her home and family. The homes were many; by moving house so often, Annie had installed in her middle daughter, Katherine, a lifelong inability to settle down at one address.

Annie's perpetual moves between England and New Zealand meant that the Beauchamp family were constantly split up during Katherine's formative years. Finally, in late 1898, the family settled for a couple of years in Wellington, New Zealand, in a large, elegant white house, typically Victorian in style and feel. The children were predominantly cared for by Granny Dyer, who provided inspiration for Katherine's grandmother character in *Prelude*. The wealthy Beauchamps gave the parties that were to inspire their daughter's famous and evocative story, *The Garden Party*, which memorably details the social stereotyping of that era. Servants did the cooking, cleaning and gardening while Annie Beauchamp entertained her husband's admirers, so Katherine grew up aware of the class divide between herself and the staff who referred to her as 'Miss Katherine'. She attended three schools during the period she lived in New Zealand, and developed a passion for reading from the age of eight, when she proudly wore spectacles that did little to aid her perfect sight.

In 1903, the family uprooted yet again and took the older Beauchamp girls, including Katherine, to Europe, where they were left in the care of relatives from London while their parents returned home to New Zealand. Katherine was enrolled at Queen's College, Harley Street, where she studied French, English, singing and music. Boarding in rooms at the top of the college, she met the girl who was to become a devoted friend for the rest of her life – Ida Baker, melancholy and plain, but gentle and kind. Katherine remembered the three years at school in London with affection in later years, although she reluctantly had to return home to New Zealand in 1906 to face both a dull, constrictive existence with her parents, sisters and little brother, and the death of her beloved grandmother. Initially the Beauchamps were reluctant to indulge Katherine's craving to return to England, but as they began to understand their daughter's potential and see the lack of good colleges and libraries at home, they eventually arranged for her to lodge respectably in Paddington, with an allowance to keep her in some comfort. So, in 1908, Katherine, aged twenty, arrived back in England.

At this stage in her life, the differences between Katherine's existence and that of the 26-year-old Virginia Stephen were many. Katherine had travelled, been embroiled in love affairs both with men and women, been indulged and expected to pleasure-seek by her family, benefited from formal schooling and, as a teenager, enjoyed robust good health. Virginia, on the other hand, had only recently escaped the insular world of 22 Hyde Park Gate, had travelled to Europe infrequently, relied solely on the library of her father for education, stayed chaste despite interest from various suitors, had endured unwanted molestation from her half-brothers, borne the brunt of four close bereavements, and had suffered two episodes of nervous breakdown. She had only one close friend, Violet Dickinson, whose advice and love she craved and desired, always in the knowledge that her feelings were reciprocated. Katherine had *her* close friend, Ida Baker, but usually dismissed poor Ida's efforts to help her, using and then dropping the devoted young woman, safe in the knowledge that Ida would each time come crawling back in the end.

On paper, these differences between Virginia and Katherine, made it seem unlikely that the two would ever meet, but despite their different upbringings, both the thin, nervous Virginia Stephen and the podgy, rebellious Katherine Beauchamp, wanted to break free of the Victorian/Edwardian repressions and limitations that had plagued the two of them since birth. More importantly, each woman had a passion for writing and an all-consuming ambition to succeed in the literary world.

By the time she first met Virginia in 1916, Katherine had changed her surname to 'Mansfield'. It was her middle name, and she thought it a more appropriate name for a writer. She had survived several unsuccessful love affairs, and had even been married briefly to George Bowden in 1909, leaving him shortly afterwards, all the time coping with a gradual decline in health, which manifested itself initially with bouts of peritonitis and gonorrhoea. She had already established herself as a successful author with the inclusion of several short stories in *New Age* magazine. She met John Middleton Murry, editor of a pioneering new literary magazine, *Rhythm*, in 1911, and began an affair with him. This was to be the one serious relationship of her life, although it was by no means conventional and often proved far from idyllic.

Virginia had the security that Katherine envied in her marriage to Leonard Woolf, was living between Richmond and Sussex, had recently recovered from the most serious yet of her breakdowns and had published *The Voyage Out* to considerable acclaim. The first meeting between the Woolfs and Katherine, accompanied by Murry, was not a success; neither couple thought much of the other, and Katherine preferred her subsequent meeting with D.H. Lawrence and his wife, Frieda, with whom she felt relaxed enough to laugh and be irreverent.

Still wary of one another, in 1917, when Katherine and Virginia spent time alone together at Asheham, they discovered that they were working towards similar goals. Virginia, becoming stronger and more ambitious by the day, witnessed the first of Katherine's painful descents into illness, watching her struggle to recover from the rheumatism that delayed the publication of *Prelude*. Virginia quite enjoyed the Asheham visit, but was not enthused, merely remarking to Vanessa that Katherine seemed to have lived an interesting life.

Katherine, meanwhile, was delighted to have spent a weekend indulging in just the sort of conversation she most enjoyed, and so wrote a warm letter of thanks to her hostess:

> It was good to have time to talk to you; we have got the same job, Virginia, and it is really very curious and thrilling that we should both, quite apart from each other, be after so very nearly the same thing.[17]

Ironically, as Katherine began to blossom as a writer and receive serious recognition for her work, her health began to slip away, firstly with a recurrence of gonorrhoea and then with the onset of the tuberculosis that was to kill her. Photographs record her plumpness falling away from her bones, her body becoming gaunt, her eyes looking eerily big and scared in a pale, drawn face. She was forced, by the dangers of wintering in cold England, to go to the south of France, alone and away from Murry. Her letters to him over the next three months reveal her insecurities and her bravery over illness, but also her insensitivity and selfishness. Devoted Ida Baker, arriving in France to help Katherine, was accused of being overweight, greedy and stupid. Indeed, next to Katherine, who existed on nothing other than cigarettes and coffee, it is hardly surprising that anyone else was considered gluttonous by comparison! Katherine's harshness extended into her letters to Murry, where she viciously attacked poor Ottoline Morrell while at the same time sending the subject of this wrath the most flattering, false letters of adoration. This situation was further complicated by the fact that Murry considered himself to be temporarily in love with Ottoline, but all the while kept up the charade of distaste in his replies to Katherine.

After three months in France, during which time she became even more unwell, Katherine decided that the separation from Murry was too painful to bear any longer, and came home. She was to be disappointed at their reunion; Murry, rather than embrace her with the passion she needed, turned his face aside, fearfully covering his mouth to avoid infection.

On 3 May 1918, in Kensington, Murry and Katherine finally got married. They moved to Portland Villas in Hampstead. Virginia received a visit from Katherine shortly after the wedding, and noted that she was deteriorating fast, but claiming to be very happy in her marriage. Despite such claims, Murry was ill and unhappy and Virginia noted that he seemed pale and desperate when the Murrys came to Richmond for dinner in June. Katherine also appeared haunted both by her inability to get pregnant and by the terrifying prospect that she might die, or at the very best, never be properly well again.

Virginia called in at Portland Villas in November 1919 and was shocked to see her friend hobbling about feebly with a body like that of an old woman's. She wrote in her diary that Murry and 'the monster' (Katherine's cruel name for Ida Baker) hung about helplessly, watching and irritating Katherine. Leonard Woolf recalled later on that Katherine, who could be jolly and stimulating company, seemed a different person altogether with Murry, who got on her nerves and encouraged her sharp tongue, bringing to the fore all her most unattractive qualities and making any time spent in the couple's company embarrassing and awkward. Leonard, always a good judge of character, presents us here with a very different, perhaps more valid, picture of Katherine than the one provided by loyal Ida Baker; after all, in Ida's eyes, Katherine could do no wrong. Patient Ottoline, continuing to offer hospitality to Katherine at Garsington, also tired of her guest's unpleasant behaviour:

> I certainly don't think you would have cared for Katherine, who is here now – she is too terribly unmoved – and uncaring – about everything.[18]

Virginia continued to send gifts of flowers and cigarettes to Katherine, keeping up a correspondence that at times proved entirely one-sided. Katherine became unreliable at keeping in touch with Virginia, who was hurt and baffled both by this and by Katherine's stony review of *Night and Day*, which had appeared in the *Athenaeum* during November 1919.

Swallowing her pride, Virginia continued to visit Katherine, although there was a long period of silence between the two women that lasted until the summer of 1920 when Katherine, returning from another winter abroad, allowed Virginia to call in at Portland Villas. Analysing the visit in her diary, Virginia recalled that Katherine had given her a cold welcome and had not expressed any pleasure at seeing her – until the topic of 'solitude' arose, at which point Katherine relaxed, became interested and waxed lyrical on the subject for some time, easing the situation between the two women. That is, until Murry entered the room, when Katherine became derogatory towards him.

Finally the two writers got back onto the topic of literature, and Katherine was now praising *Night and Day*, which further confused Virginia, who was still smarting slightly from the unfavourable published review. All this considered, it must have been a struggle for Virginia to stay loyal for the two years that were left of Katherine's life, but not only did she remain fond of her, she also paid her a high compliment:

> To no one else can I talk in the same disembodied way about writing; without altering my thought more than I alter it in writing here. (I except L [Leonard] from this).[19]

Katherine wrote to Virginia from France, where she returned towards the end of 1920, but only once. It was a warm letter, but even though Virginia wrote again, Katherine never did. Something in her was always to mistrust Virginia and Bloomsbury fundamentally. She moved to Switzerland and then on to Fontainebleau, where she remained until the end of her short life. She choked on her own blood and died only just reconciled with Murry, on 9 January 1923. Virginia, unaware of how ill Katherine had been, mistakenly believed her friend to be making a good recovery abroad.

Although Virginia knew other modernist writers (including T.S. Eliot and James Joyce, whose work she disliked and had refused to publish), her choice of themes and subjects was matched most closely by Katherine Mansfield. For all their differences of character, which were many, their short friendship was both encouraged and enhanced by a mutual commitment to producing superior fiction. They were united by their attitude towards literature, and on this level they had much in common. Both were prodigiously hard-working and prolific, despite being hampered by debilitating health problems; both women fought against their Victorian/Edwardian upbringings to take their writing careers to the forefront of their lives; and they were both married to their own publishers. They had many friendships in common as the two writers were connected, or intimate with, various members of the Bloomsbury Group and also with Ottoline Morrell and D.H. Lawrence.

Although Woolf and Mansfield captured their lost childhoods in their writing and were inspired by their dead relatives, using them to exorcize the pain of hidden grief, each woman still maintained a very distinctive, individual writing style; whilst Mansfield's characters are bold, comic and sometimes undignified, Woolf's appear unfailingly elegant, well spoken and thoughtful. Her fictional characters inhabit lives against a civilized backdrop of books and paintings, whereas Mansfield's characters carry props (such as flowers or handkerchiefs) full of symbolism. But, when Mansfield and Woolf craft their prose to describe scenery, each writer's words seem to mirror and complement the other's. Their use of colour, for example, vividly evokes the seaside holidays of childhood:

The sun was not yet risen and the whole of Crescent Bay was hidden under a white sea-mist. A heavy dew had fallen. The grass was blue. Big drops hung on the bushes and just did not fall; the silvery, fluffy toi-toi was limp on its long stalks, and all the marigolds and the pinks in the bungalow gardens were bowed to the earth with wetness.

'It suddenly gets cold. The sun seems to give less heat,' she said, looking about her, for it was bright enough, the grass still a soft deep green, the house starred in its greenery with purple passion flowers and rooks dropping cool cries from the high blue.

The first passage above is quoted from the short story *At The Bay* (1921) by Katherine Mansfield; the second is from a novel, *To the Lighthouse* (1927), by Virginia Woolf. The shape of the sentences in each extract, the references to temperature, the colours of grass, flower and trees, suggest a kinship in writing that each woman recognized and admired in the other. Often their short stories use similar themes – those that occur most often in both include: Victorian/Edwardian society; the oppression of women; the distress associated with eating and the female body; the hopeless pursuit of heterosexual love; and the minutiae of animal and insect life in parks and gardens.

In The Botanical Gardens (1907) is a short story by Katherine Mansfield where the opening paragraph informs us that

From the entrance gate down the broad central walk, with the orthodox banality of carpet bedding on either side, stroll men and women and children – a great many children, who call to each other lustily, and jump up and down on the green wooden seats.

This passage could easily be followed by the next, from Virginia Woolf's short story *Kew Gardens* (1919):

> The figures of these men and women straggled past the flower-bed with a curiously irregular movement not unlike that of the white and blue butterflies who crossed the turf in zig-zag flights from bed to bed.

Both writers examined the oppressive and shallow world of the society party circuit, Virginia reminiscing in fiction and also in auto-biography about the nightmarish experiences she had whilst attending balls and dinners with the Duckworth brothers. She based stories such as *The Evening Party* (1921) on the literary conversations that she remembered from the visits by Leslie Stephen's friends and colleagues to 22 Hyde Park Gate. She was also to use these themes in her novels, in particular *The Years*, with its Victorian tea-table conventions, *To the Lighthouse*, with the heart of the novel set over the Victorian dinner table, and *Night and Day*, where Katharine Hilbery is forced to choose between her role as hostess and her secret ambition to be a mathematician.

Mansfield used her wealthy family from New Zealand, with their ceaseless hosting of Edwardian luncheons and dinners, as inspiration for various stories, most famously *The Garden Party* (1921). There are also parallels between this and Woolf's *Mrs Dalloway* (1925); each deals with the preparations for a grand party, and each makes much of the contrast between the frivolity of a social scene and the horrific, tortured death of a man that occurs in the midst of all the festivities.

Woolf and Mansfield were acutely aware of the effects of serious illness on the body, and they explored this theme extensively in their fiction. Katherine Mansfield's insecurities about her appearance stemmed from living with a mother who had accused her, as a child, of being overweight. Virginia Woolf's arose from the treatment that she received at the hands of the Duckworth brothers. In their work the two writers repeatedly questioned the female societal role and issues surrounding female identity. At times their stories even had similar titles – Woolf's *The New Dress* (1925) and Mansfield's *New Dresses* (1912) both convey, through the device of clothing, the feelings of conflict between the body's outer appearance and the person's inner emotions. The female protagonists of these stories are only allowed to reveal distress through the motif of dress. Woolf's heroine, Mabel

Waring, cannot bring herself to look at her reflection, fearing herself repulsive (Woolf herself had a lifelong dislike of mirrors, believing herself to be lanky and too tall; she describes this phobia in the 1929 story, *The Lady in the Looking-Glass: A Reflection*). The heroine of Mansfield's story, Helen, has a mother who fails to boost her self-confidence; as a result, Helen creates a false self to appease her mother, finding comfort only in a new dress.

Virginia Woolf and Katherine Mansfield often expressed antagonistic views of heterosexuality in their fiction – anger that was directed particularly towards men and patriarchal oppression. Although their bitter, scornful and, at best, reluctantly affectionate attitudes towards the men they created in fiction were similar, their behaviour towards men in real life was markedly different. Katherine felt superior towards them, and had been promiscuous since her late teens, frequently using men for her own pleasure and then moving on once the initial thrill had faded. She fell in love quickly, but until Murry entered the picture, seemed not to possess the stamina needed to develop a relationship more lasting and meaningful. Even once she was married to Murry, she still envied the settled and caring relationship enjoyed by Virginia and Leonard; the manner in which Leonard provided the stable background crucial to Virginia's prolific output, or how he anxiously protected and nursed her when she was ill. Although Murry did, when the couple were together, express devotion to Katherine and try to look after her when she was unwell, his attentions seemed to bring her little benefit (in fact they caused her intense irritation). Yet during their frequent absences from one another, her letters pour forth full of love, anguish and pleas for him to rejoin her. The relationship, then, could never be like that of Virginia and Leonard, who were compatible friends, confidants and critics of each other's work. Virginia had never been promiscuous, and after a childhood dominated by the overbearing George and Gerald, the gruff, difficult Leslie and the highly sexed Jack Hills, she generally preferred the company of her sister, her women friends, or openly homosexual men such as Lytton Strachey and Duncan Grant. Often she found heterosexual men repulsive, as in fact was the case with Katherine's Murry, whom she once described as 'a posturing, Byronic little man; pale; penetrating; with bad teeth'.[20]

In her short stories, Katherine Mansfield usually portrayed men as the 'baddies', the buffoons who destroyed or threatened a woman's peace of mind. In *At The Bay*, the women of the family rejoice, after the departure of the blustering and demanding Stanley, at 'the relief, the difference it made to have had the man out of the house. Their very voices were changed as they called out to one another'.[21] In *The Lady's Maid*, the maid, who is narrating, reminisces about her fierce grandfather who had shut her fingers in a pair of tongs; she then decides to leave her husband-to-be in order to stay with her female employer, the 'Lady' whom she is in devoted service to. In *The Stranger*, written in 1920 when Mansfield was putting up with Murry's frequent assignations with other women, her heroine, Janey Hammond, returns home reluctantly from a cruise, a voyage of self-discovery, to her weak, over-devoted husband and her suffocating, insubstantial marriage.

Virginia Woolf expressed *her* views on heterosexual men and marriage in several novels, and her men, like Mansfield's, are usually bullies. As with Mansfield, there is much barely repressed anger towards men; Woolf focuses in particular on the peculiar power of the Victorian patriarch. In *The Voyage Out*, her first novel, she asks her readers to 'consider what a bully the ordinary man is . . . the ordinary hard-working, rather ambitious solicitor or man of business with a family to bring up and a certain position to maintain'.[22] In *Night and Day*, Mr Hilbery, the 'extravagant, inconsiderate, uncivilized male',[23] who is based in part upon Leslie Stephen, goes bellowing from the room, leaving his daughter Katharine in tears and the rest of the female members of the family stunned. His daughter admits to finding herself 'cheated as usual in domestic bargainings with her father and left to do the disagreeable work which belonged, by rights, to him'.[24] In *To the Lighthouse*, another fictional portrayal of Leslie Stephen, Mr Ramsay, intimidates his youngest son, shouts at his children, frustrates his wife (who longs for a moment to herself) and confuses his guests.

Woolf's views on the tyranny of men, the misery of heterosexual marriage and the terrifying prospect of motherhood are no more apparent than in her short story *Moments of Being: Slater's Pins Have No Points* (1927):

> 'They're ogres' she had said, laughing grimly. An ogre would have interfered perhaps with breakfast in bed; with walks at dawn down to the river. What would have happened (but one could hardly conceive this) had she had children?

It is little wonder, then, that it is women who emerge as the stronger, cleverer and more desirable characters in the fiction of both Woolf and Mansfield. Women, even those who are repressed by marriage and/or society, are portrayed variously as fragrant, exotic, witty, rebellious and perceptive creatures. Women in these writings desire only each other and long to be like one another, to spend time together alone and put up a united front against the angry, violent, bullying or weak men who attempt to impose restrictions upon them.

Although Katherine Mansfield was bisexual, there is no evidence of her ever enjoying anything other than a platonic friendship with Virginia Woolf. She admired Virginia, was stimulated by her company and respected her work (with one or two infamous exceptions). Virginia, in turn, seemed to love and admire Katherine, but, as she had done with Ottoline, she fluctuated between disgust and admiration; she detested Katherine's perfume and bad table manners, but admired her doll-like prettiness, exotic make-up and penchant for short skirts.

As Virginia was always the one to make more effort at correspondence than Katherine, it is tempting to imbue their relationship with more physical desire on Virginia's part than on Katherine's, but Virginia was, at this stage in her life, entirely chaste, happily married to Leonard with only her youthful fascination with Violet Dickinson to declare. Katherine had fallen in love with many women and had passionate affairs with them. Her journals refer unashamedly to the ecstasy of her physical union with these women, and after one such affair (with Edith Bendall) finished in 1907, she wrote a remarkably frank lesbian short story, *Leves Amores*. In nine brief paragraphs the story sets the scene for a seduction between two women in a hotel. Predictably, this piece of work was not included by Murry in his collection of Katherine's short stories, published after her death. The language is blunt and unadorned; the purpose of the tale is obvious:

> She told me as we walked along the corridor to her room that she was glad the night had come. I did not ask why. I was glad, too. It seemed a secret between us. So I went with her into her room to undo those troublesome hooks.[25]

When Virginia Woolf writes of love for women, it is often in a more analytical, considered fashion; it merely hints at what might lie ahead. Here, in *Mrs Dalloway*, the passage even seems, consciously or otherwise, to sum up Virginia's feelings for Katherine herself:

> It was not like one's feeling for a man. It was completely disinterested, and besides, it had a quality that could only exist between women, between women just grown up. It was protective, on her side.[26]

By 1918, Katherine Mansfield was still writing about woman-to-woman attraction, but her matured writing skills now employed much more symbolism, achieving an effect nearer to Virginia Woolf's. In *Carnation* (1918), a schoolroom setting provides the background for a French lesson on a hot, stuffy day. Read purely at surface level it is a well-written, descriptive and colourful tale of adolescence, but with more attention to the symbolism within, *Carnation* becomes a story of seduction; the deep red carnation itself is employed as an instrument of sexual temptation with which Eve 'tickled Katie's neck' before pulling it gradually to pieces, eating it one petal at a time. In 1908, Katherine had written a fore-runner to this story, in poetry form; the poem, *Scarlet Tulips*, describes the 'flowering' of the female genitalia.

Virginia Woolf's self-styled 'sapphist'[27] story, *Moments of Being: Slater's Pins Have No Points* (1927), echoes the language of Mansfield's *Carnation*. Written at the height of her affair with Vita Sackville-West, it also features a teacher/pupil schoolroom relation-ship and the awakening of a young girl's lesbian desires. The purple cloak of the teacher recalls the purple ink that symbolized Virginia's love for Violet Dickinson, and curiously, the flower used to repre-sent desire is again a carnation, just as it was in Mansfield's earlier story; the teacher, Julia, crushes it 'voluptuously' in her hands.

It is unlikely, given her writing in *Slater's Pins*, that Woolf's nega-tive reaction to the publication of Mansfield's openly bisexual story, *Bliss*, was due to any prudish disgust at the content. The story describes a married woman's burgeoning feelings for another woman – who turns out to be her husband's lover. It is far more likely that Woolf's literary sensibilities were disappointed by the hard, glib style of Mansfield's narrative after the more accessible, prosaic text of *Prelude*. However, her legendary prediction of the demise of Mansfield's career – she noted simply in her diary 'she's finished!' – proved unfounded, for after *Bliss*, Katherine went from strength to strength, publishing *The Garden Party* and *Bliss and Other Stories* to rave reviews. Woolf professed not to be jealous, but the very frequency of her mentioning this fact suggests otherwise.

Although united by their love of words, there were many times when the two women were torn apart by professional rivalry. Their opinions of each other's fiction were generally positive and encouraging, but Woolf's reviews tended to be slightly kinder. Mansfield's review of *Kew Gardens* for the *Athenaeum* in June 1919 admires Virginia's prose, proclaiming it to be bathed in beautiful light, and full of poise and colour, but Mansfield, whose fiction was fast-moving and full of sharp dialogue, never learned to appreciate the slow-moving attention to detail that Woolf excelled in, hence *Kew Gardens* was also said to 'belong to another age'. Mansfield's review of *Night and Day*, again for the *Athenaeum*, gave crueller vent to her dislike of what she saw as stuffiness, concluding with the cutting line 'in the midst of all our admiration it makes us feel old and chill: we had never thought to look upon its like again!' In addition she finds Woolf's portrayals of Mr Clacton and Mrs Denham lacking in depth and credibility, imagining that these characters were left suspended and motionless when Woolf removed her pen from the page until 'she [added] another stroke or two or [wrote] another sentence underneath'.

Mansfield compared Woolf to one of Virginia's favourite authors, Jane Austen, but the comparison was not intended to be read as a compliment. Woolf pondered this review in a letter to Clive Bell, calmly professing not to understand it. She remained, at least in letters to Katherine, without malice, writing to congratulate her on *Bliss and Other Stories* when the collection was published in 1920. Indeed, Woolf was still to recall the brilliance of this collection in 1922, although she also referred to it, in a letter to Janet Case, as 'hard', 'shallow' and 'sentimental', a combination that apparently had forced Woolf to run to her drinks cabinet and resulted in her refusing to read the follow-up, *The Garden Party*. Her envy of Mansfield's success was expressed in the one simple line 'but she takes in all the reviewers, and I daresay I'm wrong (don't be taken in by that display of modesty)'.[28]

Virginia, however, was never put out for long. In a subsequent letter to Clive, she recovers her humour sufficiently to write a paragraph parodying Mansfield's writing style, calling her version 'rather better than the original'.

The posthumous publication of Katherine's *Journal, 1914–1922*, revealed a different side of Katherine Mansfield to the public. The honest and detailed, unselfish descriptions of her daily struggle with appalling physical health painted her in a light hitherto unseen by many, including Virginia. Ida Baker had always portrayed Katherine as a beautiful, suffering martyr, but Murry, Virginia, and Katherine's family could see that her opinion had been hugely clouded by love, lust and her own low self-esteem. The *Journal* revealed Katherine, in the final months of her life, when illness had stripped away much of her bitterness and had silenced her cruel tongue and hurtful lies, as a much softer, more honest and endearing person.

In the short story that Virginia had so disliked, *Bliss*, Mansfield's heroine, Bertha, reflects on her happy life:

> They had this absolutely satisfactory house and garden. And friends – modern, thrilling friends, writers and painters and poets. And then there were books and there was music.[29]

This passage could be seen as an early version of the entry in Katherine's own journal, where Mansfield expressed, more eloquently than she had ever done so before, her desire to go on living, and how she aimed to achieve true happiness:

> I mean the power to lead a full, adult, living, breathing life in close contact with what I love – the earth and the wonders thereof – the sea – the sun ... then I want to *work*. At what? I want so to live that I work with my hands and my feelings and my brain. I want a garden, a small house, grass, animals, books, pictures, music.[30]

Woolf's review of Katherine's *Journal*, published firstly (unsigned) in the *Nation & Athenaeum* on 10 September 1927 and then reprinted in the *New York Herald Tribune* on 18 September, is written with the benefit of hindsight, reflection and the passage of time, which mellowed her memory of Katherine and the events surrounding her pitifully sad death. Woolf had admitted privately to friends that on first reading the journal she had felt a mixture of 'sentiment and horror', but she eventually wrote a kind review, stating that Mansfield had been the leader of her chosen medium, the short story, and had not been succeeded by anybody. She paid moving tribute to Mansfield's approach to her work, revealing her to have been 'sane, caustic, and austere'. It is an honest and sensitive assessment of an enigmatic, frustrating but dedicated individual and her contribution to literature.

After Katherine's death, those who had known her well continued to ponder her character and discuss her life and work for many years. Virginia immediately penned a long and revealing passage in her diary, where she described Katherine's illness, her appearance, her interest in unusual clothes, her huge brown serious eyes and the many earnest talks they had enjoyed together about the art of writing. In numerous letters over the next few years, Virginia asked her friends to give her their true opinions of Katherine's work, seemingly still regarding the dead woman as a threat to her own career. It is likely that Katherine would have greatly admired the change in Virginia's own writing as she moved towards modernism in all her great novels, but she did not live to see them written; she might have particularly enjoyed *Mrs Dalloway*, *To the Lighthouse*, *The Waves* and *Between the Acts*.

After her friend's death, Virginia concluded, rightly, that she would continue to think about Katherine for the rest of her life. Katherine even haunted her dreams for a while, as an apparition wearing a white wreath.

Other friends also continued to analyse their own particular relationships with Katherine Mansfield. As late as 1931, Ottoline Morrell, willing as always to see the good side in a person, wrote an eight-page letter to Rosamund Lehmann in which she tried to describe the friend who had alternately enchanted, abused and loved her:

> I think she found it very difficult to be *real*, for she was naturally an actress. She took on parts so easily that she didn't know what she was herself ... she had cheap taste – slightly 'Swan & Edgar' ... as a companion she was intoxicating ... she was jealous of Virginia.

But it was perhaps in the following line that Ottoline, not a writer but a perceptive and observant woman, achieved the nearest thing to a truthful, fair assessment of the complex character that was Katherine Mansfield. It is a line that Katherine herself would probably have rather approved of: 'she wasn't a fraud – she was more of an adventuress'.[31]

5 Carrington

She was everywhere, in everyone's house – and once inside, so glowing
with sympathetic magnetism and droll ideas for them all that there wasn't
a person of her vast acquaintance who did not get the impression that
she was their very best friend.[1]

Dora Carrington might at first glance seem to be an intruder in a book
that is devoted to Virginia Woolf's women. She certainly did not influence Virginia as profoundly as some of the other female contenders for
inclusion in this book, but Virginia and Carrington were friends, albeit
never close ones.

They were first brought together by their mutual love for an effem-
inate, difficult, homosexual man – Lytton Strachey. Their early friendship was based mainly on mistrust, from Virginia, and indignation,
from Carrington. It took from 1916 until 1932 for Virginia to develop
the great fondness towards Carrington that she eventually discovered
she possessed. Although the friendship never grew intimate,
Carrington's extraordinary kindness and her eccentric, loveable
personality drew out many of Virginia Woolf's softer, more endearing
traits, and it is for this reason that Carrington deserves her inclusion in
this book, for, through her, we see a different, perhaps more accessible, side of Virginia. Carrington rarely provoked Virginia's cruel
tongue, for instance – after they had ironed out their initial misgivings,
the mocking tone that Virginia often used in letters to Ottoline, Ethel
or even Violet, was markedly absent from her correspondence to
Carrington, and, scrutinized carefully, their lives reveal a remarkable
number of similarities, both personally and in their attitudes to art and
literature.

126

Dora De Houghton Carrington was born on 29 March 1893, the fourth of five children born to Samuel and Charlotte Carrington. Dora received the high school education that Virginia had missed out on, starting at Bedford High School for Girls in 1903, where she began to display her prodigious talent for art. She lived with her parents at 1 Rothsay Gardens in Bedford, and was still living there in 1910, when she won a coveted scholarship to the Slade School of Drawing, Painting and Sculpture. Here, Carrington dropped her Christian name, took up her easel, slashed her long fair hair into a thick golden bell, and began the work that was to continue for the rest of her life.

Her new-found independence was greatly at odds with the late-Victorian societal pressures that were still in evidence at her parents' house; although Carrington adored and revered her father, sketching him almost obsessively, she did not admire her fussy, martyr-like mother, who crammed the house with ornaments and devoted herself to charity work and religious causes. Eventually Samuel Carrington retreated into a weary world of his own and Carrington decided to seek lodgings elsewhere. She found them in 1912, by renting a studio in Chelsea, which she financed by selling paintings and teaching art privately.

Carrington's family situation eased slightly in 1914 when the Carringtons moved to a Georgian farmhouse in Hurstbourne Tarrant, Hampshire. There were enough outbuildings for Carrington to have her own studio, and here she began her love affair with the landscapes and scenery of the countryside, first capturing the view from her top-floor bedroom in an evocative watercolour entitled 'Hill in Snow at Hurstbourne Tarrant' (1916).

The other love affair that began at this time was with a fellow student, Mark Gertler, whom Carrington had met at the Slade just before graduating. Their twelve-year long friendship, which started so optimistically with shared trips to galleries and exhibitions, became troubled very quickly and caused both of them much unhappiness. Although passionate towards Gertler when discussing art, Carrington, at eighteen, had not yet had her sexuality awakened; her upbringing had taught her to repress her innermost feelings. She was looking for a platonic soul mate, but what she found was a man who was highly sexed and constantly irritated and frustrated by Carrington's lack of passion. The heartbreaking letters that passed regularly between them pay sad testimony to the anguish that this long relationship caused.

On graduating from the Slade, Carrington had fallen into an unhappy, confused state. She was unsure of her own identity, haplessly seeking somebody who would restore it to her. That somebody, a fellow guest at Virginia Woolf's country home, Asheham, was to be Lytton Strachey.

Strachey, along with Clive Bell, Duncan Grant and Mary Hutchinson, had been staying at Asheham, which Virginia had just leased jointly with Vanessa Bell. Attracted to Carrington from the moment he first laid eyes on her, he had boldly tried to kiss her during a walk across the South Downs, the feeling of his beard prompting an enraged outburst of disgust from the unwilling recipient. According to legend, Carrington plotted frenzied revenge, creeping into Lytton's bedroom during the night with the intention of cutting off the detested beard. Instead, she was mesmerized by his eyes, which opened suddenly and regarded her intently. From that moment on, the two became virtually inseparable.

Initially, Strachey's friends viewed the idea of Carrington and Lytton as a couple with repulsion; it was considered extremely inappropriate. Even though it was evident almost from the start that they were to enjoy a platonic relationship rather than a sexual one, the relationship was the talk of Bloomsbury for several months. They were a curious looking couple: Lytton was tall and lanky, bespectacled and with a curiously high-pitched voice, Carrington was short, chubby, eccentrically dressed and with daringly short hair. Her unconventional looks have been discussed many times in memoirs and fiction; her close friend, Julia Strachey, described her as a 'modern witch' and reminisced, after Carrington's death, on the artist's striking physical appearance:

> Carrington had large blue eyes, a thought unnaturally wide open, a thought unnaturally transparent, yet reflecting only the outside light and revealing nothing within, just as a glass door betrays nothing to the enquiring visitor but the light reflected off the sea . . . From a distance she looked a young creature, innocent and a little awkward, dressed in very odd frocks such as one would see in some quaint picture-book; but if one came closer and talked to her, one soon saw age scored around her eyes.[2]

In 1916, Carrington met the writer Aldous Huxley at Ottoline Morrell's Garsington Manor. Huxley was a favoured guest and even had his own permanent room in the house, but little did the visitors who flocked to Garsington know that Huxley, like D.H. Lawrence, was writing copy for his books about the people he purported to love and admire. Although, as we have already seen, Huxley's caricature of Ottoline was merciless, Carrington seems to have escaped with a kinder portrait, probably because Huxley fancied himself to be in love with her.

On many a hot night, Huxley and Carrington would sleep outdoors on the roof at Garsington, or talk into the early hours. The image of Carrington in her purple pyjamas found its way into *Crome Yellow* and emerged in the character of Mary Bracegirdle. The portrayal is not entirely sympathetic or flattering, but some of the character's dialogue is obviously based on Carrington's own; in the following passage, where Mary describes her ideal partner, it could be Carrington describing her search for love that ended in meeting Lytton:

> It must be somebody intelligent, somebody with intellectual interests that I can share. And it must be somebody with a proper respect for women, somebody who's prepared to talk seriously about his work and his ideas and about my work and my ideas. It isn't, as you see, at all easy to find the right person.[3]

Carrington's striking looks inspired virtually everyone she met to try and capture what they saw. Huxley was no exception, and his recognizable portrait of her in *Crome Yellow* also echoes Julia Strachey's own reminiscences:

> On his other side, the serious, moon-like innocence of Mary Bracegirdle's face shone pink and childish. She was nearly twenty-three, but one wouldn't have guessed it. Her short hair, clipped like a page's, hung in a bell of elastic gold about her cheeks. She had large blue china eyes, whose expression was one of ingenuous and often puzzled earnestness.[4]

Huxley may have been recalling one of Carrington's late-night confessions, about the complications of her platonic love for Lytton, when he gave Mary Bracegirdle a melancholy mood that results in her analysing out loud the difficulties of such love:

The difficulty makes itself acutely felt in matters of sex. If one individual seeks intimate contact with another individual in the natural way, she is certain to receive or inflict suffering. If, on the other hand, she avoids contact, she risks the equally grave sufferings that follow on unnatural repressions. As you see, it's a dilemma.[5]

Carrington was still pondering the dilemma of loving Lytton, who had already admitted to friends that he was useless at having sex with a woman, when she first encountered Virginia Woolf. Their friendship got off to a particularly awkward start: on route to Charleston, in the company of David Garnett and fellow Slade student Barbara Hiles, Carrington was forced to break into Asheham overnight when they found themselves without lodgings. Virginia's caretaker dutifully reported the break-in, and Virginia imperiously summoned a terrified Carrington to Richmond so that she could explain what had happened. Although Virginia admitted to David Garnett that she was not *really* annoyed, she confessed to enjoying the power of her reputation for being foreboding, reporting that 'Miss Carrington' had 'quaked' at the sound of her voice.[6]

Virginia must have continued with her terrifying interrogation during the first face-to-face meeting between herself and Carrington, for the latter detailed the event in a letter to Vanessa Bell:

I went yesterday to Virginia. What an examination!! But I was rigid and denied everything. I thought her indeed charming and also the grissily wolf [sic].[7]

Virginia invited Carrington to Asheham again for a short holiday in February 1917, and shortly afterwards wrote to request some of Carrington's woodcuts for the Hogarth Press's *Two Stories*, offering to pay her 15/-. Carrington's ecstatic response to this letter, sent from Tidmarsh Mill (where she was now living with Lytton), demonstrates not only her growing admiration for Virginia, but also her unique ability to poke fun without fear of rebuke:

I am only too delighted at the prospect of my humble woodcuts embellishing your literary masterpiece.[8]

Virginia was delighted with the quality of the resulting woodcuts, and wrote to tell Carrington so, ending her letter with a warm invitation to dinner. Shortly afterwards, however, Virginia turned to Vanessa and Duncan for the next set of woodcuts, complaining that Carrington had cut her margins too low. This seemed not to affect the development of their friendship, but until the end of 1918 there were some slight tensions, mainly due to Virginia's jealousy of Carrington's special relationship with Lytton. Carrington herself, aware that she could never replace Virginia in Lytton's life, seemed to accept this good-naturedly enough, being able to put Virginia firmly in her place whilst still encouraging the Woolfs to visit Lytton:

> Please write a postcard and say when we may expect you and if you dare refuse I shall pray to God to send the shingles upon your heads – and I'll never cut a blasted woodblock for you again.[9]

Virginia was more cautious, suffering pangs of jealousy as she strove to maintain her special place in Lytton's life:

> Intimacy seems to me possible with him as with scarcely anyone; for besides tastes in common, I like and think I understand his feelings – even in their more capricious developments; for example in the matter of Carrington. He spoke of her, by the way, with a candour not flattering, though not at all malicious.[10]

That entry in Virginia's diary goes on to record a conversation with Lytton in which she begged for reassurance – granted – that he still liked her 'better' than Carrington. Whether or not this conversation leaked back to Carrington is unclear, but in January 1918, there was a short period where the artist appeared to turn against Virginia, accusing her on the telephone of being depressing and unnecessarily critical of her friends. Again, no serious harm was done, and from then on, Virginia softened her opinion of Carrington.

In July 1918, Woolf admitted that she was conscious of Carrington's 'admiring and solicitous youth', perceptively expressing a fear that the young woman was becoming too reliant on Lytton as her sole source of happiness and that she appeared to be risking her own life in doing so. Later in the same month, Virginia rather patronizingly complimented Lytton for 'improving' Carrington. Lytton replied by stating that even if this were so, he must be free to 'go off' with other people whenever he so desired. Virginia's response did not 'quite please' Lytton, for she acerbically suggested that perhaps Carrington might 'follow suit' and find *her* own amusement elsewhere. Here, for the first time, is Virginia's first written acknowledgement of Carrington being a desirable and charismatic person in her own right.

By the summer of 1918, Carrington was back at Asheham for a longer visit, and both she and Virginia greatly enjoyed themselves. The latter was impressed by Carrington's complete unselfishness as a guest – Carrington spent most of her time cutting grass, pumping water or going for long solitary walks between Asheham and Charleston. Virginia noted Carrington's full, 'clever' face and concluded that although her appearance as a 'whole just misses', it also 'decidedly misses what might be vulgarity'.[11] Carrington wrote to thank Virginia for the visit in a loving, exuberant and endearing letter in which she promises to come and 'dig the garden for Leonard like an old Mole'.[12] Gifts to Virginia followed, including a large pat of butter that delighted both Woolfs.

In Gretchen Gerzina's 1989 biography of Carrington, the author states that 'not until the day before Carrington's suicide in 1932, did Virginia fully understand the depth of Carrington's devotion to Lytton and forgive her for removing him from the Bloomsbury fold'. This is patently untrue; a careful study of Virginia's letters and diaries reveals that not only did she understand Carrington's love for Lytton, but also approved of the effect that it had on him. As early as January 1919, she was writing of her fondness for Carrington and noting the calming effect that she was having on the edgy, melodramatic Lytton: 'she has increased his benignity' and 'his way of life insofar as it is unconventional, is so by the desire and determination of Carrington'.[13] Carrington never, as Gerzina claims, tried to 'remove' Lytton from Bloomsbury; she must have known that any such effort would have proved futile. Instead, his Bloomsbury friends became her friends as well and, as a couple, they entertained Virginia, Vanessa, Duncan, Maynard, David Garnett and many others, until Lytton's death.

In 1920, another person became part of Lytton and Carrington's complex relationship. Ralph Partridge was a friend of Carrington's brother, Noel, and he and Carrington soon became lovers. Ralph moved into Tidmarsh, where further emotional complications arose when Lytton became attracted to him. Lytton recognized an opportunity to see Carrington safely married, thereby removing some of her dependence on him, and so he encouraged the union. Ralph married Carrington in 1921 and, almost immediately, both partners were unfaithful, Ralph with Clare Bollard (a friend of Gertler's) and Frances Marshall, Carrington with Gerald Brenan. Virginia, keeping a beady eye on the situation, noted that Carrington seemed 'embarrassed' by Ralph and, after the wedding, she briskly recorded that 'certainly she is not in love; and he has the obdurate Anglo Indian in him'.[14] Woolf continued to monitor the relationship, and her assessment of the physical and mental changes in Carrington as she witnessed her new husband's unfaithful nature in full swing, strike a chilling note:

> Carrington is going to sit out his infidelities, which she does with her lips tight shut. She is going to paint. But she will never be a young woman again.[15]

And, even more ominously:

> Carrington as if recently beaten by Ralph. Is she really rather dull, I asked myself? Or merely a sun flower out of the sun?[16]

Carrington's self-confidence, never strong at the best of times, was being sapped away by the difficult *ménage à trois* at home. Her letter written to Gerald Brenan in 1923 wistfully states that she is far keener on the Woolfs than they are on her, and she speaks of the 'queer' love that she has for Virginia.

Every member of the Bloomsbury Group visited regularly when Lytton and Carrington moved to Ham Spray House in Wiltshire, in 1924. Here, Carrington painted, decorated, designed Lytton a library, and made a unique home in which she and Lytton continued their unusual, loving and, to Carrington, life-sustaining relationship. Despite her happiness in the new home, she was accused by Virginia of becoming dull, spending too much time in the kitchen on Sundays and being overly domestic; these were things that Virginia, with hired helps, rarely had to worry about. Carrington, who was ensnared by what she referred to as Virginia's 'lesbian soul', by now truly worshipped Virginia.

In 1929, Carrington read *A Room of One's Own* and, despite finding it 'fascinating', vocalized her own charming but bewildered opinion in a letter to Lytton:

> I still don't agree that poverty and a room of one's own, is the explanation why women didn't write poetry. If the Brontes could write in their Rectory, with cooking and housework, why not other clergyman's daughters?[17]

Virginia was viewing Carrington with some bewilderment as well; although she rarely spoke negatively about her, in a letter to Vanessa, she refers to Carrington as appearing 'slightly shrivelled' and was irritated by her 'usual stupid petticoat'.

Despite the differences in their age and physical appearance, Virginia Woolf and Carrington had more in common than perhaps is evident on first reading about them. Even from childhood there were many similarities; both had, after all, grown up in large, Victorian families with many siblings. Their mothers, Julia Stephen and Charlotte Carrington, had toiled ceaselessly on behalf of the poor, although whereas the agnostic Julia's charity work was done out of duty and a need to block out the reality of her own traumatic widowhood, Charlotte actively adored playing the martyr and 'worked off her sensual side in religious outbursts'.[18]

As children, Carrington and Virginia had adored, and been particular favourites of, their respective fathers. Leslie Stephen cherished his 'little Ginia' from the moment she was born, and Virginia understood and respected him, despite his bursts of tyranny. He, in turn, supported and encouraged her early love of books and writing, leaving her a share of his estate to help finance her writing ambitions. Carrington's father, Samuel, understood *her* need to be creative, and after his death in 1918, Carrington received a small annual legacy that enabled her to spend time on her art and proved that her father had taken her talent seriously. Shortly after his death, Carrington described her father as he had been in old age, in words that Virginia might have used to describe Leslie Stephen: 'that craggy old hoary man with his bright eyes and huge helpless body'.[19] Carrington then affectionately immortalized Samuel in her work, featuring him in numerous sketches and paintings; Virginia immortalized Leslie Stephen in *To the Lighthouse* and in her autobiography. Both women were profoundly affected by the deaths of their beloved fathers.

Virginia and Carrington also would have been able to talk about the grief of losing an elder brother; Teddie Carrington died on the Somme in 1916, and Thoby Stephen at home in 1906 from typhoid contracted in Greece. Again, their sisters paid lasting tribute to these handsome young men in their chosen art forms – Teddie featured in Carrington's pencil sketches and drawings, and Thoby inspired the character of Jacob in *Jacob's Room* (1922).

As well as sharing similar family backgrounds, the emotional health of each woman was precarious. Virginia's breakdowns and depressions had been prolonged and dramatic in a way that Carrington's were not (until the death of Lytton in later life). Nevertheless, the effects of mental illness, and its resulting vulnerability, were visible on their faces. The following passage about Virginia is by Frances Partridge, who knew both women:

> Virginia's [face] bore the stigmata that are to be seen in many who have been gravely mad – a subtly agonised tautness, something twisted. She was not at home in her body.[20]

This second passage, describing Carrington, is by Julia Strachey, a friend of Frances's, who was acquainted with both Carrington and Virginia:

> If one came closer and talked to her, one soon saw age scored around her eyes – and something, surely, a bit worse than that – a sort of illness, bodily or mental. She had darkly bruised, hollowed, almost battered sockets.[21]

Over the course of their lives, these two women suffered from a higher-than-average number of physical ailments: Carrington was forever enduring bad colds and flu, and raised temperatures and appalling, gnawing headaches continually plagued Virginia. Both of them possessed a fairly philosophical attitude to these complaints; Carrington turned hers into letter sketches to amuse her friends, and Virginia read, slept and ate at Leonard's insistence, knowing that this was the best way to regain her health.

Although in her mid-thirties Virginia Woolf became a confident, successful and sociable writer, as an adolescent she was crippled by shyness, blushing furiously whenever spoken to. As a young woman she had endured the misery of being 'mute' at the endless succession of balls and parties that the Duckworth brothers had forced her to attend. Carrington was also shy, eschewing 'society' and all that it stood for, and she remained this way throughout her life, often finding it easier to communicate with animals than with people. She suffered from physical awkwardness, turning her feet in and hanging her head. Virginia's own awkwardness stemmed from her above-average height and thin, angular body; she lacked confidence in her appearance and thought her neck particularly unattractive.

Carrington and Woolf had eccentric tastes in dress, which, although making them the objects of strangers' attention, did little to mask their attractiveness. Carrington did not care for clothes and wore long, shapeless frocks or smocks, which immediately labelled her as an artist. Virginia, descended from a mother whom she remembered as having possessed only one dress, also cared little for clothes shopping, and would pack books for the Hogarth Press dressed simply in overalls or a dressing-gown. Formal visits to dressmakers traumatized her, reminding her of the torturous trips made from Hyde Park Gate. She did enjoy dressing-up for parties or theatre visits, however, choosing unusual or boldly coloured garments that attracted much attention:

> It was very odd indeed, orange and black, with a hat to match, – a sort of top-hat made of straw, with two orange feathers like Mercury's wings, – but although odd it was curiously becoming and pleased Virginia because there could be absolutely no doubt as to which was the front and which the back.[22]

The difficulties that each woman had with her self-image and physicality were part of the reason that neither Carrington nor Virginia ever became mothers; the other, more realistic, fear was that children would hamper and restrict their ability to paint or write. Carrington was ill at ease with her femininity and hated to be reminded of it; menstruation threw her into turmoil. Virginia, after a brief time during her 1904 breakdown, when she begged Violet Dickinson to find her a baby, never again showed overly strong maternal urges. There was a six-month period after her marriage to Leonard when the Woolfs seemed to take it for granted that children would follow, but after consulting with Virginia's doctors, Leonard decided that her state of mind would not benefit from the strain of pregnancy, childbirth and rearing of a child. The matter was dropped, and although Virginia often envied Vanessa and her 'brood' of children, she also came to realize that her career as a novelist depended on uninterrupted peace and quiet, and she endeavoured to comfort herself with the knowledge that her earning potential was far greater than Vanessa's. However, a little wistfulness was always to remain, so Virginia channelled it into forging close relationships with her nieces and nephews. Her imagination and her ability as a storyteller made her hugely popular with other children, too – the sons of Vita Sackville-West, Ben and Nigel, looked forward to the great treat of Virginia coming to tea for precisely that reason.

Carrington also appealed to children and for a short time was an art teacher, which she had enjoyed, but she did not welcome children to Ham Spray, fearing that they would annoy Lytton and prevent both adults from working. She had no maternal urges whatsoever, and so on finding herself pregnant by Beakus Penrose in 1929 became suicidal with fear and depression. After a fruitless and dangerous attempt to miscarry by riding her horse vigorously over the Downs, Carrington, humiliatingly, had to allow her husband, Ralph, to pay for an abortion at a nursing home. Her elation on terminating the pregnancy was short lived and contributed, together with the constant absence of Lytton, as he grew more deeply involved with Roger Senhouse, to her worsening depression.

Virginia and Carrington had the habit of adopting nicknames for themselves and other people that they were fond of. Carrington used a selection of strange or self-effacing names when signing her letters to Lytton; two of the more frequent ones were 'Mopsa' and 'votre grosse bébé'. She later invented 'Kunak', 'Amigo' and 'Doric' (sometimes written backwards as 'Cirod') for her lover, Gerald Brenan. Virginia had a host of animal nicknames that were used in letters to Vanessa and Violet Dickinson, and she referred to herself and Leonard as 'Mandril' and 'Mongoose', or to herself, less frequently, as 'Marmot'. These nicknames imply great affection, but also suggest the strong need for petting and reassurance that both Carrington and Virginia required regularly from their partners.

The two of them were highly insecure women, suffering from separation anxiety whenever parted from loved ones; Virginia had suffered terrible agonies as a child when Julia Stephen came home later than expected. She transferred this anxiety into every close female friendship that she ever had, and also established it in her marriage to Leonard, hating their rare times apart and writing obsessively for calming words about his health and whereabouts. Her anxieties appeared to worsen if events were out of her control; when Leonard visited the doctor, she would pace the pavements outside, convincing herself of the worst. Carrington hated to be apart from Lytton and wrote him wretched, emotional letters of such intensity that Lytton was understandably reserved and apprehensive in his replies. She understood that her insecurity put pressure on Lytton, and wrote to tell him so:

> Lytton every time you come back I love you more. Something new which escaped me before in you completely surprises me. Do you know, when I think of missing a day with you it gives me proper pain inside. I can't help saying this at a risk of boring you.[23]

Such insecurities gravitated outwards, affecting each woman's chosen field of work. Carrington was always to be prodigiously hard-working and prolific, taking on many commissions as well as painting portraits and oils on a daily basis and decorating her friends' fireplaces, walls and doors. She also made glass pictures, signboards and bookplates, and decorated tiles. Yet she would doubt her own talent to the end. Virginia tried to boost Carrington's confidence by encouraging her to provide original woodcuts for the Hogarth Press, and she praised the results. Although both Roger Fry and Clive Bell could have used their influence in British art circles to help progress Carrington's career, it is significant that neither of them did; after a consultation in 1916 with Roger about her work and future as an artist, Carrington felt discouraged. She lost faith and confidence in her painting and refused to exhibit, writing to Lytton of her frustrations:

> I wish I wasn't so 'tied up in knots' over my painting. I feel as if I was painting behind iron bars, in a cage, unable to do really what I want to do.[24]

Virginia might have understood this sentiment better than anyone. She wrestled throughout her life against restrictions imposed upon her writing by ill health and by the repressive ghosts of Julia and Stella, and in particular against the torturous self-doubt, inherited from Leslie, combined with ruthless perfectionism, that caused agonies of despair both prior to and after publication of each of her novels:

> I have finished my book [*The Waves*] – yes – but it is a failure. Too difficult: too jerky: too inchoate altogether.[25]

When Carrington felt unable to paint, or was unhappy with the result, she channelled her energy into looking after Lytton, tidying the house or cooking. Virginia, waiting for publication of a novel, cooked, walked, embroidered or, at the end of her life, energetically scrubbed floors. Neither woman was good at being idle, as idleness would immediately encourage too much damaging self-analysis. Instead, by frenetically throwing themselves into practical activities, these two highly sensitive and talented women attempted to hold the dark shadows of insecurity, despair and depression at bay. Each of them had a pronounced tendency towards these darker moods, which were often heightened by absence from loved ones and a fear of the onset of old age. This did not prevent them from being sought-after company, as both were also capable of enjoying themselves and spreading much good humour. Virginia loved conversation and parties, and Carrington would play the clown, to make her friends roar with laughter.

These gregarious qualities were totally at odds with the private, emotional attachment that both women had for the peace and tranquillity of the English countryside. Carrington spent her happiest times at Ham Spray in Wiltshire, reading under the trees with Lytton at her side, or riding her white horse Belle over the Downs as a release from stressful situations (particularly in the wake of her destructive affair with Gerald Brenan). Virginia also took to the Downs in times of stress, walking vigorously for miles whilst she composed fragments of fiction in her head. Monk's House, with the almost constant companionship of Leonard, became her favourite dwelling-place and, like Carrington, she eventually came, with age, to view London with some ambivalence; the complexities of urban life, however exciting, could not compete with the inspirational beauty of the countryside. Carrington painted the landscapes and farmland that she loved; Virginia captured her beloved garden at Rodmell in prose that was as visually colourful as the fruits of Carrington's paintbrush:

The opals on her finger flushed green, flushed rosy, and again flushed orange as the sun, oozing through the apple-trees, filled them. Then, when the breeze blew, her purple dress rippled like a flower attached to a stalk; the grasses nodded; and the white butterfly came blowing this way and that just above her face.[26]

Nowadays Carrington is known predominantly for her art, but her talents as a correspondent should not go unnoticed. She was a prolific and considerate letter writer; even when coping with the agonizingly slow death of Lytton, she still took time to respond to each and every one of the letters written by his concerned friends, including Roger Senhouse, Lytton's last lover. Although her diaries can be difficult to read, being so honest and self-effacing, her letters to friends shine with vigour and wit:

I, after breakfast, was walking over the bridge across the little duck stream, in rather a bad temper and vague mood and walked off the edge and fell with my bucket of duck's food into the stream. This for some reason drove me into such rage that I ran into the hen's house and cried and in my rage tried to hit a hen on the head with a wooden spoon.[27]

As an ardent correspondent herself, Virginia appreciated and encouraged Carrington's letters. They were often charmingly illustrated with little sketches of animals that must have reminded Virginia of Leslie Stephen's own illustrated letters to his children. Carrington wrote letters to keep her relationships alive, even when it was obvious that they perhaps should have been allowed to fade gently – she had a great fear of losing people. Virginia's letters also flattered, seduced, cajoled and amused her many friends, as indeed they were intended to; to receive a letter from Virginia was to be almost immediately inspired (or provoked) into replying. She, like Carrington, demonstrated her inherent sense of fun far more succinctly in letters than in the personal and ruthlessly self-analytical diaries. A letter to her nephew, Quentin Bell, reveals Virginia as a probing, teasing aunt with a sense of the ridiculous not dissimilar to Carrington's:

You admit your trousers have holes in them. Why at Lewes station you had to be covered with a potato sack in order to save the blushes of the young women who sell violets.[28]

But Carrington's letters could also, at times when Lytton was away, display a terrible pathos that was less evident in Virginia's correspondence. Carrington seemed truly unable to hide her misery:

I talk with Julia all day, on rather painful topics and get rather gloomy. I do not know what to advise, for I have very little faith in there being any happiness for human beings on this earth.[29]

The greatest similarity between Carrington and Virginia Woolf was, of course, that they both loved, and were loved by, the same man – Lytton Strachey. Virginia had come to know Strachey long before Carrington came onto the scene, when, as a friend of Thoby's from Cambridge, Strachey had begun to visit 46 Gordon Square for tea. His early and astute impressions of the young, eccentric Virginia Stephen, recorded in this 1904 letter to Leonard Woolf, were already positive:

The latter is rather wonderful, quite witty, full of things to say, and absolutely out of rapport with reality.[30]

Lytton was attracted to Virginia's ethereal, otherworldly countenance, her intelligence and her asexuality. She in turn became fond of him, finding him an inspirational and comforting companion. Despite his obvious homosexuality, Virginia accepted his proposal of marriage, and then, recoiling with horror, they both realized that they were about to make a dreadful mistake and so discarded the whole idea at once. Carrington must have been aware, after meeting Lytton some ten years later, that a very special place in his heart was reserved solely for Virginia, who was beautiful as well as clever, and also that she, Carrington, was unlikely ever to receive a marriage proposal from Lytton. Nevertheless, oddly enough, when jealousy did arise, it was not from the big-hearted Carrington, but from Virginia, who constantly asked Lytton to reassure her that she was his favourite correspondent and confidante.

There were, of course, a few very marked differences between Virginia and Carrington, one of the obvious ones being sexuality. Although both were at times attracted to members of the same sex, Carrington had been experimental with men and women both before and after she met Lytton. She was impulsive in affairs of the heart, but somehow succeeded in remaining friends with all her ex-lovers, a feat in no small way due to her total lack of maliciousness. She was not, unlike Virginia, faithful to her husband, nor he to her.

Another very clear difference between Carrington and Virginia was the reactions they had to social occasions. Virginia could be intimidating, sometimes intentionally, towards people she considered not to be on her own level, but Carrington was always easy company to be with and helpful almost to the point of subservience. Whilst Virginia enjoyed 'holding court' in a circle of admirers, Carrington was more likely to be serving drinks to the group, or sitting quietly at the side. She put visitors at their ease and saw to their every need. She was not snobbish and was unconcerned with 'class' and, in the absence of regular hired help, fetched and carried for Lytton devotedly, submissively, in a manner that Virginia would not have done for Leonard.

A poignant section of archive film footage entitled 'Carrington – Home Movies 1929' has preserved one of the last happy times that Carrington and Lytton were to have together at Ham Spray. A smiling, barefoot Carrington rides Belle, or swims nude in the water on top of a huge plastic swan; Ralph and Lytton sit happily on a first-floor windowsill, waving to the camera; a group of artist friends frolic in fancy dress. Although there were, as usual, hidden complications behind the smiles (Carrington was embroiled with Beakus Penrose; Lytton and Ralph spent much time in London), there is no hint of the rapid descent into illness and death that was to begin over the next two years.

Sadly, at the beginning of 1930, the situation at Ham Spray began to deteriorate. Carrington had a new servant, Flo, but she was difficult to manage; the house was full of too many guests, shrieking and staying up late, expecting meals and entertainment; every morning, poor Carrington had to suffer the indignity of hearing her husband, Ralph, giggling and splashing in the bathroom with his lover, Frances Marshall; and Lytton was hardly ever at home. In addition, Beakus Penrose had become nastily critical of Carrington's clothes and appearance. She developed insomnia, and even her work began to depress her; nearly all her energy had to go into the painting of tiles, which was lucrative but unfulfilling.

In March 1931, Lytton turned fifty-one and Carrington thirty-eight. Beakus, still an important part of her life, became less so after he developed jaundice at Ham Spray and expected her to become his full-time nurse. This she did, with some exasperation, for it killed all the passion that had existed between them. Lytton's affair with Roger Senhouse was also turning sour, which brought him back to Carrington newly affectionate, with the result that she grew closer to him again, but they had little time to enjoy this – by the end of 1931, Lytton was at Ham Spray in bed with a very high fever.

Lytton's illness was serious. Nurses were called in, and the real cause of his pain, stomach cancer, was not diagnosed until after his death. The illness was presumed to be typhoid. Shocked and worried, all of Lytton's friends rallied round. Carrington replied to the letters that flooded in, including some from Ottoline, Sebastian Sprott, Vanessa and Clive Bell, and Virginia, whose concerned letter clearly reveals the extent of her genuine affection not only for Lytton, but also for the terrified Carrington:

> We're so unhappy to hear that Lytton is ill. We didn't know it. If you or Ralph could ever let us have a card to say how he is we should be more than grateful. Our best love. If there was anything I could do you would let me know wouldn't you.[31]

Sadly, there was nothing that Virginia or anyone else could do. Lytton's illness progressed rapidly throughout Christmas 1931 and into the New Year. In a series of heartbreakingly sad letters to his lover, Roger Senhouse, Carrington bravely and unselfishly charted the final days of the man whom she loved more than life itself:

> Darling Roger,
>
> Lytton loved your flowers. He asked to hold them in his hands and for a long time buried his face in them, and said, how lovely. He sends you his fondest Love . . . the Doctor said Lytton's state was much the same this morning. He couldn't say there was any improvement. The Diet is to be altered today. Perhaps it will have a good effect on the digestion. Leonard and Virginia dropt [sic] in today. It was nice to see them. Your freesias look so beautiful against the dull green-yellow wall in a pewter mug.[32]

In her diary entry for Friday, 1 January 1932, Virginia rightly predicted that Carrington would try to commit suicide. Nobody was prepared, however, for Carrington's first attempt at suicide to take place *before* Lytton's actual death. She was saved – Lytton was suffering a bad attack at the time, which roused the household early and caused Ralph to realize her absence. He found her in the car, in their garage, with the engine running, and dragged her free. Carrington remained in bed until lunchtime on 21 January, when she crept back into Lytton's room and found that her soul mate with the beady eyes and high-pitched laugh was dying. She heard a bird singing outside the window and then Lytton drew his final breath. There was no funeral, and nobody recalls what became of Lytton's ashes, which were given to his brother James.

Carrington's grief was all-consuming and catastrophic. She poured her thoughts out into her diaries, in the form of long, pathetic letters to the dead Lytton. Wide-eyed and pale, she drifted around Ham Spray, constantly attended by Ralph or by well-meaning friends; they all knew that there was a high risk of her committing suicide. Virginia initially thought that suicide seemed a 'quite reasonable' option for Carrington. Her letters to the grieving, lost child-woman were supportive, loving and demonstrated her own sizeable sorrow at the loss of Lytton, and his enormous influence on her life and work:

> I hope you don't mind me writing to you sometimes – it is such a comfort because there is nobody to talk to about Lytton who knew him as you did . . . one so hates the feeling that things begin again here in London without him. I find I can't write without suddenly thinking Oh but Lytton won't read this, and it takes all the point out of it.[33]

Carrington's response to this letter was typically selfless and must have comforted Virginia:

> Thank you so much for your letter. There are only a few letters that have been any use. Yours most of all because you understand . . . I can't quite bear to face things or people. But you are the first person I'd like to see when I come to London.[34]

Shortly afterwards, at Virginia's request, Carrington sent some photographs of Lytton. Virginia, aware that Carrington was now hanging onto life by a thin thread, tried to get her interested in providing some new woodcuts for one of Julia Strachey's novels; but

Carrington could not look that far ahead, although she made some half-hearted entries in her appointment diary. She continued to churn out letters to friends, changing from her usual illustrated notepaper, with its sketch of Ham Spray, to a more austere and formal one. A letter in faint, spidery writing to her dear friend Dadie Rylands demonstrates the futility of all attempts to console her:

> I am sorry not to have written before but you understand I expect. There is nothing anyone can say that is any comfort. For everyone, in their different way, has lost something irreplaceable.[35]

Carrington carefully copied out a paragraph from David Hume's *Essay on Suicide* (1777) into her diary, concentrating on the sentences that seemed particularly relevant to her own situation. The following paragraph, with its tone of great reasonableness, must have made a particular impact:

> A man who retires from life does no harm to society. He only ceases to do good. I am not obliged to do a small good to society at the expense of a great harm to myself. Why then should I prolong a miserable existence . . . I believe that no man ever threw away life, while it was worth keeping.

Although Ralph had refused to leave Carrington's side for the five weeks since Lytton's death, she finally managed to persuade him to leave her on her own at Ham Spray. She was there, alone, when Virginia and Leonard called on 10 March to see how she was. Virginia's painfully honest account of that meeting is detailed in her diary. The three of them had gone into Lytton's study and gazed in sad silence at all his treasured books. Later, in the sitting room, Carrington had burst into floods of tears as Virginia held and tried to comfort her. She gave Virginia a little box of Lytton's as a keepsake.

On leaving, the Woolfs tried to get her to commit to a return visit at Rodmell. She would not. As they reluctantly left, Carrington turned round to wave goodbye. It was the last time anybody would see her alive. By the time Ralph, Frances and Bunny had rushed back from London the next morning, Carrington lay dying on the floor, wearing Lytton's dressing-gown and with a gunshot wound to her thigh – she had missed her heart. She had borrowed a gun, ostensibly to shoot rabbits, and on seeing Ralph's distress, the dying Carrington assured him that it had been an accident. Three hours after having raised the gun, she died. A letter that Virginia had written on returning home the day before was probably delivered too late. In it, Virginia, terribly worried, begs Carrington to hold onto life.

Although it was obvious to her friends that Carrington's death was far from being an accident, the coroner, remarkably, pronounced a verdict of 'accidental death'. It is possible that the question of why Carrington was left dying on the floor for three hours, rather than moved to a hospital, was discussed among her wider circle of friends. The answer, in all probability, is that Ralph, worn down and fully aware of Carrington's mental anguish, respected the fact that she only wanted to die, and thus let her be. At any rate, Ralph and Frances were shocked and numbed by Carrington's harrowing death. They later married, as she had wished. Frances, still alive today, possesses and treasures some of Carrington's most beautiful paintings.

Virginia was haunted by the image of Carrington, pale and tragic, on that final evening, and by the events of the following morning. She immediately tightened her own grip on life, proclaiming in her diary that she was

> Glad to be alive and sorry for the dead: can't think why Carrington killed herself and put an end to all this.[36]

Nine years later, almost to the day, Virginia wrote her own suicide notes and took the lonely walk to the River Ouse.

6 Vita

Over my head the years and centuries sweep,
The years of childhood flown,
The centuries unknown;
I dream; I do not weep.[1]

'The trouble is that the best has always been published, and in this case
the archive has been ransacked more than once ... all biographers
want unpublished material – what the French call 'la joie de l'inédit'.'
These words, written to me by Vita's son, Nigel Nicolson, reinforced
what I already suspected, but made the task at hand seem more daunt-
ing. It is true, certainly, that the life and work of Vita Sackville-West
have been thoroughly and expertly explored in Victoria Glendinning's
outstanding biography *Vita* (1983). The relationship between Vita and
her husband, Harold Nicolson, has been documented by the publication of their letters, and more intimately still, in Nigel Nicolson's
Portrait of a Marriage (1973), a book that also offers frank insights
into Vita's relationships with other women, including Violet Trefusis,
Virginia Woolf, Mary Campbell, Hilda Matheson and Evelyn Irons.
The letters of Virginia to Vita, edited by Mitchell Leaska (1984), reveal
yet further the intimacy between these two remarkable women, and
when in 1993 Suzanne Raitt published her excellent, in-depth analysis
and critique of the friendship and working relationship between Vita
and Virginia, it seemed that no further books could, or would, reveal
any hitherto unpublished material on Vita.

However, with such a wide-ranging choice of books, letters and
portraits to draw upon, it is still possible for the contemporary biographer to extract, here and there, a nugget of new information or a
sliver of truth perhaps previously left unexplored; after all, the friend-

ship between the two writers lasted for nineteen long and eventful years. There is still room here for some new argument; for instance, much has been made in nearly every biography about them of the 'maternal protection' that Vita offered Virginia, yet despite Virginia's own admission that this was the case, Vita's son, in his own biography of Virginia Woolf, categorically denies it.

Vita Sackville-West's grandfather, Lionel Sackville-West, met but could not marry – she was already married – a Spanish gypsy dancer, Pepita, in 1858. They had seven illegitimate children together, one of whom, Victoria, was destined initially to take Washington society by storm, and then to return as mistress of Knole, the largest stately home in England.

When Lionel Sackville-West was appointed British Minister to Washington, his beautiful daughter Victoria joined him, to take on the role of hostess to the British Legation. As she was unable to speak English fluently, was naïve, convent-educated and, of course, illegitimate, the wives of the secretaries of state had many reservations about her appointment. But Victoria took charge of the situation as if she had been born to do it – her beauty quickly became legendary; men fell in love with her, proposed and were rejected on a regular basis. This continued for seven years until fate intervened, and Lionel was informed that he had succeeded his brother to become Lord Sackville. He was now expected to return to England and take his place at Knole.

His daughter, by now an experienced hostess, stepped into her next role, as Mistress of Knole, with very little need for readjustment. To ensure her future in the house that she loved, she married her first cousin, another Lionel Sackville-West; conveniently, he was the next heir to Knole. They married in the chapel in 1890 and by 8 March 1892 had their first and only child, a daughter. By being a girl, the child, named 'Victoria Mary' but nicknamed 'Vita', automatically became ineligible to inherit Knole, which would pass down the male line of the family. This was to become a huge sorrow and cause of much frustration to Vita who, from the moment she first staggered across the Green Court at the age of one, fell totally and irreversibly in love with this most romantic and historic of great houses.

Another source of frustration for Vita was her mother's tendency to ignore her, belittle her or be absent from the important events of Vita's life. Victoria started this habit from the very day of her daughter's christening, claiming depression and staying in bed instead. The scene was already set for a difficult and fiery relationship between mother and daughter, and it was to last right until Lady Sackville's death in 1936. Victoria was not a calm, reassuring mother, but an infuriating, temperamental and spiteful woman.

On better days, she could appear beautiful, loveable and great fun to spend time with; like Julia Stephen, Victoria was blessed with exceptional looks, the sort that begged to be captured on canvas or portrayed in photography. She was overly fond of clothes, shopping, jewellery and anything else that allowed her to exercise her vanity. So Vita, like Virginia, grew up in the shadow of a beautiful, revered mother who was always to be the central figure of the household.

Lady Sackville seemed to love Vita as a baby, but as the baby grew into an awkward, gangly teenager, Victoria's cruel tongue got the better of her on too many occasions. The gentle Lionel, tiring of his volatile wife, withdrew to the study, or outside to manage his huge estate, leaving Vita in the company of a mother who grew bored with her daughter's company, or constantly picked fault:

> I had very long legs and straight hair, over which Mother used to hurt my feelings and say she couldn't bear to look at me because I was so ugly.[2]

Vita analysed her relationship with her mother many years later when she wrote *Pepita*, the story of her ancestry. A pathetic picture is drawn of a little daughter desperate for affection from a mother who changed mood even faster than she changed her outfits:

> How my mother puzzled me, and how I loved her! She wounded and dazzled and fascinated and charmed me by turns. Sometimes she was downright unjust, and accused me of things I had never done, lies I had never told.[3]

It is hardly surprising that Vita, by the time she turned twelve, was spending many of her days alone in that huge house, roaming from one end to the other. She did not resent her loneliness, finding romance and inspiration in the stories of her ancestors, whose images still hang on the walls and staircases today. Knole is largely fifteenth-century, although older buildings on the site still exist, and has some three hundred and sixty-five rooms, although no one, including Vita, has ever been able to confirm this figure exactly.

The house sits in a great deer park, the gates of which open onto the small town of Sevenoaks. Vita used her favourite memories of the house in one of her novels, *The Edwardians* (1930), referring to it as a 'mediaeval village' that had one hundred chimneys and contained many small shops. There were at least fifty full-time servants in residence at Knole, working in a kitchen that was as high as a cathedral and many beautiful rooms, including three state bedrooms which were kept as museum pieces.

The Prince and Princess of Wales were regular guests while Vita was growing up; in the midst of all this splendour, the 12-year-old was writing passionate, rambling, historical novels. Elsewhere, in Kensington, London, a 22-year-old woman called Virginia Stephen was about to move to Bloomsbury, having made a name for herself as a professional reviewer and journalist for the *Guardian* and the *Times Literary Supplement* whilst churning out descriptive travel pieces in the back of her diary. She had already suffered and survived the indignities that Vita was still to experience, attending smart social parties and balls in an agony of shyness and defiance, returning home with relief to read by the light of a candle.

Vita suffered similar tortures when she turned eighteen and was expected to make an appearance at all the best country-house balls:

> The only good thing that could be said of me is that I wouldn't have anything to do with my kind. Seeing that I was unpopular (and small wonder for a saturnine prig), I wouldn't court popularity. I minded rather, and used to cry when I went to bed after coming home from a party, but I made myself defiant about it.[4]

As Vita turned from a lanky teenager into a beautiful young woman, suitors from all the grandest stately homes appeared, to offer their hands in marriage, but Vita remained resolutely unimpressed. She turned them all down, even Lord Lascelles, the dashing heir to Harewood House, for by this time (1912) she had begun to fall in love with Harold Nicolson, a junior official in the Foreign Office. Quiet and unassuming, but confident, handsome and with a boyish charm, he made an immediate impression on the 18-year old Vita when they first met at a dinner party in 1910:

Everything was fun to his energy, vitality and buoyancy. I liked his irre-
pressible brown curls, his laughing eyes, his charming smile and his
boyishness.[5]

Harold was duly invited to Knole for a weekend, and he and Vita
continued to meet at London parties. Her first letter to him is friendly,
but not intimate:

I have been asked to 'ask a man' to dine on Thursday with Mrs Harold
Pearson and go to a dance, so would you like to come? I promise you
shan't be made to dance![6]

By Christmas 1911, Harold was at Knole again, in love with Vita,
who was hoping for a proposal before he left for Constantinople. They
attended a ball at Hatfield House early in 1912, where Harold professed
his love. This sent Vita into a panic, and she asked him to wait at least a
year before marrying her. Lady Sackville later had a long talk alone with
Harold, confirming that he and Vita could not be engaged for over a
year. He then left straight away for his six months in Constantinople.
Vita took to her bed, but eventually arose and continued the affair she
had been having with Rosamund Grosvenor; it never occurred to her
that there was anything amiss in writing miserable letters to Harold
whilst spending the spring of 1912 in Florence with Rosamund. Harold
returned from Constantinople newly determined to marry Vita, and
stated that he wanted the wedding to take place in April 1913. Lady
Sackville had other ideas, and the wedding did not take place until 1
October of that year. Although she had finally given the couple her
blessing, Victoria did not attend the wedding, choosing instead to stay
in bed all day, thus causing a mixture of relief and regret in her family.

The married couple took a train to Coker Court, the home of
Dorothy Heneage who had decided to lend them her house for the
start of their honeymoon, and they then spent their first month
together in Constantinople. In September 1914, their first son, Ben,
was born, and the Nicolsons returned to England and set up home at
Ebury Street in London. Lady Sackville continued to cause them difficulties; furious that Vita wanted to christen the child 'Benedict Lionel'
as opposed to 'Lionel Benedict', she caused terrible scenes at Knole until
Vita was forced to concede to her mother's wishes and christen the
child as Victoria demanded. It made little difference – Vita immediately

151

reverted to calling her baby 'Ben', and so Lady Sackville stormed off to London, where passionate, angry letters shot back and forth between herself and Vita; in many ways, their relationship was like that of two tempestuous, insecure lovers.

Shortly after the First World War began, Vita spotted and fell in love with a house deep in the heart of the Kent countryside, setting the pattern for the rest of her life. Long Barn, only a short drive from Knole, was the perfect setting for Vita and Harold to write in, with its long, low rooms hung with great oak beams. Here, for the first time in her life, Vita began to develop an interest in gardening. She was pregnant again, only four months after the birth of Ben, but the pregnancy was difficult and the baby was eventually several weeks overdue. On 1 November 1915, the doctors confirmed that the child she was carrying had died in her womb. Despite their terrible grief, this tragedy brought Vita and Harold onto a new level of emotional intimacy. Although the words that Vita chose in her autobiography to recall her love for Harold at this time could have been written by any young woman in love, in the context of her later life they inevitably recall the words used by Virginia Woolf in her suicide note to Leonard:

> I should think it was hardly possible for two people to be more completely and unquestioningly happy. There was never a cloud, never a squabble. I knew that if Harold died, I should die too; it all made life very simple.[7]

On 19 January 1917, Vita gave birth to her second son, Nigel, at Ebury Street. This time, for once, Lady Sackville was acquiescent on the subject of names and there were no arguments. By the end of the year, Vita was a published poet, with inclusions in *Country Life* and a volume, *Poems of East and West*, published by The Bodley Head, but her private life was becoming turbulent. Although her love for Harold remained strong, the revelation that he had contracted a venereal disease threatened to rock their happiness badly. Vita had thrown her soul and all her passion into the early years of their marriage, but this realization of Harold's homosexuality had, unsurprisingly, a negative effect on the physical side of their relationship. Despite this blow, Vita continued to give him unconditional love and support, which goes some way to explaining Harold's later, remarkable tolerance of her significantly more high-profile affairs with other women.

Vita hid her unhappiness behind hard work, rewriting and finishing *Heritage*, her first novel. Harold went back to the Foreign Office, which meant that he was often away during the week. Lonely and needing a shoulder to cry on, Vita opened up her heart one night to her childhood friend Violet Trefusis; Violet, who had been in love with Vita for years, saw this vulnerability as her chance to pounce, and the infamous affair that changed Vita's life began at Long Barn on 18 April 1918.

By this time, the relationship between Vita's parents was also suffering, and all pretence of happiness had long since diminished, leaving a strained and artificial situation. Lady Sackville had been accepting vast sums of money from her devoted friend Sir John Wallace ('Seery'), and was to inherit a large fortune upon his death. She had also opened an interior furnishings shop in London, and her life consisted of one endless round of shopping, spending, ordering and designing; the once-beloved Lionel felt hurt and ignored, finding consolation in his mistress, Olive Rubens. To Lady Sackville's horror, he installed Rubens and her husband in apartments at Knole.

In 1919, when Lady Sackville finally, and unexpectedly, in a blaze of temper, left Knole forever, Vita and Lionel were truly stunned. Victoria, despite her temper, had been the lynchpin around which they all functioned. Vita watched in helpless grief as her mother stormed about, organizing the packing and servants. The departure from Knole of this vibrant, tempestuous woman, was almost like a bereavement, as it was in Virginia Stephen's childhood home at 22 Hyde Park Gate, where her mother-figure had been the central, life-giving force behind everyday existence. Vita described her parents many years later in a manner that brings to mind something of the early years of marriage between Julia and Leslie Stephen:

> I loved them both equally, though in different ways, my mother as the more brightly coloured figure, my father as the dear, steady, yet wistfully poetic one.[8]

Lord Sackville remained at Knole and Victoria bought herself not one, but three adjoining houses in Brighton, which she had knocked into one enormous mansion. She then rattled around bad-temperedly in it with only her servants for company. Although she was proud of Vita's *Heritage* when it came out in 1919, and proved herself a very pro-active publicist on her daughter's behalf, Lady Sackville was outraged during the following year to read the proofs of *Challenge*. Vita had based this novel on her love affair with Violet Trefusis; Harold, for once agreeing with his mother-in-law, ensured that publication was postponed and that the book was never published in England. For the next two years, Vita tested to the limits the patience of both her mother and her husband. The affair with Violet was all consuming; any event that Violet did not attend was condemned by Vita as being 'boring'. Violet had married Denys Trefusis at the very height of this affair, and the two women had then foolishly eloped to Amiens in France before their long-suffering husbands flew out and brought them home.

The passionate phase of Vita's affair with Violet Trefusis finally subsided in 1921. Vita threw herself into her home, her work and her children. Her new collection of poetry, *Orchard and Vineyard*, came out in 1922. She turned thirty, retaining her striking beauty; in reminiscences by Lady Sackville, written that year, Vita is described as having a complexion that is 'beautiful; so are her eyes, with their double curtain of long eyelashes'.

Another beautiful woman, Virginia Woolf, had turned forty that same year, and her brother-in-law, Clive Bell, had recently become a friend of Vita's. In November 1922 he handed Vita a copy of *Jacob's Room*, which she confessed to having read with interest but slight bewilderment. She relayed her admiration back via Clive, and on 14 December 1922, the two women met at one of Clive's dinner parties. Although Vita did not record her first impressions on paper, Virginia noted in her diary that she was 'muzzy-headed' following this meeting, but that Vita was 'not much' to her 'severer taste'. A return invitation to Ebury Street was politely issued from Vita, for 19 December – this time Virginia did not record the event, but Vita, already falling under her spell, wrote about that same evening to Harold; the passage below gives a revealing portrait of Virginia Woolf, aged forty, and also an indication of Vita's frank, accessible writing style:

> Mrs Woolf is so simple: she does give the impression of something big. She is utterly unaffected: there are no outward adornments – she dresses quite atrociously. At first you think she is plain; then a sort of spiritual beauty imposes itself on you, and you find a fascination in watching her. She was smarter last night; that is to say, the woollen orange stockings

were replaced by yellow silk ones, but she still wore the pumps. She is both detached and human, silent till she wants to say something and then says it supremely well. She is quite old (forty). I've rarely taken such a fancy to anyone, and I think she likes me. At least, she's asked me to Richmond where she lives. Darling, I have quite lost my heart.[9]

Before the dinner at Richmond took place on 10 January 1923, Vita began to bombard Virginia with books for her to read, and the recipient duly noted this in her diary together with a summation of Vita as 'the new apparition'. Their first dinner alone together passed without further comment from Virginia, but Vita was yet again both euphoric and resigned to her fate in this letter to Harold (who by now must have been hearing familiar warning bells):

I dined alone with Virginia Woolf last night. Oh dear, how much I love that woman.[10]

Before their next dinner together, the Nicolsons dropped in unexpectedly to Hogarth House. Virginia analysed Vita's appeal in her diary, concluding that part of the attraction was her ancestry. She also made reference to her new acquaintance being a 'pronounced Sapphist' and deliberated as to whether she herself was to become the next love object; but at this stage, Virginia was only amusedly toying with ideas. Despite her admiration for Vita's dashing, aristocratic manner and also for her prolific output as a writer, she had reservations about Vita's intelligence. Virginia, on the other hand, greatly excited Vita:

Dined with Virginia at Richmond. She is as delicious as ever. How right she is when she says that love makes everyone a bore, but the excitement of life lies in 'the little moves' nearer to people.[11]

Vita was obviously hoping for some 'little moves' to be made in her own direction, but, unbeknown to her, Virginia was recording yet more doubts about Vita's personality in her diary, judging both Nicolsons to be 'incurably stupid' after a dinner party at which Nessa, Duncan and Lytton had been scathing of the new guests.

The two women appear to have met only these three times in 1923, according to their diaries and letters; this is not as odd as it seems, given that towards the end of that year Vita had become embroiled in two new love affairs, one with Geoffrey Scott and the other with Dorothy Wellesley.

In March 1924, Leonard and Virginia moved to Tavistock Square, near their old haunts in Bloomsbury, taking the Hogarth Press with them. Vita was among the first to visit, but was horrified by the décor, referring to Vanessa and Duncan's painted panels as being 'of inconceivable hideousness'. She submitted her new book, *Seducers in Equador*, for Virginia's perusal. Virginia was impressed by the book and began to see Vita in a new, more flattering light. Vita set up a meeting for Virginia and Lord Sackville at Knole, and, never averse to an evening of aristocratic splendour, Virginia admitted to having greatly enjoyed the whole experience.

An admiring letter from Vita, sent on holiday in Italy during July, displayed her growing feelings for Virginia, her infamous 'wanderlust', her insecurity, her dislike of Bloomsbury and, significantly, the laying of 'bait' for Virginia to take if she chose:

Will you ever play truant to Bloomsbury and culture, I wonder, and come travelling with me? No, of course you won't. I told you once I would rather go to Spain with you than anyone, and you looked confused, and I felt I had made a gaffe, – been too personal, in fact, – but still the statement remains a true one, and I shan't be really satisfied until I have enticed you away.[12]

In the same letter, Vita, trying to presume intimate knowledge of her new friend, attributed Virginia's keen interest in human relationships to her needing to acquire 'copy', i.e. material for novels or short stories. Whatever truth there may have been in this observation, it stung Virginia enough for her to reply, admitting that she felt much pain and that such pain must, she realized, be the 'first stage of intimacy'. Although no serious harm appeared to have been done, Virginia remembered this comment of Vita's for a long time and sought subtle revenge two years later with this less than friendly analysis of Vita's *own* character:

Isn't there something obscure in you? There's something that doesn't vibrate in you: it may be purposely – you don't let it: but I see it with other people, as well as with me: something reserved, muted – God knows what ... it's in your writing too, by the by. The thing I call central transparency – sometimes fails you there too.[13]

This clever, but hurtful assessment of Vita's tendency to distance herself emotionally in her writing, caused Vita to analyse herself with some anguish in a letter to Harold.

Vita came for her first visit to Monk's House on 13 September 1924, and stayed overnight. The visit was innocent enough – Leonard was present, they all discussed literature, and Ottoline, and Virginia noted how her beloved Monk's House suddenly became a 'ruined barn' in comparison to Vita's luminosity and grandeur. The party walked to Charleston, which seemed 'grey' and 'shabby' in the shadow of Vita's illuminating presence.

The final meeting during 1924 between the two women caused Virginia to lapse into uncharacteristic vulgarity; in a letter of 26 December to Jacques Raverat, she proclaimed that Vita's *real* claim to uniqueness was neither the fact that she strode over her own land, surrounded by hounds, nor her prolific output as a novelist, but rather her *legs*, which Virginia described as 'running like slender pillars up into her trunk'. In this way, the year finished on a note of excited anticipation.

During the first part of 1925, the two writers met infrequently. Vita was shaking herself free from the clutches of the enamoured Geoffrey Scott and was also writing *The Land*, which would become her most famous, prize-winning poem. Virginia was starting to write *To the Lighthouse*, although she was plagued by headaches and minor illnesses. Vita and Virginia gradually grew closer over the summer, inspired by their common interest in literature. They wrote to one another regularly, in letters that flattered and teased, or were wistful and then provocative. Vita wrote with growing respect to her friend as she realized the multifarious nature of Virginia's daily schedule:

You seem to combine in yourself at least six whole-time jobs: novelist, journalist, printer, publisher's reader, friend, relation. Each of these an occupation in itself.[14]

But it was not until December, after Harold had left for Persia, that Virginia spent a long weekend with Vita at Long Barn. She arrived on the Wednesday and spent the next three days and nights alone with her, before Leonard arrived to collect her on the Saturday. Whilst her guest enjoyed breakfast in bed, Vita wrote to console and reassure Harold:

Please don't think that

a) I shall fall in love with Virginia
b) Virginia will fall in love with me.[15]

The physical aspect of Virginia and Vita's relationship, which began during this visit, was tentative, sporadic and not always successful. Virginia never alluded to it with anyone else, but Vita confided to Harold that although they *had* slept together, on this and subsequent occasions, their relationship was based mainly on companionship and deep affection. This was a far safer option for Vita, who was terrified of tipping Virginia into a mental breakdown. Virginia, unable to commit the details of their physical union to paper with quite the same frankness, still managed to convey the vibrant image of Vita striding into the grocer's shop at Sevenoaks in her pearls, confiding to her diary that this difficult year had been finished in 'great style', and even attributing her newly passionate relationship with Vita to Leonard, claiming that he had encouraged her to write to Vita in the first place.

What Leonard made of this claim is not known, but what is clear is that after a few initial misgivings, he saw no great harm in the friendship, rarely questioning it and, in time, realizing Vita's positive effect on Virginia's health, vitality and creative output. After Virginia's death, Vita was one of the first people allowed to visit Leonard, and they continued to treat one another with great affection.

The correspondence between Vita and Virginia increased in intensity when Vita departed for Persia with Dorothy Wellesley in January 1926. Only one day after her departure, Vita was already 'reduced to a thing that wants Virginia'[16] and Virginia's letters reciprocated the agony of being apart. After four months abroad, Vita returned to England and the two women spent a night alone together at Monk's House. Vita, as usual, sought to reassure Harold:

Virginia, not a muddle exactly; she is a busy and sensible woman. But she does love me, and I did sleep with her at Rodmell. That does not constitute a muddle though.[17]

By October 1926, Vita was seeing more of Dorothy Wellesley than she was of Virginia – a fact that she tried to conceal – but a visit to Tavistock Square in November forced her once more to analyse, with uncanny accuracy, Virginia's future and their friendship:

> I know Virginia will die, and it will be too awful (I don't mean *here*, over the weekend, but just die young) . . . oh Hadji, she *is* such an angel; I really adore her. Not 'in love', but just love – devotion.[18]

The exact form that this 'devotion' took, and the role played by each woman, is in a sense less clear than the issue that, until recently, was far more fascinating to the general public: whether or not Virginia Woolf and Vita Sackville-West were actually lovers in the true sense of the word. As we have seen, Vita herself admitted to having slept with Virginia, and Nigel Nicolson, Vita's son, made reference to the 'physical element' of their relationship in his *Portrait of a Marriage*, although he also states that to call this union an 'affair' would be a 'travesty of their relationship'.

It is abundantly clear that the key elements of the relationship were not sexual ones, but the far more enduring qualities of love, friendship, inspiration and respect; but how far the common assumption of Vita being 'maternal' towards Virginia is true has recently become less certain. Vita's son Nigel offers, in his latest biography of Virginia, an opinion that clashes with those of all Vita's and Virginia's biographers to date:

> It was said that Vita was like a mother to Virginia, but I can find no evidence of this. Their relationship, though tentative at first, was always on the level, protective, perhaps, on Vita's side, but not maternal, nor submissive on Virginia's. They were mutually solicitous and provocative.[19]

Nicolson's claim that there is 'no evidence' is puzzling; Virginia herself wrote in her diary that Vita 'lavished on' her the 'maternal protection'[20] that she needed from the women in her life. Perhaps Nicolson's opinion was influenced by the sometimes *less* than maternal attitude that Vita had towards both her sons, or perhaps he, more than most, has reason to suspect Virginia of exaggerating matters in her diary. Nonetheless, he stands alone with this particular theory; for Vita herself described incidences at Tavistock Square where she sat with Virginia at her feet, rumpling her hair in an obviously maternal manner. Virginia wrote to Vita that 'like a child, I think if you were here, I should be happy',[21] thereby imbuing Vita with the qualities of a surrogate mother. In his *The Interrupted Moment – A View of Virginia Woolf's Novels* (Stanford, 1986), Lucio Ruotolo claims that Virginia's *Orlando* was written to reclaim this maternal love of Vita's, and that Vita 'enjoyed the role of protectress and found Virginia's fragile dependence a source of some attraction'.

Although Nicolson's comments make it seem unlikely that Virginia received enough maternal affection from Vita to compensate for the losses of Julia and Stella during her childhood, what can certainly be deduced is that Vita went some way towards restoring the confidence that Virginia lost so traumatically at the hands of her half-brothers in the claustrophobic atmosphere of 22 Hyde Park Gate. After years of having a complex about looking in mirrors (stemming from an occasion where the young Virginia had seen, or imagined, the distorted reflection of an animal looking over her shoulder), Virginia purchased an antique mirror on her trip to France with Vita in 1928. The author Helen Dunmore sees the relationship between Vita and Virginia as providing 'solace, perhaps for the wounds which were inflicted upon Woolf's sexuality and sense of herself as a sexual being in childhood and youth'.[22]

Early in 1927, a delighted Virginia accepted the invitation to stay with Vita at Knole. Lord Sackville, together with his mistress Olive Rubens, patiently answered Virginia's endless questions, as she no doubt gained inspiration for the new novel that was beginning to shape itself in her head as respite from *To the Lighthouse*, which was published in May of that year. Vita loved *Lighthouse* and, years later, borrowed the poem *Luriana, Lurilee* that Virginia had included in the novel, for her own anthology of poetry, *Another World Than This* (the compilation was also to include a few lines from Virginia's *Orlando*).

By July 1927, however, Vita's affections became seriously diverted from Virginia as a new attraction arrived in the form of the beautiful poet Mary Campbell. Vita concealed the affair from Virginia, and their correspondence continued to be full of affection and declarations of love; Virginia still believed that her only rival for Vita's affection was Dorothy Wellesley. Thinking about Dorothy made Virginia insecure, and on 16 September, it provoked her to write Vita an uncharacteristically terse letter, which made no secret of her jealousy:

I won't belong to the two of you, or to the one of you, if the two of us belong to the one. In short, if Dotty's yours, I'm not. A profound truth is involved which I leave you to discover.[23]

Vita replied casually, but in the very last line of her letter she implored Virginia not to become too distant, adding that she, Vita, depended on her.

On 5 October, after a time of uncertainty for Virginia, the balance of power in this unpredictable friendship shifted back in her favour. Finally aware of the existence and importance of Mary Campbell to Vita, Virginia recorded, firstly in her diary and then in a letter to Vita, her ideas for *Orlando*, to be based on Vita's life and her Knole ancestry. Vita was enchanted and ensnared once more, and Virginia, for the meantime, was assured of her devoted attention:

> My God, Virginia, if ever I was thrilled and terrified it is at the prospect of being projected into the shape of *Orlando*. What fun for you; what fun for me. You see, any vengeance that you ever want to take will lie ready to your hand.[24]

Virginia's letters from thereafter, regained their coquettishness; she appeared to be doing everything possible to ensure that Vita still found her desirable above all other competition. Her letter of 5 December playfully discusses what might happen if she were in Vita's bed. Vita responded, as intended, with a desperate request for a visit, but even as she received that letter she was composing three passionate sonnets, not for Virginia, but for Mary Campbell. Vita's duplicitous nature was once more in full swing. In addition, she was writing letters that were economical with the truth to Harold; although she did tell him about Roy Campbell's dramatic suicide bids, she failed to reveal the reason for them – namely, that Roy had found out about Mary and Vita's affair.

By the summer of 1928, as Virginia finished writing *Orlando*, her relationship with Vita finally began to settle into fond friendship. She still loved Vita, but was aware that Vita's heart belonged elsewhere. Since breaking with Mary Campbell, Vita's new love was Hilda Matheson, the Head of Talks at the BBC; ironically, Vita and Harold did a BBC radio interview at around this time, in which they discussed the virtues of marriage(!).

All Vita's other distractions were temporarily forgotten when she first opened her copy of *Orlando*. She was truly humbled on two levels; as a writer, she was impressed by Virginia's literary achievement, and on a personal level, she was deeply flattered at the comparisons between herself and the dashing *Orlando*. She wasted no time in thanking Virginia:

> Darling, I don't know and scarcely even like to write, so overwhelmed am I, how you could have hung so splendid a garment on so poor a peg.[25]

Orlando, started almost as a joke and intended to provide Virginia with some light relief between her two difficult novels *To the Lighthouse* and *The Waves*, achieved fame instead for being an open declaration of her love for Vita. With this novel, Virginia returned Knole to her friend, giving her back the inheritance that she had been denied, and eulogizing Vita's connection with this lovely and ancient house. *Orlando* has been described by Nigel Nicolson as Virginia's 'most elaborate love letter', which indeed it is, but others see a more technical reason behind it.

Lucio Ruotolo claims that *Orlando* represented an 'important break in Woolf's literary development, an escapade, as she put it later, from the more demanding task of formulating new directions from the novel'.[26] Suzanne Raitt sees the novel as being 'about the loss, and the recovery, of maternal care'.[27] Discussing the diversity of performances by actors who have played *Orlando*, both in terms of text and also of gender, Brenda R. Silver maintains that the novel's connection with Vita has ensured that *Orlando* has always had a following among those who know the real story behind its 'encrypted lesbianism'[28] She also states that the playing-down of this lesbianism in Sally Potter's 1992 film, was the reason why British filmgoers praised and accepted the film whilst some Americans disappointedly complained that it was not properly a 'lesbian film' at all. And Vita's mother, Lady Sackville, was outraged at the book's publication, with its revelation of the affair between her daughter and that 'madwoman' Virginia Woolf.

With the writing of *Orlando*, Virginia exorcized some of her more painful feelings for Vita and eased her draining obsession with keeping her love. She also inspired her friend to work harder on her own historical novel, *The Edwardians* (published in 1930 by the Hogarth Press),

which was again based on Knole and the Sackville family. It is a romantic story, conveying Vita's love of traditional values coupled with her
dislike of Edwardian ones. The book was a bestseller, making money for
both author and publisher, but Virginia preferred *All Passion Spent*,
Vita's next book, which was based on the whimsical reflections of an old
woman at the very end of her life. It can be seen as a feminist novel and
was likely to have been influenced by Virginia's *A Room of One's Own*,
based on two lectures given at Cambridge, one in the company of Vita.

In 1930, Vita and Harold purchased Sissinghurst Castle in Kent
after finding out that it had Sackville family connections. They did not
move in until 1932, after much renovation work had been done, but
here, with a tower she could use as a writing-room and other cottages
and outbuildings to provide enough bedrooms and sitting-rooms for
the family, Vita found further consolation for the loss of Knole. Soon
after moving in, she wrote a poem, 'Sissinghurst', and dedicated it to
'V.W.', again enraging Lady Sackville, who was still fuming about the
publication of *Orlando*. 'Sissinghurst' reveals a calmer, more reflective
side of Vita, as she takes stock of her new surroundings:

> So plods my stallion up my evening lane
> And fills me with a mindless deep repose
> Wherein I find in chain
> The castle, and the pasture, and the rose.[29]

Vita's love of the countryside and the trees, plants and wildlife
within it, became stronger every day, and the famous Sissinghurst
gardens began to take shape, providing a source of comfort and shared
pleasure for Harold and Vita. There were always animals around, as
Vita loved dogs and had given one of hers, Pinka, to Virginia.
Surprisingly, given her aristocratic upbringing, Vita abhorred cruelty
to animals and forbade any hunting or shooting on her land. The
following poem reveals both her anger and the softer, more endearing
side of her nature:

> Within the acres that I rule
> The little patch of peace I vaunt
> Where ways are safe and shadows cool
> Shall come no scarlet-coated fool
> To tease my foxes from their haunt.[30]

Vita's newfound happiness at Sissinghurst occupied her fully for a while, but in Virginia's life, significant changes were occurring. By the time she first visited Sissinghurst, Virginia was becoming involved in an absorbing new friendship with the composer Ethel Smyth. In addition, she was deeply immersed in writing *The Waves*. The pattern of friendship between Virginia and Vita was settling into something less disruptive and of more benefit to both of them. Their letters continued to be loving, genuine and intimate right up until Virginia's death in 1941, but in 1931, after finishing *All Passion Spent*, Vita predictably fell in love again, this time with the journalist Evelyn Irons.

Evelyn returned her passion wholeheartedly, and the two became lovers, sleeping together at Sissinghurst. As was usual with Vita, complications occurred; Evelyn was already living with another woman, Olive Rinder. The inevitable happened – Olive went to Sissinghurst to inspect her rival, promptly falling in love with her. Vita, unable to resist flattery, and still desperately needing to be loved and desired, carried on seeing *both* women! Evelyn's infatuation, demonstrating the incredibly powerful effect that Vita had on so many women, can clearly be seen in one of her earlier letters:

Darling, shall I say 'I am completely happy. I don't miss you much. I don't think I love you quite as passionately as I did yesterday'? No, I'll give you the truth – I can't live without you and I'll love you till I die.[31]

Vita responded, typically, with an overly sentimental poem:

Since in each other's arms they sleeping lay
Towards each other had no need to turn
When love was interwoven night and day.[32]

In the spring of 1931, no doubt curious about Evelyn, Virginia asked if she could watch a newspaper being printed at the *Daily Mail*, where Evelyn worked. Virginia did not record this visit, which also included Vita and Leonard, and it is difficult to gauge her reaction to Evelyn, as some seventy letters from Virginia to Vita written during this year later went missing; but the visit made a notable impact on Evelyn, who wrote her account of it some thirty years later in a 1963 issue of the *New Yorker* magazine. The piece is worth including here, for it gives a poignant, affectionate and witty picture of the *Daily Mail*'s two striking female visitors. Vita was forty, Virginia fifty:

> But there they were, perched round the room like unfamiliar night birds: Vita Sackville-West, tall, intensely handsome, wearing her usual long, dangling earrings and smoking through a paper cigarette holder; Leonard Woolf, a dark brooding man with aggressive eyebrows; and Virginia Woolf, recalling the moon in the daytime sky – ethereal, bone-pale, the eyes set deep in the skull. She was fifty, but age had nothing to do with her appearance; she might have looked like that forever. You might as well show those clattering presses to a ghost, I thought, but she had asked to be shown them . . . Mrs Woolf put on a pair of steel-rimmed spectacles and looked at this scene with intense interest. We inspected everything, down to the circle of telephone booths in the centre of the roll . . . as we left the plant on our way to supper at the Jardin des Gourmets, one of the printers from the composing room who had come out onto the sidewalk to take the air grabbed my arm, drew me aside and asked, 'Who's that lady that was asking all the questions up there?' 'Virginia Woolf,' I answered. 'That's her husband and they run the Hogarth Press.' 'Oh,' he said in a disappointed voice. '*Books*.'

Although Vita and Virginia stayed in touch, their correspondence became less frequent from 1932 onwards. Despite Virginia's success as a writer and the extraordinary amount of anguish and mental energy that she poured into *The Years* (not published until March 1937), Vita's lapse as a correspondent hurt Virginia enough for her to complain to Ethel Smyth that she 'never heard a word from V., which rather hurts me'.[33] Her relationship with Vita up until that point had still been influencing her writing, and a recognizable portrait of Vita was drawn in the character of Kitty in *The Years*; Kitty has a commanding presence and a dashing, aristocratic manner reminiscent of Vita's. She 'strides' rather than walks, drives a large car, loves gardening and loses her inheritance because she is female. Virginia used Kitty to reflect on Vita's grief at losing Knole:

> Spring was sad always, she thought; it brought back memories. All passes, all changes, she thought, as she climbed up the little path between the trees. Nothing of this world belonged to her; her son would inherit; his wife would walk here after her.

But, like Vita, Kitty is 'in the prime of life; she was vigorous. She strode on'.[34]

Mitchell Leaska sees Vita's character in Virginia's last novel, *Pointz Hall* (published posthumously as *Between the Acts*). It is certainly true that Mrs Manresa is confident, ebullient, and at times, too much to handle. Virginia's description of this character brings to mind her earlier observations, noted in her diary, concerning Vita's admirable command of hounds, children and land:

> Vulgar she was in her gestures, in her whole person, over-sexed, over-dressed for a picnic. But what a desirable, at least valuable, quality it was – for everybody felt, directly she spoke, 'she's said it, she's done it, not I', and could take advantage of the breach of decorum, of the fresh air that blew in, to follow like leaping dolphins in the wake of an ice-breaking vessel.[35]

There was no doubt that Vita did, at times, appear oversexed and bumptious compared to the slender, refined Virginia. Vita's life from the age of twenty up until she was in her sixties had been a permanent struggle between her desire for 'wanderlust' and her deeply engrained notions of how an aristocrat should behave. She never lost the insecurity that stemmed from her childhood, and frequently felt pressured by the need to conform to the behaviour that was expected of women who had come of age in Edwardian society. These conflicting voices within her, and the determination to try and maintain, at least outwardly, her respectable, heterosexual marriage whilst simultaneously indulging in a series of unsteady love affairs, caused endless misery to herself, Harold and a host of other people. She possessed a duality of nature that is accurately caught in Lillian Faderman's *Surpassing the Love of Men*:

> There was a split in her personality all right, but not the kind she imagined. Rather it was the split of an individual deceiving herself with a notion of her freedom and bohemianism, entrapped by the moral shibboleths of her day, which limited her perspective as surely as if she had been a model of conformity.[36]

Vita grew more reclusive as she aged, and her love affairs diminished, to be replaced by contentment and a peace of mind previously unobtainable. She withdrew into her private world at Sissinghurst, wrote a gardening column for the *Observer* and continued to write poetry and articles, although the cultivation of her gardens became, in old age, her preferred occupation. Her marriage to Harold survived all the years of uncertainty and emotional turmoil, partly due, no doubt, to his great gentleness and understanding, and it remained solid and a source of much shared happiness until their deaths.

Virginia's affection for Vita continued. Her last extant letter to Vita was written on 22 March 1941, a week before her death, and in it she offered, somewhat vaguely, to come to Sissinghurst. The visit never took place.

Vita mourned Virginia with anguish after her death, writing to Harold in 1949 that the two people she missed most were Virginia, and Geoffrey Scott, but pointing out that whereas Scott had proved to be a 'nuisance', Virginia had never been a 'nuisance, but only a delight'.[37]

By 1953, however, with the benefit of hindsight and the passing of time, Vita's positive memories of Virginia were becoming tinged with doubts. She became able, on publication of extracts from Virginia's diary, to glimpse the other side of Virginia's character. It was the side that had rarely surfaced with Vita, but had the power to hurt and shock from beyond the grave, for the diaries contained spiteful and malicious references to many friends, herself included. How sad that, in the following paragraph, Vita's great love for Virginia has been reduced to the word 'like':

> I can't get over Virginia's diary – so self-pitying, so vain in a way so malicious. The envy is difficult to understand. One realizes that she must have been far more mad than that calm exterior suggested. It doesn't make me admire or like her less. But it will surely create a bad impression on those who never saw her great dignity or witnessed the wit and curiosity that rendered her animated. It really has left me with a puzzle.[38]

The other 'puzzle' that Vita was left trying to solve was whether or not she, better than anyone, could have persuaded Virginia not to kill herself. It seems unlikely that her involvement would have made any difference; such intense depression could not have been lifted by a friendly word. Vita must later have re-read her own poem, 'Sissinghurst', written in 1930 and dedicated to Virginia, with a shudder, for, in retrospect, the opening lines appear not only to have somehow predicted her friend's weary descent into depression and death, but also even to recall Virginia's own description of Julia Stephen's exhausted demise back in 1895:

> A tired swimmer in the waves of time
> I throw my hands up: let the surface close.

7 Ethel

It is sometimes a relief to meet a primitive animal such as Ethel, a rogue elephant disobedient to the herd.[1]

By the time Ethel Smyth burst into the life of Virginia Woolf at the age of seventy-two, her career as a working composer was largely over, and she had devoted herself to writing her autobiography. Virginia, aged forty-eight, was established as a successful author, with *The Voyage Out*, *Night and Day*, *Jacob's Room*, *To the Lighthouse*, *Orlando*, *A Room of One's Own*, *The Common Reader* and *Mrs Dalloway* all published to acclaim. She was working on *The Waves* and dividing her time between Tavistock Square in Bloomsbury and Monk's House, Rodmell. Her life, although punctuated by headaches and influenza, was fairly sedate.

Into this ordered calm, on 20 February 1930, exploded the extraordinary character of Ethel Smyth. Over the last decade of Virginia's life, she was to become both a much-needed tonic and a dose of the worst possible medicine. There is little doubt that she brought love, friendship and inspiration into Virginia's life, but Ethel often brought these gifts only when *she* chose to, causing great interruption to Virginia's endless quest for a peaceful, productive writing day. Nevertheless, it was an endearing and enduring friendship, which tested Virginia's patience to the limit at times, but also enabled her to put down on paper many private thoughts and emotions that had lain hitherto unconfessed. It was also to be the last great friendship of Virginia's life.

Ethel Mary Smyth was born in London on 23 April 1858, to Lt. Col. John Hall Smyth and Emma Stracey. From the start, she was encouraged to indulge her interest in music, although she did not develop a real passion for it until the age of twelve, when a governess played her a Beethoven piano sonata. Shortly after Ethel left school in 1875, her elder brother died unexpectedly in a hunting accident, and Ethel, who had decided that she must aim to study music at the Leipzig Conservatorium, found herself trapped at home instead, with a clutch of young siblings to care for. Her desire for Leipzig persisted; her father opposed the idea, but Ethel, true to form, argued her case with great stubbornness, for it seemed a much better opportunity than studying in London at the Royal Academy, which at the time did not offer the same high level of training given at Leipzig.

While Lt. Col. Smyth tried to find reasons to keep his daughter at home, Ethel was introduced to Judy Ewing, a children's author and the wife of the composer of 'Jerusalem the Golden', a popular Victorian hymn. Mr Ewing took one look at Ethel's compositions and realized that he was witnessing an exceptional musical talent. He relayed this to Ethel's parents and requested that he might start to teach her the rudiments of harmony and music theory. With the encouragement of her mother, Ethel went to Mr Ewing for classes in composition, and to Mrs Ewing for some literature classes. This agreeable arrangement went drastically wrong after only a short time when Lt. Col. Smyth became convinced that Ewing's intentions towards his daughter were not just professional, but dishonourable. Ethel tried to convince him that he was wrong, but to no avail.

It took two years for father and daughter to reach an uneasy truce, until finally, on 26 July 1877, Ethel Smyth, aged only nineteen, left for the Leipzig Conservatorium – the triumphant conclusion to her seven-year wait. Already showing signs of the boundless enthusiasm that was to render her such an exhausting friend in later years, she arrived several weeks before term started and wandered around Leipzig in a haze of happiness, admiring the architecture and standing with reverence in the church where Bach had once held the post of organist.

Once term had started, Ethel was taken under the wing of a musical family, the Röntgens, who recognized and encouraged her talent; flatteringly, they compared her first efforts at writing a piano sonata to one written by Mozart. The first term threatened Ethel's individuality – as anyone who has attended a music college will have experienced, there is something humbling about finding oneself surrounded by three hundred equally talented musicians – but Ethel continued to shine at composition, and although she never learned how to position her hands correctly on the piano, she demonstrated a talent for singing that more than compensated.

Ethel met and befriended the daughter of the composer Felix Mendelssohn, Lili Wach, a friendship that stayed warm and close until Lili's sudden death in 1906. Another beautiful friend, Lisl von Herzogenberg, became the object of Ethel's desire, and, because she was childless, enjoyed lavishing maternal protection on Ethel, who, in turn, would be demanded by Virginia Woolf to *supply* this protection to her in later years.

Through Lisl, Ethel was introduced to Brahms, an event she looked forward to greatly. Unfortunately, on showing the great composer one of her own fugal compositions, Brahms, quite reasonably, offered her some constructive criticism, whereupon Ethel lost control and challenged him on some minor detail, causing Brahms to finish his analysis by expressing contempt for this outspoken young woman. As she was to do so often in life, Ethel interpreted the snub as a sexist one; because she, a girl, had interrupted the great maestro, he had been reminded that she was after all, a mere female, someone not to be taken as seriously as a male composer. In fact, she was wrong – although Brahms did not hold a very high opinion of women in general, on this occasion he was irritated purely by Ethel's obsession with a minor detail in the music. But the damage was done; although she was always to remain heavily influenced by his work, Ethel became fond of recalling that Brahms, when confronted by a pretty woman, had a 'way of pushing out his lips' that she found immensely irritating.

In 1880, during a vacation in England, Ethel formed a close friendship with Rhoda Garrett, a member of the 'Women's Movement' that would, many years later, become an integral part of Ethel's life. (Rhoda's cousin was Elizabeth Garrett-Anderson, who was to achieve fame as an ardent Suffragette). But Ethel, wrapped up in her music and the development of her composing career, was not to take the Garretts and their struggles for equality seriously for another thirty years.

In 1882, after four years of intensive study, Ethel decided to spend the winter in Italy. While baby Adeline Virginia Stephen was being introduced into the Stephen family nursery in Kensington, Ethel was touring Italy. Smyth began an unhappy affair with Lisl's brother-in-law, Harry Brewster, and entered into an enormous correspondence with him; Ethel's later letters to Virginia Woolf pale into insignificance beside the length of her letters to Brewster – some of them ran to over five thousand words. Returning to Leipzig, Ethel found herself without Lisl's friendship, but in the company of several new acquaintances, including Tchaikovsky. Her chamber music was performed for the first time, to a clutch of disparaging reviews. Never one to remain disheartened for long, Ethel began composing her first important work, the *Mass in D* and on 26 April 1890, she made her debut in England with a performance of her orchestral work, *Serenade*. This piece was well received, and Ethel now had reason to feel positive about her future career.

The *Mass in D* was premièred in 1893 at the Royal Albert Hall to a wildly enthusiastic reaction from the audience and also from *The Times*, which noted that 'this work definitely places the composer among the most eminent composers of her time,' but then goes on to add 'and easily at the head of all those of her *own sex*' (my italics). 'Is a great female composer possible?' scathingly asked *The Star* newspaper. George Bernard Shaw, in his early, less well-known vocation as a music critic, made snooty reference to the 'appallingly commonplace preparatory passages'. In her own memoirs, Ethel recalled yet another galling comment:

> The only other unofficial comment I recall is that of Archbishop Benson, who overhearing bits of it at Addington, remarked afterwards that in this Mass, God was not *implored* but *commanded* to have mercy.[2]

Ethel was forced to wait a staggering thirty-one years before her *Mass* was performed again in public. The wait was not due, despite what Ethel liked to believe, to her being a woman, but because her music was vigorous, personal and unique, in a way that frightened the majority of critics.

The public did not welcome new English music, a prejudice that continues to some extent today, but listening to the *Mass* now, it is almost impossible to understand the neglect of this outstanding piece of music. Devoid of the militant tendencies that overshadowed and dated much of Ethel's later work, her *Mass* remains timeless, one hundred years after its composition. The fiery, passionate score owes much to the influence of Ethel's much-maligned Brahms, and its lyrical beauty is Victorian in flavour, but not overly so. The *Agnus Dei* is particularly beautiful, with spine-tingling passages of exquisite suspense before the full chorus explodes into a dramatic conclusion that leaves the listener shaken and unsettled. But this work, with its great, dark, dramatic overtones, benefits the listener further if he or she knows something about the character of the composer who created it; Ethel Smyth, at thirty-four, was passionate, emotional, determined and highly individual. During her thirties she was also fervently religious; all in all, she possessed a myriad of qualities that produced music both disturbing and profoundly moving.

In 1910, Ethel began *The Wreckers*, her opera inspired by the Cornish coast, for which she, like Virginia Woolf, had a great passion. As with her *Mass*, Ethel's opera demonstrates her deeper, more profound side. She sent the score to Delius, who told her that he appreciated the vigour apparent in this composition, a vigour rarely to be found in British music. Ethel travelled around Europe in her role as a travelling sales-composer, trying to find someone who would put on a performance of *The Wreckers*. Eventually she returned to England where, to her delight, Thomas Beecham finally agreed to conduct it at Covent Garden. Her joy was short-lived – Beecham did not give the performance the attention that she thought it deserved, saving his energies instead for compositions by Strauss and Delius. Edward VII turned up at this concert and attempted to kiss Ethel, which she did not take kindly to. The disappointment and her struggle for recognition were to continue.

The year 1911 was an important turning point in Ethel's life. She met Emmeline Pankhurst and fell in love with her, joining the Women's Social and Political Union (WSPU). After some initial qualms as to how her composing would be affected by this commitment, she threw herself with Ethel-style determination into the cause, giving two years of her life to the militant Suffrage movement. Sylvia Pankhurst gives us a glimpse of Ethel as she appeared to others at that time:

Individualised to the last point, she had in middle age little about her that was feminine. Her features were clean cut and well marked, neither manly nor womanly; her thin hair drawn plainly aside, her speech clear in articulation and incisive rather than melodious, with a racy wit. Wearing a small mannish hat, battered and old, plain-cut country clothes . . . she would don a tie of the brightest purple, white and green [these were the official colours of the WSPU] colours she was so proud of, which shone out from her incongruously, like a new gate to old palings.[3]

Ethel also composed a special piece for the WSPU, still available as a recording today. In marked contrast to her earlier work, this *March of the Women* is militant, patriotic, rousing and regimental. It is controlled, rigid and rather forceful in a way that the passionate, rambling *Mass* is not. But the *March* recalls an important and nostalgic period in women's history and can instantly summon up the image of Suffragette rallies, although to the contemporary listener there is something dated and a little ridiculous about the pomposity of the music. At the time, though, Ethel's *March* brought her fame and notoriety as a composer, and it became the official accompaniment to all Suffragette marches. On being imprisoned for throwing a stone at the window of a Cabinet Minister, Ethel, as Thomas Beecham was fond of recounting, conducted her two hundred fellow prisoners with a toothbrush as they paraded around the courtyard, leaning from an upper window whilst beating time.

Ethel was unrepentant for her stone throwing, but her time as a Suffragette ran its course, and the two years spent away from music resulted in her longing to get back to life as a full-time composer. She took a trip to Egypt, hiding away in a pavilion to work on her new opera, *The Boatswain's Mate*, with only a piano for company. In 1914 she once more took the role of a travelling saleswoman, peddling her scores around Vienna for the new opera and for *The Wreckers*; she returned to England triumphantly clutching contracts for the performances of both works at two leading continental opera houses. But, as so often in Ethel's eventful life, things did not go according to plan, and the First World War inconveniently put a stop to the concerts going ahead.

Never deterred for long, Ethel put on her own performance of *The Wreckers*, at the Shaftesbury Theatre in London, conducting the opening night herself and then handing over to Thomas Beecham for a further six performances. Finally, in 1924, Ethel's *Mass in D* was resurrected at the Queen's Hall, and conducted by Adrian Boult. George Bernard Shaw, somewhat hypocritically given his criticism thirty years earlier, wrote to congratulate Ethel, giving his opinion that 'the originality and beauty of the voice parts are as striking today as they were thirty years ago'.[4] Other parts of his letter meant more to Ethel, as they dwelled flatteringly on her new reputation as a successful female composer who could hold her own against any male contemporary.

After *The Wreckers*, Ethel produced several more works, including some chamber music, organ preludes and songs with piano or orchestral accompaniments. Her last great work was *The Prison* (1930), based on her published memoir of Henry Brewster. In 1931, in Edinburgh, Ethel conducted the first performance at one of Donald Tovey's symphony concerts. It was unanimously declared to be a triumph by the critics and the audience. A less successful performance in London shortly afterwards had a negative effect on both the audience and Ethel; the work, which finishes with the *Last Post*, was scheduled for the same programme as another funereal work called *The Last Things of Man*. The audience came out gloomy, depressed and annoyed (those who lasted the entire performance, that is – many walked out halfway through).

Adrian Boult, who had produced this performance, found his friendship with Ethel severely tested as a result; Ethel had the usual trouble finding further venues for the work to be performed in, and *The Prison* was eventually performed for her seventy-fifth birthday tribute at the Royal Albert Hall. Some thought this concert the best performance to date of Ethel's work, with Thomas Beecham conducting magnificently. The sad irony was that Ethel, stone deaf by then, was unable to hear her own compositions.

Although Virginia Woolf and Ethel Smyth did not meet formally for the first time until 1930, Virginia had made her first appraisal of Ethel far earlier, in November 1919 when they were both in the audience for a concert at the Wigmore Hall. Ethel's striking appearance did not escape Virginia's critical eye:

> Near at hand one sees that she's all wrinkled and fallen in, and eyes running blue on to the cheeks; but she keeps up the figure of the nineties to perfection.[5]

With this description, included in a letter to Lytton, Virginia included her witty opinion of Ethel's first volume of autobiography, just published, concluding that 'Ethel's passion for the W.C. (it occurs in every chapter) is of the highest merit'. 'Friendships with women' she added prophetically, 'interest me'. In 1921, Virginia published a glowing review of the second volume of Ethel's autobiography, *Streaks of Life*, in the *New Statesman*, paying particular tribute to the writer's enthusiasm, originality and wholehearted dedication to the pursuit of female friendship.

The first serious attempts to schedule a meeting between Virginia and Ethel ran similarly to Ethel's attempts to get her music performed; delays, last-minute cancellations and letters of apology abounded, mainly from Virginia who was suffering from influenza during the first few weeks of February 1930. She was also under considerable stress whilst writing *The Waves*. Ethel had written to Virginia saying how much she had enjoyed *A Room of One's Own*, and had included a special edition of her own autobiography as a gift. Virginia was pleased with both letter and gift, and wrote a warm reply. As in Ethel's operas, this introduction had already given a flavour of the performance yet to come; the scene appeared to be set favourably for the development of an interesting friendship.

On 20 February 1930, Ethel quite literally burst into the room where Virginia was lying quietly, recovering from a morning visit made by Marjorie Snowden, who had been maudlin and full of complaints about her life. Ethel could not have presented more of a contrast. She wore her trademark three-cornered hat and grey tailored suit, and was clutching a notebook in which to write the answers to the many questions she had lined up for Virginia. Ethel demanded to know Virginia's family history, wanting details of all the Pattle relatives and the names of their various daughters, until tea interrupted the flow, after which the two women continued to talk until seven, when Leonard entered. His early impressions of Ethel were far from favourable; he detested her vulgarity and saw her as a threat to Virginia's health and peace of mind.

The general topic for discussion during this first meeting had been – Ethel herself! She waxed lyrical about her musical career (in particular the struggles she was currently undergoing whilst orchestrating *The Prison*), about golf, cycling and her life in Woking. She also complimented *A Room of One's Own* again. Virginia, despite herself, was enchanted, and concluded in her diary that Ethel was 'a fine old creature'. Act One, Scene One had thereby contained the highest entertainment value possible; the rest of the performance, during which the friendship between Ethel and Virginia would develop further, seemed destined to pass successfully.

Ethel instantly developed a great partiality to Virginia, although she did not admit this until June, confiding in a letter to Vanessa Bell that 'it will be hard not to get attached to V.'.[6] But attached she immediately became, musing on her feelings in one of the hundreds, possibly thousands, of letters that she dashed off to her new love-object, Virginia, in a way that demonstrated her intelligence, insight and sincerity. It would have been difficult for the following letter not to appeal to both the vain side of Virginia, that which craved success, flattery and approval, and her insecure side, the one that doubted her own beauty and genius:

> Odd as it may seem to you I did love you before I saw you, wholly and solely because of *A Room of One's Own*. There is that in it – most of it far away in the background, the inmost core of your book, that (as I once found out) is your essence. Then I saw you and was glad – as I think I told you – that I had felt all that before I had seen you – because your beauty is an unescapable [sic] factor unless (as in the case of Mrs Ramsey [sic] it was remarked) you were born stone blind.[7]

In the same letter, Ethel's poignant reminiscences of her own mother, who died not long before Virginia's, must have struck a powerful chord with Woolf, who had spent most of her adult life reflecting on the enigma that was Julia Stephen:

> I can never think about her without a stab of real passion and amusement, tenderness, pity, admiration are in it and pain that I can't tell her how I love her.

As well as yearning for Virginia's friendship, Ethel also fell passionately in love with her, making no secret of it. She analysed her feelings in some depth in a series of short, written pieces describing Virginia in intimate and unflinchingly honest terms; she often refers to Virginia's vanity, not about her writing, but her looks, thus instantly shattering the belief held by many that Virginia Woolf did not much care for clothes or about how she appeared to others. Whilst Vanessa Bell rarely wore anything other than artists' overalls at Charleston, living in the general chaos of children, lovers and paintbrushes that fulfilled her needs, her insecure younger sister obviously still keenly felt the need for reassurance about her looks:

> She is very vain, and tries not to be, but can't help it. If she heard that someone thought her books very overrated, she wouldn't care at all. But if she heard these snooks [sic] had said her eyes were too close together (which they are perhaps) she would be thoroughly annoyed.[8]

It was not long after they had first met before Ethel, however entertaining she was, suffered the sharper side of Virginia's tongue, and noted the experience, without resentment, in her diary:

> Only her passion of fury – the slightly insane streak in her on which I am convinced her terrific gift depends – has to expend itself. She can be cruel then, and may say something that lashes one across the face, but she has to give that flick . . . fortunately in the new epoch the flick no longer hurts.[9]

As with Violet Dickinson and Vita Sackville-West beforehand, Virginia initially believed Ethel to be a new source of that much-needed motherly love. This was not due solely to the significant age gap between the two women; in fact, Ethel's old age and elderly appearance came to repel Virginia, unhealthily feeding her own obsession with age, dying and death, and Ethel did not at first seem to be the most maternal of people, never having had children of her own and being abrupt, rather than tender, in her manner. But Smyth's very real, honest personality held many attractions for Virginia, and it was her loyalty and genuine care for the younger woman that provoked, yet again, the occasional demand for this matermal love:

> You are, I believe, one of the kindest women, one of the best balanced, with that maternal quality which of all others I need and adore.[10]

After the first year of their friendship, Virginia came to admire Ethel for other reasons; she was an excellent confidante, a successful female artiste, witty, big-hearted and inspirational. Virginia summarized a diary entry analysis of Ethel in August 1903 with reference to her 'certain smile, very wide and benignant'. She enjoyed Ethel's infectious enthusiasm and boundless ambition. This first year of friendship with Ethel, whilst it contained a few fiery sparks, proved intriguing and refreshing to Virginia.

Unfortunately, given Ethel's monstrous egotism and Virginia's sensitivity, an argument seemed inevitable. At the end of February 1931, Virginia had just completed *The Waves* and was severely depressed, remembering Thoby's death and suffering from her usual post-book 'back wash'. On 24 February, the Countess of Rosebery gave a party at Berkeley Square in order to celebrate Ethel's first performance of *The Prison*. Ethel took Virginia along, but the party, full of aristocrats and well-to-do society ladies, no doubt reminded the vulnerable Virginia of being dragged by George Duckworth to similar events as an unwilling teenager. She had a violent over-reaction to this party, proclaiming it to be 'that awful Exhibition of insincerity and insanity'.[11] She wrote about the evening in her diary and also in letters to Ottoline, admitting to not having been able to sleep a wink after-wards, and to Ethel herself in an angry letter, describing the 'indignity' of having to make polite small talk and suffer the attentions of butlers and peers, and, oddly, of having to drink champagne. Virginia reported that she had resorted to taking a sleeping draught afterwards and complained of being made an exhibit of. This letter is indicative of her severely stressed state of mind at the time rather than revealing any blame on the part of poor Ethel; after all, Ethel had merely invited her friend to a party, presuming that she might enjoy it. Virginia, to punish Ethel further, retreated back into her safe relationship with Vita Sackville-West, writing to her as 'honey', requesting a visit to help soothe her damaged nerves.

In May 1931, Ethel fell out badly with Adrian Boult over the production of *The Prison* for the BBC. He then refused point blank to conduct it, so Ethel stomped round to Virginia for comfort, regaling her with the long story of her life with all its various persecutions, swamping Virginia with demands for sympathy. Her weary friend, suffering a bad headache and longing to get down to Rodmell for some peace and quiet, lost her temper and shouted at Ethel, protesting that unless she shut up, one or other of them would probably burst into flames and spontaneously combust.

Ethel then sent Virginia a copy of an article she had written for the *New Statesman* in which she had complained about her own bad treat-ment as a woman composer. With her patience already wearing

terribly thin, Virginia immodestly replied that if *she* had had the originality and drive to set up her own publishing press, why couldn't
Ethel create and manage her own orchestra? Woolf's reply becomes
even more insensitive, comparing Ethel to a large, hairy Cornish pig
that was using Virginia as its scratching-post. Not surprisingly, Ethel
exploded with rage and Virginia suffered more visits during which
Ethel, ranting and bombastic, insulted Virginia, who now was beginning to refer to these occasions as an insult to the 'celebrated sensibil-
ity' of her nervous system.

Their friendship did actually survive the storminess of 1931, but
Virginia's tone in her letters to Ethel changed, taking on an ironic
wisdom and a faintly mocking tone. She remained fond of Ethel, and
confided in her more openly than with any other woman, discussing
sex, masturbation and other topics that she had never before been able
to mention. However, she also referred more frequently in her diary
to 'old Ethel's' advancing years, her unattractiveness, her unpleasant
way of chomping through food, her red-facedness and her ability to
wind Virginia up into a frenzy. Ethel was by now almost completely
deaf, which meant that she did not compose any more major works
after *The Prison*, but she was pleased about a revival of *The Wreckers*
in 1931, and invited Virginia to attend the performance – which she
did, even managing to enjoy it.

Virginia Woolf was not the only woman who simultaneously
adored and was frustrated by Ethel Smyth. Vita Sackville-West, who
still loved Virginia and often resented Ethel for stealing her away so
often, did not enjoy Ethel's visits all that much, and reacted to her
egotism with weary resignation. In August 1931, in the throes of her
new love affair with Evelyn Irons, Vita complained to Evelyn that:

> Now old Ethel Smyth wants to come to stay at Sissinghurst. What am I
> to do? I adore Ethel, but I don't want to give up an evening to her. Very
> difficult. She will talk about life and how impossible it is for women to
> play in orchestras. And although she is a damned good writer I have a
> suspicion that she is a damn dull musician . . . one cannot hurt the feel-
> ings of people of 73.[12]

Vita continued to demonstrate both her respect for the elderly, and
her frustration at Ethel's monopolization of Virginia in a cross letter to
the latter:

Isn't it enraging that of all people in the world, your own particular
Ethel should be the one to prevent me dining with you tomorrow? But
there it is – the engagement has been arranged for weeks past – I get
letters fairly trumpeting with excitement from Ethel by every post –
supplemented by post cards and telegrams, and so I felt I simply couldn't
put her off – much as I longed to. Anyone else – any herring griller –
could have gone to hell. But Ethel, I reflected, is 75 and one cannot play
fast and loose with the old.[13]

Ethel, Vita goes on to say, has 'defrauded' her of an evening with
Virginia. Despite her exhaustion, Vita did love Ethel dearly and
enjoyed her humour as much as Virginia did.

Looking back, after Ethel's death, Vita gave a recognizable portrait
of the woman who frustrated, pestered and amused her closest friends,
and a taste, in turn, of what it was like for Virginia to be loved by
Ethel:

And how angry she would get when her friends didn't answer her
letters in detail. Poor Virginia Woolf, endlessly patient under this loving
persecution, had to endure long questionnaires: 'You haven't answered
my questions one, two, three, four – right up to twenty. Please reply by
return of post'. Ethel seemed to command endless time, and to expect
her friends to command equal leisure. Blinkered egoism could scarcely
have driven at a greater gallop down so determined a road. But although
a nuisance, Ethel was never a bore.[14]

Ethel certainly never bored children, for whom she held great
appeal, either. Vita's son, Nigel, has recorded his own impression of
Ethel:

I just remember Ethel. She often came to Long Barn, dressed like a
coachman in cloak and tricorn hat and she was vigorous in a way that
didn't frighten children, bursting through the weeks like paper hoops, a
woman whose pertinacity was irresistible. Deafness, which can make
people tedious to their friends, was for Ethel an asset. She told us to yell
at her, and we yelled with an exuberance unequalled when talking to
normal people. Once she insisted, when sitting on our terrace at Long
Barn, on hearing a nightingale. A bird sang its heart out in the garden,
but not a note penetrated to Ethel until it obligingly perched on the

table in front of her and gave her a solo performance. How we cheered! How we adored her![15]

Ethel continued to confound and exasperate Virginia over the eleven years that they knew one another, bringing interruptions, some welcome, many not, to Virginia's work process and flow of inspiration. It cannot be denied that on many an occasion the libretto from one of Ethel's own compositions seemed remarkably appropriate to Virginia's mixed feelings about the earthquake that was Ethel:

> Again you think you'd like to see a friend
> but if the friend turns up to spend the day
> you cannot imagine what madness made you suggest it.[16]

Despite the trail of exhaustion and frustration that Ethel often left in her wake, she also had a hugely important and positive influence on Virginia's writing between 1930 and 1941. Her own reactions to Virginia's work were mixed. She loved *To the Lighthouse*, referring to the 'submergence, stupification, awe and a lot of other things'[17] that she gained from reading it. She enjoyed the spirited feminist tone of both *A Room of One's Own* and *The Common Reader*, but on reading, or attempting to read, *Flush* (1933), she wrote to Vanessa Bell in horror, admitting that '*Flush* is the sort of book that gives me the kick-screams to think of, indeed I only read a chapter and could read no more'.[18] Ethel also found it difficult to read *The Waves*, which was finished during the second year of her friendship with Virginia. She expressed her doubts a couple of years after its publication, in her diary:

> I can't get on with *The Waves*, and I rather doubt the judgement of those, mainly quite young people, who rave about it. But her second volume of *The Common Reader* is superb.[19]

However, after *The Waves* had first come out, during the second half of 1931, Ethel had written to Virginia not of her disappointment, but of her enjoyment of some of its more alluring and enduring qualities:

> The book is profoundly disquieting, sadder than any book I ever read and because it has no adorable human being in it (like the *Lighthouse*, sad as it is) there is no escape from its sadness.[20]

Ethel's effect on Virginia's writing was also liberating and intense; Virginia realized that, like her Suffragette friend, she had a right to free speech, and the anger that she had suppressed, or masked with humour, in *A Room of One's Own*, was at last fully unleashed as a direct result of her many conversations with Ethel Smyth. Ethel's passion for life, music, her commitment to the WSPU, her carving of a niche for herself in a male-dominated field, her rebelliousness and fiery belief in careers for women, all contributed to Virginia's sudden, vigorously angry voice of protest, clearly heard in *The Years* and *Three Guineas*.

Virginia had described Ethel as a 'burning rose' in a passionate letter to her, written in 1930 – a rose that was thorny, flushed and pink. In *The Years*, Virginia's exploration of the nature of patriarchy in public and private guises, she resurrects the rose imagery and lets it grow into the character of Rose Pargiter, a full-blown tribute to Ethel. Rose, 'thorny Rose, brave Rose, tawny Rose',[21] is unmarried, unconcerned with clothes, good-looking in a 'ravaged way', stout and possesses Ethel's unwavering faith in her own beliefs:

> 'Well, I'm proud of it!' said Rose, brandishing her knife in his face. 'I'm proud of my family; proud of my country; proud of . . .'
> 'Your sex?' he interrupted her.
> 'I am,' she asseverated.[22]

Ethel, of course, approved of this book greatly and although she admitted to having initially found it 'unintelligible', she later decided, on re-reading it, that the book was 'superb' and rang Virginia up to tell her so.

Three Guineas, published in 1938, owes much to Ethel's feminist militancy. Virginia's book set out to answer an imaginary letter from a barrister, asking how war might be prevented. Her response proved her to be a major pacifist, a feminist, and a woman who had been angry for far too long at the inequality of the sexes. It included much historical reportage on the women's reform movement and, inevitably, provoked a huge and varied postbag from the general public; letters that made 'a valid contribution to psychology', as Virginia ironically commented to Ethel.

Despite *Three Guineas* provoking more correspondence than any of her others, Virginia complained that none of her closest friends or relations bothered to write to her about it. Indeed, many of them were shocked and uneasy at its content and at the angry tone of the author. The exception to the rule, as ever, was to be Ethel. Delighted, she wrote to Virginia that 'your book is so splendid it makes me hot'.[23] To Ethel, *Three Guineas* must have seemed the equivalent of her own *March of the Women*.

Virginia was again to use Ethel as her inspiration for a character, in her last novel, *Between the Acts* (1941). Miss La Trobe, the creative director of the summer pageant, is a lesbian, mannish in behaviour and appearance. The following passage may well have been inspired by Virginia's very first sighting of Ethel at that concert in the Queen's Hall: Miss La Trobe's 'deep-set eyes' and 'very square jaw' are undoubtedly Ethel, as is the following description:

> Outwardly she was swarthy, sturdy and thick set; strode about the fields in a smock frock; sometimes with a cigarette in her mouth; often with a whip in her hand; and used rather strong language – perhaps then she wasn't altogether a lady? At any rate, she had a passion for getting things up.[24]

Virginia admired and enjoyed the things that Ethel herself 'got up', in particular her life as a musician and composer. Although not talented musically in any way, Virginia had been surrounded by music from childhood, due largely to Stella's ability to play the piano and violin. There had been music played in the drawing-room at Hyde Park Gate, or at Talland House, and Stella had played in an orchestra and regularly attended concerts. As a young adult, Virginia had often gone to the Queen's Hall, witnessing the great Henry Wood conduct some significant premières of orchestral work; in February 1905 she had taken her seat for the very first performance of Richard Strauss's *Symphonia Domestica*, a work she judged as beautiful and slightly unintelligible, before returning home where Cordelia Fisher played the pianola for the family.

During this same month, she attended a performance of Brahms and Beethoven at the Queen's Hall, proclaiming it to be first-rate. She saw Edward Elgar conduct his own music, including *Pomp and Circumstance*, and shortly afterwards attended another performance of Beethoven, Elgar and Bach. This pattern of regular concert-going was to continue up until her marriage in 1912 and then became more spasmodic as music became more 'modern'. Ethel would no doubt have been annoyed to hear that, in 1917, Virginia had admitted to walking out of a concert at the Aeolian Hall in Bond Street when the 'English piece came on'.

Virginia realized, without regret, that her enjoyment of music was limited, and noted in her diary that at certain concerts her musical friends, such as Saxon Sydney-Turner, listened 'critically, supercil-iously, without programmes'[25] whilst she, no doubt, needed the writ-ten explanation of each piece to aid her understanding. She continued to display a certain awe and respect for concert musicians, such as the ones who played their way through a Beethoven Festival Week in April 1921:

> Do I dare say I listened? Well, but if one gets a lot of pleasure, really divine pleasure, and knows the tunes, and only occasionally thinks of other things – surely I may say listened.[26]

Virginia not only listened, but also began to use musical imagery in her diary as a consequence of frequently attending orchestra concerts. In October 1924 she referred to Lytton as an 'exquisite symphony', full of deep, rumbling first violins. Sometimes she used her diary for 'doing my scales', implying that she 'warmed up' for the serious writing of the day in much the same way that an instrumentalist did before a concert. With these 'scales' completed, Virginia then used musical rhythm as a way of forming and shaping her sentences; she walked over the South Downs making up words that fell in strict time with her footsteps. Music continued to be a pleasure and an inspiration for her writing; in 1924 she confessed that 'it's music I want; to stimulate and suggest'.[27]

One early result of Virginia's fascination with music, the players and their audience, was the short story A String Quartet (1921), in which the thoughts of the audience are captured as the music inspires their imagi-nations to unfold and takes them on a journey back through their memories. As the four musicians simultaneously lift their bows and place them on the strings and the music commences, the reader gains a taste of the many images that must have flitted through Virginia's own mind as she sat in the audience at the Queen's Hall:

> Flourish, spring, burgeon, burst! The pear tree on the top of the moun-tain. Fountains jet; drops descend. But the waters of the Rhône flow

swift and deep, race under the arches, and sweep the trailing water leaves . . .[28]

Virginia used musical imagery to describe Ethel, three months after their first meeting, writing to Smyth, her 'burning rose', that 'the thorn hedge is the music; and I have to break my way through the violins, flutes, cymbals, voices to this red burning centre'. Spending time with Ethel forced Virginia to re-evaluate the process of musical composition and see it in a new light. Rather than merely listening, she now had an intimate insight into the mind of a professional composer. Virginia admired Ethel's way with notes immensely, although she did not always enjoy live performances of her friend's music, in particular *The Prison*, which left her horrified. She did greatly appreciate and learn from Ethel's own descriptions of how she composed music, drawing instant parallels with her own literary process:

> She says writing music is like writing novels. One thinks of the sea –
> naturally one gets a phrase for it. Orchestration is colouring. And one
> has to be very careful with one's 'technique'.[29]

Virginia was taken with the way that profound and passionate music poured from the practical-natured Ethel straight on to a manuscript page, where it was quickly notated for posterity. She analysed Ethel's skill in her diary:

> I am always impressed by the fact that it is music – I mean that she has
> spun these coherent chords harmonies melodies out of her so practical
> vigorous, strident mind.[30]

But Virginia's admiration for Ethel stretched beyond music and into writing. During a speech that she had to give to the London National Society for Women's Service, Virginia paid tribute to Ethel's other skill:

> When I read what Dame Ethel Smyth writes I always feel inclined to
> burn my own pen and take to music – for if she can write as well as all
> that, why shouldn't I compose, straight off – a masterpiece?[31]

Virginia could not, of course, have stepped down from the lectern and written a symphonic masterpiece – but much of her writing continued to take music as its inspiration. Ethel was quick to see this, and wrote to Virginia using a series of highly flattering comparisons between her and the great composers that Smyth so admired:

> First of all I think of you as a creator. I mean of what you stand for, than of anyone I have met. I felt like that about Brahms when I was young – and I was quite right . . . there is something in your vision no one else has ever seen and it affects me like music.[32]

Two weeks later, she made a further musical comparison, one that must have fed Virginia's ego immensely:

> Look here: to certain qualities to you as a writer I can swear and I am going to put very moderately: sense of beauty (top marks), sincerity – ditto – a mastery of language like Toscanini's mastery over orchestral players.[33]

Perhaps as a result of listening for so many decades to the work of Beethoven, Virginia's *To the Lighthouse* seems to demonstrate her knowledge of classical sonata form. There is the Exposition, or main theme, 'The Window'; this is further explored in the Development, 'Time Passes'; the third and final part of the novel, 'The Lighthouse', is a Recapitulation of the first theme, and can even be seen to have a Coda at the end (the arrival by boat at the lighthouse). These three sections neatly come full circle, as do the movements of a Beethoven or Mozart piano sonata.

The Waves explores Virginia's experiences as a concertgoer, this time in a negative manner: the author juxtaposes the themes of music and greed, imbuing the experience of sitting in the audience with a nasty, sordid undertone. Here, older, more cynical, aware of imminent old age and with her mind awash with thoughts of patriarchal oppression as she was preparing to experiment with ideas for *The Years*, Virginia now condemns the sort of people who attended the lunchtime concerts she once sat through so regularly:

> Here is a hall where one pays money and goes in, where one hears music among somnolent people who have come here after lunch on a hot afternoon . . . we lie gorged with food, torpid in the heat.[34]

In *The Waves*, the four players who featured in *The String Quartet* appear to have been resurrected, but whereas once they were the innocent 'four black figures', now, ten years later, they represent a nightmarish unreality; here is the negative effect of music on an unsettled mind:

> Then the beetle-shaped men come with their violins; wait; count; nod; down come their bows. And there is ripple and laughter like the dance of olive trees and their myriad-tongued great leaves when a seafarer, biting a twig between his lips where the many-backed steep hills come down, leaps on shore.[35]

In the same way that the *Gloria* of Ethel Smyth's requiem *Mass* catapults the entranced listener towards death with all guns blazing, leaving him in stunned silence, Virginia's momentous final paragraph of *The Waves* ('Against you I will fling myself, unvanquished and unyielding, O Death!') leaves the reader reeling from the effect of this equally dramatic sentiment; in mood and feel, the conclusions of both works are strangely similar.

In 1938, whilst Ethel was battling with old age, deafness, forgetfulness and a bad temper, still pestering Vita with visits to Sissinghurst ('she arrived in a state. Her hair was coming down and she mistook her muffler for a handkerchief'[36]), Virginia was still musing on the connections between life, music, writing and art as she prepared to write her autobiographical *A Sketch of the Past*, concluding that

> The whole world is a work of art; that we are parts of the work of art. Hamlet or a Beethoven quartet is the truth about this vast mass that we call the world. But there is no Shakespeare, there is no Beethoven; certainly and emphatically there is no God; we are the words, we are the music; we are the thing itself.[37]

Virginia's last extant letter to Ethel, written during her final month alive, was characteristically affectionate and teasing. In it, she promised to visit Ethel on 'a Wednesday'. Ethel found this odd and analysed it in a letter to Vanessa written shortly after Virginia's death; Virginia had not been in the habit of making such vague arrangements, and her mind, mused Ethel with the benefit of hindsight, must have been elsewhere. Woolf had always been genuinely glad to hear from

Ethel, who had given her over a decade of spirited friendship and who encouraged her to be frank and honest about subjects that had been left buried and untouched for far too long. Although Ethel had long since got over the obsessive side of her passion for Virginia, and indeed had fallen in love with somebody else as she entered her eighties, her own last letter to Virginia written a month before Woolf's death, was truly affectionate. However, with its conclusive tone, Ethel almost seemed to pre-empt the terrible event that would shortly follow:

> Darling Virginia – Pay no attention to my grumble of yesterday. After all, you have given, and give me the greatest joy of my latter end. As it said in that wonderful American poem: 'I am content,' said the soldier. Yes, by God I *am*. Bless you, my dearest.[38]

Ethel, shaken and terribly dismayed by her friend's suicide, continued to write to Vanessa and Vita, offering the two them her support and sharing with them her memories of Virginia.

Ethel Smyth died three years after Virginia Woolf, in May 1944, quietly and uneventfully, at home in Woking. She was eighty-six. Many of her friends expressed surprise that this spirited woman, who wrote, composed and lived with 'violence, passion, indignation, loyalty, integrity, incorruptibility, shameless egoism, generosity, excitability, energy, a hundred horse-power drive',[39] had actually been extinguished at all.

One such disbeliever, Vita, paid tribute to her in a poem that surely would have echoed the thoughts of their mutual friend, Virginia, had she lived longer:

> You were marked out to meet a violent end
> You should have matched the violent young men
> Stormers of evil in all elements
> Earth, water, air, and in the daring mind.
> They were your peers; their life, their death were yours:
> Not in a Surrey villa, of old age,
> Where you who greatly lived have gently died.[40]

8   Virginia

Take away my love for my friends and my burning and pressing sense of the importance and lovability and curiosity of human life and I should be nothing but a membrane, a fibre, uncoloured, lifeless.[1]

Throughout the previous chapters, we have met a selection of women who profoundly interested Virginia Woolf not only as friends, but also as role models for many of the female protagonists in her fiction. By studying her correspondence and relationships with these women, several diverse aspects of Virginia's personality have come to light: her insecurity, sense of repression and aversion to physical passion (Julia, Stella); her capacity for strong, enduring and all-consuming love, (Violet, Vanessa, Vita); her fervent, angry beliefs in equality for women (Ethel); her strange capacity to demonstrate fascination simultaneously with repulsion, cruelty and snobbery (Katherine, Ottoline); and her ability to empathize (Carrington). We have gradually been able to build up a picture of Virginia Woolf as a real, if complex, woman. But there are gaps still left unfilled; Woolf's early life, for instance, is less well documented generally and yet, once probed, it yields a most rewarding and intimate glimpse not only into late-Victorian Britain, but also into the heart, mind and ambitions of an extraordinary young woman.

To those who know little about Virginia Woolf other than from reading snippets of sensationalist reportage about her suicide and sexuality, or witnessing the tired portrayals in books and films of a 'mad' woman obsessed with suicide, the predominant image called to mind when the name 'Woolf' is mentioned will be that of the haunted, elderly, fragile lady of her later photographs. It is an unavoidable and frustrating fact that, to many people, the most interesting fact about her life is how she chose to end it.

But Virginia Woolf lived for fifty-nine long, rich, event-filled years, and whilst it is often, sadly, only the last of those years that are recalled and debated, it is the early ones, between 1895 and 1906, that prove to be far more fascinating; partly because they are less explored to date by contemporary biographers, but primarily because these are the years when Woolf's raw emotions, burgeoning writing talent and development as a woman were all being shaped and affected by the harrowing experience of living as a young Victorian under the restrictive conditions at 22 Hyde Park Gate.

None of the other women featured in this book suffered anything approximating the incredible chain of bereavements, breakdowns and traumatic events that Virginia had endured and survived by the time she had reached her mid-twenties; aided by conventional education, great wealth or liberal-minded families, most of them in fact enjoyed relatively unremarkable childhoods. Therefore it is even more astonishing that Virginia, formally uneducated, insecure and almost permanently in mourning during her teenage years, should have managed to fight back from such a difficult beginning; she not only survived life at Hyde Park Gate, but also was able to use it as inspiration. She rose up into and maintained a position of great literary success, becoming more famous than any of her female friends and contemporaries. For this reason, whilst it is sometimes difficult to feel much warmth towards Virginia Woolf as a person (for, like most people, she could be cruel, dishonest and impatient), it is much more difficult not to respect her achievements.

If the persistent researcher or reader is interested in delving beyond the commonly known facts of Woolf's life, widely available in her fiction and the many biographies about her, with the intention of revealing more about her as a person than as a writer, although it is of course impossible to separate fully the former from the latter, there are a few further routes that he or she might decide to take, which I will explore here. The most immediate, fascinating and corporeal route is via the scrutiny of early, unpublished archive photographs. Another, more widely followed way is to read her intimate diaries and letters, now published in their entirety. A visit to the Sussex archives that contain the honest reminiscences (soon to be published) of those who, after Virginia's death, wrote in sympathy to her husband and sister, will help to fill in many further details. Finally, by visiting and spending time in the key places where Virginia once lived and worked, it is possible to achieve some additional insights, however transitory, into her personality.

Many of the popular photographic images of Virginia Stephen/Woolf, particularly those taken by George Beresford, Gisèle Freund and Man Ray, are overly familiar to us, having been reproduced endlessly in biographies and documentaries, on stationery and gallery posters; but it is not these photographs, but rather the other, far earlier ones, which lie scattered between America and England, unprobed and largely forgotten about in dusty archives, that most poignantly and accurately chart the remarkable change of Virginia Stephen from a chubby child, through nervy adolescence, into a reluctant yet successful adult. Studied in conjunction with her own diaries and journal pieces of the time, these photographs give us a fascinating insight into what it was like to be a girl, and then a young woman, growing up in Victorian Kensington.

The camera lenses during the latter half of the nineteenth century were unforgiving, with few special effects, and so here, raw and uncensored, is Virginia Stephen as she transforms from that painfully thin, plain-featured teenager into the ethereal, strong-featured beauty called Virginia Woolf. Many of the early photographs show her as a young girl who did not enjoy being the focus of attention; shy, modest and uncomfortable with her appearance, she is more often than not gazing at the ground or fiddling with a book or newspaper.

As a very young child, Virginia Stephen had impressed virtually everyone she came into contact with. As a picture of her nestled up against Julia Stephen shows, she was plump, robust and vivacious, charming the grown-ups at Hyde Park Gate, prodigiously eloquent and aware of how to flirt with her father even before the age of two; she always managed to burrow her way into the coveted place by his side or on to his lap. She was a happy, confident toddler; in the very few extant photos from this time, she is almost unrecognizable as the forerunner to the skinny, angular child of only a few years later.

Whereas Virginia's sister, young 'Nessa', already possessed, by the age of four, something of the solemnity, gravity and solidity that were to stay in her expression for life, Virginia's physical appearance was to change drastically after the age of six. Even her bright, button eyes, full of mischief and sparkling with fun, were to take on a fraught and serious melancholy from the age of seven onwards. Much of the little girl's physical change of appearance was attributed to a bout of whooping-cough, an ailment from which all the Stephen children suffered; but although her siblings recovered fully, Virginia never gained back the weight that she had lost, emerging from the illness quieter, thinner, more thoughtful and lacking in self-confidence. The growing contrast between Vanessa, always full-figured and statuesque, and Virginia, also tall, but thin and awkward, was already in place by the early 1890s, and despite their facial resemblance to one another, each sister was uniquely and differently beautiful.

With only Stella Duckworth's scribbled appointments diary for 1896 to give us any consistent written record of Virginia's health, activities and emotions during this difficult year (during which she suffered from an early breakdown following on from Julia's death), it is remarkable and gratifying to find that old photographs still survive from the 1896 Stephen family summer holiday at Hindhead House, Haslemere. These astonishing pictures show a thin-faced but pretty 14-year-old Virginia, still in mourning for her mother who had died the previous year. Sporting a black armband, she is shy, awkward, chisel-featured, with a long tight plait of hair down her back. Other pictures show her looking pale, with huge anxious eyes in a sensitive, slender-boned face. Vanessa, by contrast, often appears stubborn, resentful, and almost bulldog-like in her silent, stony resolution. Perched on the roof-terrace of Hindhead House, her hands protectively clasped around her knees, Virginia, a gentle, sensitive-looking child, averts her eyes from the camera. During this same holiday, it is possible to gauge her worried reaction to the engagement of Stella and Jack. This event was captured in a photograph that when enlarged several times, shows the newly unwrapped wedding rings of the engaged couple resting on the grass at their feet.

During a holiday to Boulogne in the company of their Aunt Minna, later in the year, another photograph leaves us with a breathtakingly clear picture of the two Stephen sisters; in their black travelling capes, unsmiling, gloved (it was November), they are still visibly scarred by their mother's death. Virginia's long plait weaves snakily out from under a beret; Vanessa, aged sixteen, has been allowed to wear her hair up. Again, Virginia avoids the camera's gaze; Vanessa, challengingly, meets it head-on.

After Stella's traumatic death in 1897, a picture taken only three weeks later remains pitiful and poignant to the eye of the contemporary researcher. Skinny, hunched over and clad in black Victorian mourning dress, Virginia sits on a step at The Old Vicarage in Painswick, Gloucestershire. Two walking canes lie beneath her feet, suggesting that she was frail enough not to be able to walk unaided. Her eyes look up beseechingly towards the camera, imploring it not to take a photograph. Never did Virginia's later nickname of 'Sparroy' seem so terribly appropriate; in this mournfully sad photo, she resembles a fledgling that has fallen out of the nest away from its mother (indeed Virginia herself had been weaned too early from Julia). The picture confirms what we know of Virginia's life in the dark days after Stella's death, but it still comes as a shock to witness it so clearly in black and white; Virginia, at the age of fifteen, was a sickly invalid.

During this stressful holiday at Painswick, Virginia kept a few brief, disjointed entries in her diary that help us to understand better her pathetic appearance, although many of the entries make little direct reference to Stella's death. The agony and frustration of the emotional repression required of the time is visible in Virginia's anguished features, for it was not the 'done thing' for young Victorians to speculate emotionally, on paper or otherwise. Virginia was inevitably recalling the limitations that her upbringing imposed at this time, when she wrote *Orlando* (1928):

> The sexes drew further and further apart. No open conversation was tolerated. Evasions and concealments were sedulously practised on both sides.[2]

Virginia's arrested development and the mental turmoil that she experienced during this holiday do occasionally show through in her diary accounts. With a writer's technique, albeit subconsciously, she manages to convey maximum distress with the minimum of words:

> Nessa and I walked round and round the tennis lawn after dinner (our custom nowadays) and discussed everything. It is hopeless and strange.[3]

Even more hopeless was the plight of Stella's widower Jack Hills, who joined the family on this holiday expecting constant support and sympathy. It was left to Virginia and Vanessa to sit with him in the

194

summer house while he gripped their hands and they stared at a barren, leafless tree. This tree appeared to symbolize for Virginia the loss of Stella, and although it was never mentioned, Stella's unborn child. Jack bemoaned loudly his lack of a sexual partner and wrung his hands. By her own admission, Virginia was becoming patently 'ill-adjusted; growing painfully into relations that her death had distorted'. It was not a healthy growing-up process for a 15-year-old girl and Virginia was unable to record her feelings succinctly at the time. Only in 1939 could she fully explain what that dreadful holiday had meant, and why she had appeared so wretched in those photographs:

> But trees do not remain leafless. They begin to grow little red chill buds. By that image I would convey the misery, the quarrels, the irritations, half covered, then spurting out, the insinuations, which as soon as family life had started again began to prove that Stella's death had not left us more united; as father said.[4]

Virginia did not record details of the next Stephen family summer holiday, taken at Ringwood Manor in the New Forest during 1898, but a photograph taken during that holiday conveys its mood. Happily, there is a marked difference between the scowling, pitiful girl photographed in 1897 and the young lady now seen sitting in a chair reading the newspaper. Here, for the first time, is a clear indication of Virginia Stephen's ambitions as an aspiring journalist, as she avidly reads a broadsheet, taking no notice of the photographer. Her face is serene, contemplative; she seems to be moving, without further interruption, towards adulthood. The shock of the deaths of Julia and Stella appears to have abated.

The process of Virginia changing from a teenager into a young woman is even more evident pictorially in a photograph of Virginia taken at Warboys, Huntingdonshire, during summer 1899. With her hair pinned up under an elegant, wide-brimmed hat, her dress no longer black but light and edged with lace, Virginia Stephen has clearly passed into adulthood. Her journals reflect this newfound maturity as well; the prose becomes expansive, acutely observant, carefully shaped. The Warboys journal is descriptive, yet still slightly detached. It demonstrates the slightly self-conscious and endearing pomposity of a young woman determined to make her name as a serious writer;

for instance, she writes that Vanessa had the nerve to 'insinuate, with some pertinacity'[5] that Virginia had stolen her scissors.

By the time she turned twenty-one, Virginia had entered fully into early Edwardian society, as a photograph taken at Netherhampton House, Salisbury, shows. In this 1903 posed shot, Virginia is seated on the grass amongst a group that also includes Vanessa, (who was now very beautiful), and the laid-back Thoby Stephen, his arms stretched casually behind his head. Virginia gazes away from the lens, as she usually does, towards the ground, perhaps at the book on her lap, which she was probably longing to get back to. The journal that she kept during this holiday at Salisbury is a mature and elegant piece of travel writing, full of signs that she was now finally beginning to move on from the dreadful late 1890s and towards a confident future as a writer.

Even when this holiday, much enjoyed by the whole family, came to an end and Virginia was forced to return to her dreaded 'cage' at Hyde Park Gate, she accepted the situation pragmatically, turning her hand to writing a series of descriptive pieces about London and Kensington Gardens. Unfortunately, fate was to deal yet another blow. Soon after their return from Salisbury, Leslie, who had been ill with stomach cancer for some time, took a turn for the worse and died. His death in February 1904 catapulted Virginia straight into another breakdown and worst of all, it put a further obstacle in the path of her development as a woman. She degenerated into illness with periods of psychotic behaviour and regression, and took nearly two years to recover, only to be hit within another two years by the early death of Thoby.

It was not until these bereavements had happened, been mourned and some sense of reality restored, that Virginia Stephen could continue to take the steps needed to ensure her place as a great writer. Even her first job as a reviewer for the *Guardian* and subsequent work for the *Times Literary Supplement*, were marred by what amounted almost to another bereavement: the marriage of her beloved Nessa to Clive Bell. Therefore it was not until 1909, when Virginia had left the house at 46 Gordon Square to Vanessa and Clive, and was living with Adrian at Fitzroy Square, that she finally began to live confidently as an independent, money-earning journalist.

Virginia Stephen was at the height of her unusual and mesmerizing physical beauty in her early to mid-twenties. The infamous Beresford photographs of 1902 clearly portray a woman blessed with classical features and a gentle, ethereal loveliness, but a far more seductive image of Virginia Woolf the *real* woman is given (unwittingly) by her brother Adrian in his diary for 1909. Virginia, we are told, has attended a fancy-dress ball at the Botanical Gardens, dressed as Cleopatra:

> She looked very fine in long flowing robes with her hair down, though more like Isolde than Cleopatra.[6]

Her beauty continued to attract admirers, among them Clive Bell, Lytton Strachey, and Philip Morrell, Ottoline's amorous, unfaithful husband, and, of course, Leonard Woolf, whom she married in 1912. As Virginia entered her forties, her good looks, whilst still feminine, took on a severer quality, reminiscent of her mother's, and those who knew her continued to regard her as beautiful well into middle age, although as with Julia Stephen before, her appearance became tainted with the legacy of weariness and depression. However, photographs of Virginia in later life, according to her nephew Quentin, did scant justice to their subject:

> The extraordinary beauty of her face, it was very austere in a way, angular, odd, quite unlike most of the early photographs. The face itself is indescribable I think because it – it owed so much to its movements.[7]

In later life, Virginia began to resemble Julia Stephen more noticeably. David Cecil remembered Virginia's face as being that of a 'mocking Madonna', a description eerily similar to Elizabeth Robins's reminiscence of Julia Stephen, whom she said would say something 'so unexpected, from that Madonna face, one thought it *vicious*'.[8]

As a writer, Virginia Woolf was rigidly self-disciplined, training her mind to produce tightly written copy by walking, reading, studying, and writing letters and diaries. Her nephew, Cecil Woolf, witnessed this astonishing dedication to the written word on a visit to Rodmell:

> I remember on one visit to Monk's [House] taking my aunt's breakfast tray up to her and seeing perhaps a dozen scraps of paper lying on the floor round the bed. When I remarked on this – probably offered to put them in the waste paper basket – she told me that she often made such

notes – sometimes no more than a single word or name, or a phrase – for her current work during the night.[9]

But as a person, Virginia was not always so self-disciplined. Never overly concerned about her appearance, bits of her clothing would fall off in public, hairpins plopped into her soup, her skirts were held up by safety pins, and she could be scatty, forgetful and vague. To the local village children of Rodmell, she was a figure of fascination. The actor Dirk Bogarde, who grew up in the neighbouring village of Lullington, recalled his boyhood sightings of Virginia:

Used to see her marching about the water-meadows quite often. Hair wispy and caught into a loose sort of knot, a big stick or sometimes a brightly coloured umbrella furled. A golf umbrella, I imagine, a droopy cardigan. She sometimes wore a big floppy straw hat and we all thought she was a witch. Or could put spells on you ... there was a strange décontracté air about her which made us all uneasy ... she never spoke to us, but sometimes sang to herself, a sure sign that she was 'barmy' as we said ... and picked little bunches of wild flowers.[10]

Despite these rather endearing traits, she still possessed enough dignity and elegance of behaviour to provoke the following recollection from E.M. Forster, giving us a humorous insight into how Virginia viewed *herself* as a female:

She felt herself to be not only a woman, but also a lady, and this gives a further twist to her social outlook. She made no bones about it. She was a lady, by birth and upbringing, and it was no use being cowardly about it, and pretending that her mother had turned a mangle, or that Sir Leslie had been a plasterer's mate.[11]

Virginia's marriage to Leonard, although seen by many as unconventional due to its emphasis on intellectual companionship rather than passion, brought out many of her best qualities, not least of which were loyalty, commitment, frankness and love. On occasion, Leonard's treatment at the hands of his over-sensitive wife could be brutal, but he was patient, and Virginia was well aware of her deficiencies as a partner, chronicling them honestly (though it has to be said, without much shame):

I hear poor L. driving the lawn mower up and down, for a wife like I am should have a label to her cage. She bites! And he spent all yesterday running round London for me.[12]

On the rare occasions when Leonard expressed displeasure with their relationship, Virginia had enough of a conscience, as well as a fear of gaining his disapproval, to show contrition:

Also I can, by taking pains, be much more considerate of L's feelings; and so keep more steadily at our ordinary level of intimacy & ease.[13]

After her death in 1941, and even to the present day, the legend of Virginia Woolf as an unsmiling, sickly, sexless depressive who was obsessed with suicide has continued to gain momentum, aided by a clutch of negative biographies and a tendency by biographers to publish pictures of Virginia that predominantly show her looking frail, or sad. Countless books have attempted to analyse her depressive moods, and television documentaries proclaim her 'tragic' story with dour, funereal music to accompany them. Whilst it is undoubtedly true that Virginia, during the early part of her life, suffered far more tragedy and bereavements than most, it is forgotten that, as a friend, she brought happiness, stimulation and humour into the lives of all those who knew her intimately. Fortunately, some of their tributes, soon to be published, pay moving testimony to the lighter, more endearing side of Virginia Woolf. Disproving the image often associated with her of a fragile, dour and humourless woman, Nigel Nicolson remembers that 'almost to the end Virginia was capable of much enjoyment and intensive work'.[14] Elizabeth Bowen, the writer, remembered Virginia laughing 'in this consuming, choking, delightful hooting way' – that observation was made only a few weeks before Virginia's death.

After Virginia's suicide in March 1941, shocked letters of condolence flooded on to the doormats of Leonard Woolf and Vanessa Bell. Very few people made reference to Virginia's struggles with mental illness, or to her darker moods, but chose instead to celebrate the life of a woman who, despite the attempts of many to portray her otherwise, had enjoyed life to the full and tossed back, with considerable vigour, all the challenges that it had thrown at her. Amongst the hundred or so letters that Vanessa Bell received after her sister's death, the following handful, are particularly revealing about Virginia:

I think she had a rich enjoyment of much in life – her affections, her reading, her view of humanity, her own powers gave her a great deal of happiness – but the bodily fabric and the brain were not tough enough to withstand the volcano within. *Marjorie Strachey*

She was, among other things, as beautiful to look at as her works were to read – I have never seen anyone of more perfect distinction. *Osbert Sitwell*

I think that anybody who knew Virginia felt that the world was suddenly impoverished and darkened. *Raymond Mortimer*

I expect it was all too much for her acutely sensitive spirit and that it is best she should be at rest. *Violet Mannering*

I can see Virginia lying back in her chair, the lovely head and beautiful features, the smile and delicious laugh. *Sybil Colefax*

So much has left the world with poor Virginia – distinction, a peculiar charm, a rare kind of beauty, a genius. *Edward Sackville-West*

The old cook from 22 Hyde Park Gate, Sophie Farrell, was terribly distressed by Virginia's death and died herself only a couple of weeks after writing her letter of condolence to Vanessa. She had watched 'Miss Ginia' grow from a talkative, mischievous little girl into a highly successful author, and she found it hard to believe that Virginia had really gone for good:

> I have known and loved her very much since she was 4 years old. I can't bear to think that she has strayed away from you all.

Photographs, letters and reminiscences aside, the only other way to gain a more personal glimpse of Virginia is to visit the houses that influenced and affected her development. Three, more than the rest, possess a haunting feel; these houses are places where, armed with an imagination and some knowledge of their history, it is possible to believe that Virginia Woolf has just passed out of a room, seconds before you entered it.

To indulge in these literary pilgrimages is to understand something of the pleasure that Virginia herself used to enjoy, albeit rather guiltily, as she visited the homes of *her* favourite writers. Although she tried to justify her curiosity at Haworth Parsonage, the home of the Brontës, by proclaiming that 'the curiosity is only legitimate when the house of a great writer or the country in which it is set adds something to our understanding of his books', she also rhapsodized over Charlotte's tiny shoes and admitted that she temporarily forgot 'the chiefly memorable fact that she was a great writer'.[15] To the many of us who peer around at Monk's House hoping to find not only the clues to her life as a writer, but also some personal thrill by gazing guiltily at Virginia's narrow bed and embroidered shawl, there is doubtless some comfort in reading her words.

Talland House, Virginia's childhood holiday home in Cornwall, still looks much as it did then, with an additional extension to the roof and the side. The vast lawns and orchards that once surrounded it have sadly been taken over by a car park and several ugly Victorian villas. However, with a knowledge of Virginia's reminiscences about her childhood holidays, described in *Moments of Being* and fictionalized in *To the Lighthouse*, it is still possible to stand on one of the old wrought-iron balconies that Julia and Leslie, with their children, would have stood on in order to look out at Godrevy lighthouse.

Talland was immensely important to Virginia, not just as a place of childhood idyll, but in retrospect, as a key aid to the development of her senses and observation skills, and thus to her development as a fine writer. As the only place where she was truly, consistently happy, St Ives remained in her imagination for the rest of her life, proving far more superior, as she was to recall, than holidays in the paltry Isle of Wight or Sussex. Whereas her permanent home at 22 Hyde Park Gate was suffocating, repressive and imposed great limits upon such an imaginative child, Virginia was allowed to roam relatively freely at Talland House, around the house, garden and beach. Here, amidst the vast, rugged landscape of the Cornish coast it was possible to have great adventures, and to feel, think, experience and listen in ways that were not possible at home.

Talland House was the most important of Virginia's childhood dwellings, and she realized this by writing about it and returning on several visits as an adult, to creep up the carriage drive and peer at the lighted house through a gap in the escallonia. Talland was a magical place for Virginia because it was one of the few places not directly associated with a family bereavement, although after Julia's death in 1895, the children never returned to stay there. In the lush gardens there, Julia, Stella, Vanessa, Virginia and their friends and family had relaxed and entertained, and experienced some hope for the future.

At the other end of the spectrum, and at the other end of Virginia's life, was Monk's House in Rodmell. Although a place of beauty, owing to its setting in a picturesque village nestled away in the South Downs, the house itself is ordered and sparse, seeming to represent the austere, mature and calm side of Virginia Woolf. The rooms at Monk's House have been carefully arranged by the National Trust to have a similar atmosphere to the one that would have existed in Virginia's day; slightly sober, basic, unsentimental. They represent the necessary clearing-out of a mind filled with the frivolities of the London social scene; they reflect the ability that Virginia possessed to attain and maintain a focused frame of mind. Monk's House symbolizes the life of a worker, a prolific and serious writer. Although Rodmell provided a much-needed calm, when the church bells rang or schoolchildren chanted, Virginia often despaired.

Monk's House was a holiday home to the Woolfs, but also a house to work in; unpretentious, with a writer's view and a writer's lodge. Unconstrained beauty is not found in the rooms, with their low ceilings and simple Omega furniture, but in Leonard's garden which, although much changed, still presents a pleasing excess of colour and shape to the visitor's eager eye. Despite the many changes both in and outside Monk's House, it remains surprisingly personal in atmosphere, with an old set of Virginia and Leonard's bowling balls stashed away under the staircase as if they are still waiting for use.

The one house that was never viewed as a place where much pleasure was experienced, the 'house of all the deaths', the 'cage' of Virginia's youth, still stands rather forebodingly at Hyde Park Gate. Even now, some hundred or more years after the unhappy deaths of Julia Stephen and her daughter Stella, the external appearance of 22 Hyde Park Gate manages to convey something of the gloom, claustrophobia and stifling Victorian repression of Virginia's childhood. Inside, on the narrow, winding stairs, the visitor can still smell her fear, her longing to escape the confines of existence in this house where privacy was rarely to be had. The basement hallway, now containing an attractive flat, still gives off a musty smell of damp. The attic stairs, leading to a luxury flat in what was once Leslie Stephen's study, can seem bare and chill. All the negative aspects of Virginia's childhood that caused her to be over-sensitive, nervous and tortured in later life are still impregnated into the walls and foundations of 22 Hyde Park Gate.

The lease of this house remained with the Stephen family until 1928, when it was finally sold. Extraordinarily, the original mortgage deeds, drawn up shortly after Leslie's death, recently turned up in a collectors' shop in Bournemouth and have now been returned to the owner of one of the six private flats that make up No. 22. Elaborately written in black ink on yellow parchment, signed and sealed in wax by the four Stephen children and witnessed by Jack Hills, they are a poignant reminder of the many years that Virginia spent at Hyde Park Gate.

Years of being run first as a hotel and then as 'flatlets' until 1958, resulted in the house becoming shabby and run down. At one point in 1966, it accommodated fourteen people, nearly as many as during Virginia's childhood. Converting it into six larger flats, a businessman eventually rescued the house in the 1970s. Nowadays, sympathetic ownership has ensured that the house is pleasantly decorated inside and well maintained. A member of the Virginia Woolf Society of Great Britain lives in one of the flats and runs the Residents' Association. A smart coat of white paint on the front of the house hides what used to be a red-brick façade in the Stephens' day. The back of the house, with smaller windows, looms up towards the sky largely unchanged, apart from the addition of an ugly lift shaft to the side. It is still possible to see the little glass room where Vanessa and Virginia once painted and wrote, planning their futures. Inside the house there are sections of the original staircase balustrade remaining, but the layout of the house has changed greatly.

Apart from the chill in the basement, the house feels warm and welcoming where once it was foreboding, crowded and filled with tortuous grief. The original front door to the house is now filled in, but it is visible from the inside. There is no grand front hallway, where once there would have been a table, coat hooks, visiting cards and umbrellas. Leslie and Julia's large bedroom, where so many dramatic moments of life and death occurred, is now divided into an attractive sitting-room and a smaller bedroom; the ancient and heavy mirror that stood near Leslie and Julia's bed is still on show at Charleston, once the home of Vanessa Bell. The corridors at Hyde Park Gate, so dark and gloomy in the 1880s, are now white and airy. On the half-landings, where the water closets and tin bath would have stood, are the modern day lifts.

Despite so many changes, it is still possible, when alone, to stand for a moment on the narrow staircase and hear the ghostly sounds of the tall, dark house as it might have been in the 1880s, when Julia Stephen was mistress of the house and eighteen people, including Virginia Stephen, lived out the dramas of daily life in stifling proximity.

Two doors down, Stella's house, 24 Hyde Park Gate, stands solid and silent.

Afterword

Only four of the women discussed in this book outlived Virginia herself. Violet Dickinson, on hearing of Virginia's death, wrote at once to Vanessa, admitting that she was experiencing 'a feeling of the deepest thankfulness that she's no longer tired and depressed'[1] and praising Vanessa for the care and love that she had always provided for her sister.

Vita Sackville-West also wrote to Vanessa immediately, offering the most comfort that she possibly could have, with the following words:

> I should like you to know that (at your request) I did tell her what you had said about the comfort she had been to you over Julian – and I have never seen her look more pleased and surprised.[2]

Vita lived on until 1962, dying peacefully at Sissinghurst. Harold, heartbroken, never recovered from her death, first giving up writing and then, eventually, reading. He died six years later, in the same cottage that his beloved 'Mar' (Vita) had died in.

Ethel Smyth retreated, in her final few years, to her house at Woking. On hearing the news of Virginia's death, she was not altogether surprised, having received, as mentioned earlier, that vague, uncharacteristic letter from Virginia a few days previously. She wrote to Vanessa Bell:

> I . . . you see, it is not only (I did not tell her this) that I loved her, it was that my life [was] literally based on her . . . it was the constant amazing contact with a mind of genius.[3]

Ethel, showing a great depth of understanding for her late, treasured friend, added: 'I believe she chose her end wisely.'

Vanessa Bell did not completely break down, as many feared she would, on hearing of her sister's death. She began to age quickly; her once-robust body became thin and emaciated and her features grew in severity and began to take on a pronounced resemblance to the long-dead Julia Stephen. She withdrew still further into that world of her own making at Charleston, spending the next twenty years surrounded mainly by Duncan, Clive, her children and grandchildren, and dear old friends such as Maynard Keynes. She painted, no doubt remembering herself as the young woman who had bicycled, hair and cape flying, to Arthur Cope's School of Art and, later, to the Slade; she observed the heavy-lidded eyes and graceful features of Julia Stephen starting to appear on the faces of her children and grandchildren; she kept in touch constantly with Leonard and Vita into their old age; and, with more difficulty, she buried, deep inside, her private memories of Virginia, the little sister who had joined her in the twilight world under the nursery table at 22 Hyde Park Gate whilst the 'Angels in the House', Maria, Julia and Stella, wrapped their dark, protective, heavy wings around the shoulders of the unsuspecting Stephen girls.

Select Bibliography

Anderson, Gwen, *Ethel Smyth, The Burning Rose* (Cecil Woolf, London, 1997)

Barrett, Michèle, *Virginia Woolf On Women & Writing* (The Women's Press, 1996)

Bell, Quentin, *Virginia Woolf* (Pimlico, 1996)

Bell, Vanessa, *Sketches in Pen and Ink*, ed. Lia Giachero (The Hogarth Press, 1997)

Bishop, Edward L., *Jacob's Room, The Holograph Draft* (Pace University Press, 1998)

Bogarde, Dirk, *A Particular Friendship* (Penguin, 1990)

Bonnerot, Luce, *The Sayings of Virginia Woolf* (Duckworth, 1996)

Burden, Joy, *Winging Westward* (Robert Wall Books, Bath, 1974)

Carrington, Dora, *Carrington, Letters and Extracts from her Diaries*, ed. David Garnett (Jonathan Cape Ltd., 1970)

Caws, Mary Ann, *Carrington and Lytton, Alone Together* (Cecil Woolf, London, 1999)

Channon, Joyce, *The St. Ives Weekly Summary 1889–1910* (St. Ives Printing & Publishing Company, 1987)

Curtis, Vanessa, *Stella and Virginia – An Unfinished Sisterhood* (Cecil Woolf, London, 2001)

De Salvo, Louise & Leaska, Mitchell A., *The Letters of Vita Sackville-West to Virginia Woolf* (Virago, 1992)

De Salvo, Louise, *Virginia Woolf – The Impact of Child Sexual Abuse on her Life and Work* (The Women's Press, 1989)

Dell, Marion, *Peering Through The Escallonia: Virginia Woolf, Talland House and St. Ives* (Cecil Woolf, London, 1999)

Denny, Barbara & Starren, Carolyn, *Kensington Past* (Historical Publications Ltd., 1998)

Duckworth, Stella, *Stella Duckworth's Diary for 1893* (in the ownership of Anne Olivier Bell)

——, *Stella Duckworth's Diary for 1896* (Berg Collection, New York Public Library)

Dunn, Jane, *Virginia Woolf and Vanessa Bell – A Very Close Conspiracy* (Pimlico, 1990)

Faderman, Lillian, *Surpassing the Love of Men* (The Women's Press, 1997)

Forster, E.M., *Virginia Woolf – The Rede Lecture 1941* (Cambridge University Press, 1942)

Garnett, Angelica, *The Eternal Moment* (Puckerbush Press, 1998)

Gerzina, Gretchen, *A Life of Dora Carrington* (Pimlico, 1989)

Gillespie, Diane F. & Steele, Elizabeth, *Julia Duckworth Stephen, Stories for Children, Essays for Adults* (Syracuse University Press, 1987)

Gillespie, Diane F., *The Multiple Muses of Virginia Woolf* (University of Missouri Press, 1997)

Glendinning, Victoria, *Vita, The Life of V. Sackville-West* (Weidenfeld & Nicolson, 1983)

——, *Jonathan Swift* (Pimlico, 1998)

Gordon, Lyndall, *Virginia Woolf, A Writer's Life* (Oxford University Press, 1986)

Heilbrun, Carolyn G., *Lady Ottoline's Album* (Alfred A. Knopf, 1976)

Hill, Brian, *Julia Margaret Cameron – A Victorian Family Portrait* (Peter Owen, London, 1973)

Hill, Jane, *The Art of Dora Carrington* (The Herbert Press, 1994)

Holroyd, Michael, *Lytton Strachey and The Bloomsbury Group* (Penguin 1971)

Hussey, Mark, *Virginia Woolf A to Z* (Facts on File, New York 1995)

Huxley, Aldous, *Crome Yellow* (Flamingo, 1994)

Jacobs, Peter, 'Virginia Woolf and Music' from Gillespie, Diane F., *The Multiple Muses of Virginia Woolf* (University of Missouri Press, 1997)

Kennedy, Richard, *A Boy at The Hogarth Press,* (Penguin, 1972)

Kirkpatrick, B.J. & Clarke, Stuart N., *A Bibliography of Virginia Woolf* (Clarendon Press, Oxford, 1997)

Lawrence, D.H., *Women in Love* (Guild Publishing, 1978)

Leska, Mitchell A., *Granite and Rainbow, The Hidden Life of Virginia Woolf* (Picador, 1998)

——, *The Pargiters: The Novel-Essay Portion of The Years* (The Hogarth Press, 1978)

Lee, Hermione, *Virginia Woolf* (Vintage, 1997)

Mansfield, Katherine, *Collected Stories of Katherine Mansfield* (Constable, 1945)

——, *The Journal of Katherine Mansfield 1914–1922* (Constable, 1927)

——, *New Zealand Stories* (Oxford University Press, Auckland, 1997)

McNeish, Helen, *Passionate Pilgrimage – Katherine Mansfield: A Love Affair in Letters* (Hodder & Stoughton Ltd., 1976)

Morrell, Ottoline, *Ottoline at Garsington: Memoirs of Lady Ottoline Morrell 1873–1915*, ed. Robert Gathorne-Hardy (Faber, London, 1963)

Nicolson, Nigel, *Portrait of a Marriage* (Guild Publishing, 1990)

——, *Virginia Woolf* (Weidenfeld & Nicolson, 2000)

——, *Vita and Harold* (Weidenfeld & Nicolson, 1993)

Partridge, Frances, *Memories* (Gollancz, 1981)

Plomer, William, *The Autobiography of William Plomer* (Jonathan Cape, London, 1975, and Taplinger, New York, 1976)

Raitt, Suzanne, *Vita and Virginia – The Work and Friendship of V. Sackville-West and Virginia Woolf* (Clarendon Press, 1993)

Rothenstein, William, *Men and Memories, A History of the Arts 1872–1922* (Tudor Publishing Company, New York, 1932)

Ruotolo, Lucio P., *The Interrupted Moment, A View of Virginia Woolf's Novels* (Stamford, 1986)

Russell, Bertrand, *The Autobiography of Bertrand Russell* (George Allen and Unwin Ltd., London, 1967)

Sackville-West, Vita, *Collected Poems Vol.1* (The Hogarth Press, 1933)

Seymour, Miranda, *Ottoline Morrell, Life on the Grand Scale* (Hodder & Stoughton, 1992)

Silver, Brenda R., *Virginia Woolf Icon* (University of Chicago Press, 1999)

Smyth, Ethel, *Memoirs*, ed. Ronald Crichton (Viking 1987)

Somerville, E.O., and Ross, Martin, *Irish Memories* (Longmans, Green & Co., New York, 1917)

Spalding, Frances, *Duncan Grant, A Biography* (Pimlico, 1998)

——, *Vanessa Bell* (Phoenix, 1994)

Spielman, M.H., & Layard, G.S., *The Life and Work of Kate Greenaway* (Bracken Books, 1986)

St. John, Christopher, *Ethel Smyth, A Biography* (Longmans, 1959)

Stape, J.H., *Virginia Woolf, Interviews and Recollections* (Macmillan, 1995)

Stephen, Leslie, *The Mausoleum Book* (Clarendon Press, Oxford, 1977)

——, *Selected Letters of Leslie Stephen, Vol. 2*, ed. John W. Bicknall (Macmillan, 1996)

Strachey, Julia & Partridge, Frances, *Julia* (Phoenix, 2000)

Tranter, Rachel, *Vanessa Bell, A Life of Painting* (Cecil Woolf, London, 1998)

Whelan, Robert, *Octavia Hill and the Social Housing Debate* (IEA Health & Welfare Unit, 1998)

Woolf, Virginia, *A Passionate Apprentice*, ed. Mitchell A. Leaska (The Hogarth Press, London, 1992)

——, *A Room of One's Own* (Penguin, 1945)

——, *Between the Acts* (The Hogarth Press, London, 1941)

——, *Collected Letters of Virginia Woolf Vols I–VI*, ed. Nigel Nicolson/Joanne Trautmann Banks (The Hogarth Press, 1975)

——, *The Common Reader* (Pelican, 1938)

——, *The Complete Shorter Fiction*, ed. Susan Dick (Triad Grafton Books, 1991)

——, *The Death of the Moth* (The Hogarth Press, London, 1947)

——, *The Diaries of Virginia Woolf Vols I–V*, ed. Anne Olivier Bell (The Hogarth Press, London, 1980)

——, 'Friendship's Gallery' from *Twentieth Century Literature* (Vol. 25, 1979)

——, *Jacob's Room* (The Hogarth Press, 1990)

——, *Moments of Being*, ed. Jeanne Schulkind (Harcourt Brace, 1985)

——, *Mrs Dalloway* (The Hogarth Press, London, 1950)

——, *Night and Day* (Penguin, 1992)

——, *Orlando* (Penguin, 1993)

——, 'Professions for Women', from *The Crowded Dance of Modern Life* ed. Rachel Bowlby (Penguin, 1993)

——, *To the Lighthouse* (Penguin, 1964)

——, *To the Lighthouse* (Penguin, 1999)

——, *The Voyage Out* (Penguin, 1992)

——, *The Years* (Grafton, 1977)

Notes

Abbreviations used in the following notes:

VW   Virginia Woolf
VSW   Vita Sackville-West
VB   Vanessa Bell
LW   Leonard Woolf
APA   Virginia Woolf, *A Passionate Apprentice*, ed. Mitchell A. Leaska (The Hogarth Press, 1992)
MOB   Virginia Woolf, *Moments of Being*, ed. Jeanne Schulkind (Harcourt Brace, 1985)
LI–LVI *Collected Letters of Virginia Woolf, Vols I–VI*, ed. Nigel Nicolson/Joanne Trautmann Banks (The Hogarth Press London, 1975)
DI–DV   *The Diaries of Virginia Woolf, Vols I–V*, ed. Anne Olivier Bell (The Hogarth Press, London 1975)
MHP   Monk's House Papers, University of Sussex Special Collections
CP   Charleston Papers, University of Sussex Special Collections
KCLC   King's College Library, Cambridge
BC   Berg Collection, New York Public Library

Introduction

1   Virginia Woolf, *A Writer's Diary*, 1 November 1924
2   Virginia Woolf, 'Professions for Women' from *Killing the Angel in the House: Seven Essays*, ed. Rachel Bowlby (Penguin 1995), p.5
3   VW, *The Voyage Out*, ed. Jane Wheare (Penguin 1992), pp.238–39
4   VW, *DIII*, 31 May 1929, p.230

Chapter 1 – The Angels in the House

1   VW, 'Professions for Women', from *Killing the Angel in the House: Seven Essays*, ed. Rachel Bowlby (Penguin 1995), p.3
2   VW, *A Sketch of the Past*, unpublished fragment, MHP
3   *Sir Leslie Stephen's Mausoleum Book* (Clarendon Press, Oxford, 1977), p.47
4   Letter from Leslie Stephen to Julia Stephen, 23 January 1883, BC
5   VW, *MOB*, p.39
6   VW, *To the Lighthouse*, (Penguin 1999), p.34
7   Ibid., p.35
8   VW, *MOB*, p.83
9   Ibid., p.96
10 Ibid., p.90
11 Letter from Maria Jackson to Stella Duckworth, c.1873, Sussex

12   Letter from Maria Jackson to Julia Duckworth, 1874, Sussex
13   Letter from Stella Duckworth to Maria Jackson, 1881, Sussex
14   Letter from Maria Jackson to Julia Stephen, c.1881, Sussex
15   Louise De Salvo, *Virginia Woolf – the impact of childhood sexual abuse on her life and work* (The Women's Press, 1989), p.42
16   *Sir Leslie Stephen's Mausoleum Book* (Clarendon Press, Oxford, 1977), p.59
17   VW, *MOB* p.96
18   Louise De Salvo, *Virginia Woolf – the impact of childhood sexual abuse on her life and work* (The Women's Press, 1989), p.44
19   VW, *MOB*, p.97
20   Octavia Hill, 1838–1912, born in Wisbech; radical campaigner for and manager of working-class housing estates. Founded the Charity Organisation Society and also the National Trust in 1895.
21   *Stella Duckworth's Diary for 1893*, by permission Anne Olivier Bell (hereafter referred to as SDD 1893).
22   SDD 1893
23   SDD 1893
24   SDD 1893
25   Louise de Salvo, *Virginia Woolf – the impact of childhood sexual abuse on her life and work* (The Women's Press, 1989), p.51
26   SDD 1893
27   VW, *MOB* p.94
28   Ibid., p.45
29   Ibid., p.48
30   VW, *A Sketch of the Past*, MHP, A5c
31   Ibid.
32   VW, *MOB,* p.45
33   *Stella Duckworth's Diary for 1896*, BC
34   Jack Hills, 1867–1938, was at Eton with George Duckworth, trained as a solicitor and married Stella Duckworth in 1897. After her death he re-married, but not until near the end of his life (1931), one Mary Grace Ashton. On his death the legacy from his marriage to Stella was given to Vanessa Bell, Virginia Woolf and Adrian Stephen.
35   VW, *MOB,* p.47
36   VW, *MOB,* p.104
37   VW, *LI,* p.496
38   VW, *A Sketch of the Past*, MHP, A5c
39   *Selected Letters of Leslie Stephen*, Volume 2, ed. John W. Bicknall (Macmillan, 1996).
40   VW, *APA*, p.80
41   Ibid.
42   Ibid., p.115
43   VW, *The Voyage Out* (Penguin, 1992), p.196
44   VW, *Night and Day* (Penguin, 1992), p.426
45   Ibid., p.426
46   VW, *To the Lighthouse* (Penguin 1964), p.134
47   Ibid., p.151
48   VW, *The Years* (Grafton 1977), p.18
49   Ibid., p.104
50   Ibid., p.428
51   VW, *A Sketch of the Past*, MHP, A5c

52 William Rothenstein, *Men and Memories, A History of the Arts 1872–1922* (Tudor Publishing Company, New York), p.97

Chapter 2 – Vanessa

1   VW, *MOB*, p.54
2   VW to VB, *LVI*, no. 3708, p.485
3   VW, *A Sketch of the Past*, MHP, A5c
4   VB, *Sketches in Pen and Ink*, ed. Lia Giachero (The Hogarth Press), 1997, p.57
5   VW, *MOB*, p.56
6   VW, *MOB*, p.171
7   VW, *A Sketch of the Past*, MHP, A5c
8   VW, *LI*, no. 305, p.250
9   Ibid., no. 333, p.273
10 Ibid., no. 438, p.357
11 VW to Violet Dickinson, *LI*, no. 620, p.500
12 VB to Leonard Woolf, September 1913, MHP
13 VB to Leonard Woolf, January 1913, MHP
14 VW to VB, *LII*, no. 985, p.289
15 VW to VB, *LII*, no. 1000, p.312
16 VW to Leonard Woolf, *LIII*, no. 1382, p.30
17 Angelica Garnett, *The Eternal Moment* (Puckerbrush Press, 1998), p.52
18 VW, 'Julian Bell', included in Quentin Bell's *Virginia Woolf* (Pimlico, 1996), p.257
19 VB to VW, 4 February 1938, BC
20 Angelica Garnett, *The Eternal Moment* (Puckerbrush Press, 1998), p.54
21 VB to LW, 6 March, year not known, MHP
22 VB to LW, Charleston, undated, MHP
23 VB to LW, Charleston, 1959, MHP
24 VW to Violet Dickinson, *LII*, no. 655, p.15
25 Lyndall Gordon, *Virginia Woolf, A Writer's Life* (Oxford University Press, 1986), p.130
26 VW to VB, *LII*, no. 923, p.232

Chapter 3 – Violet

1   Joy Burden, 'The Dickinsons', from *Winging Westward* (Robert Wall Books, Bath, 1974)
2   Ibid., p.138
3   VW, Notebook, A26, MHP
4   VW to Violet Dickinson, *LI*, no. 75, p.72
5   VW, *Friendship's Gallery*, MHP
6   Violet Dickinson Autograph Album, BC
7   VW, *LI*, no. 177, p.139
8   Ibid., no. 178, p.140
9   Ibid., no. 77, p.73
10 Ibid., no. 189, p.153
11 Ibid., no. 229, p.191
12 M.H. Spielman, *The Life and Work of Kate Greenaway* (Bracken Books, 1986), p.188
13 VW, *LI*, no. 251, p.211

14 Ibid., no. 310, p.253
15 VW, *Friendship's Gallery*, MHP
16 Ibid.
17 Jean Thomas to Violet Dickinson, 14 September 1913, BC
18 Ibid., 19 April 1915
19 VW to Violet Dickinson, n/d 1937, MHP
20 VW to Violet Dickinson, 8 September 1940, MHP
21 Lillian Faderman, *Surpassing the Love of Men* (The Women's Press, 1997), p.16
22 Ibid., p.159
23 Ibid., p.164
24 E.O. Somerville and Martin Ross, *Irish Memories* (Longmans, Green and Co., New York, 1917), p.236
25 VW to Violet Dickinson, *LI*, no. 57, p.60
26 Quentin Bell, *Virginia Woolf* (Pimlico, 1996), p.83
27 Joy Burden, letter to the author, January 2001
28 Violet Dickinson, fragment of letter, n/d, CP

Chapter 4 – Ottoline and Katherine

 1 William Plomer, *The Autobiography of William Plomer* (Jonathan Cape, London, 1975, Taplinger, New York, 1976), pp.254–9
 2 *The Early Memoirs of Lady Ottoline Morrell 1873–1915*, ed. Robert Gathorne-Hardy (Faber, London, 1963), p.179
 3 Ibid., p.178
 4 *Ottoline at Garsington: Memoirs of Lady Ottoline Morrell 1915–1918*, ed. Robert Gathorne-Hardy (Faber, London, 1963), p.179
 5 *The Early Memoirs of Lady Ottoline Morrell 1873–1915*, ed. Robert Gathorne-Hardy (Faber, London, 1963), p.183
 6 Ibid., p.204
 7 Ottoline Morrell to VW, 1912 n/d, MHP
 8 *Ottoline at Garsington: Memoirs of Lady Ottoline Morrell 1915–1918*, ed. Robert Gathorne-Hardy (Faber, London, 1963), p.179
 9 Ibid.
10 *The Autobiography of Bertrand Russell* (George Allen and Unwin Ltd., London, 1967), p.205
11 D.H. Lawrence, *Women in Love* (Guild Publishing, 1978), p.9
12 Aldous Huxley, *Crome Yellow* (Flamingo Modern Classics, 1994), p.5
13 Ottoline Morrell to VW, 16 May 1919, MHP
14 Ottoline Morrell to Molly McCarthy, 1928 n/d, McCarthy mss., Manuscripts Dept, Lilly Library, Indiana University
15 Ottoline Morrell, *A Farewell Message*, n/d, BC
16 VW, *The Voyage Out* (Penguin 1992), p.181
17 Katherine Mansfield to VW, August 1917, from *The Letters of Katherine Mansfield Vol.1*, ed. J. Middleton Murry (Constable & Co., 1928), p.80
18 Ottoline Morrell to VW, 25 May 1919, MHP
19 VW, *DII*, 31 May 1920, p.44
20 VW, *LII*, no. 1228, p.515
21 Katherine Mansfield, 'At the Bay', from *Collected Short Stories of Katherine Mansfield*, Constable & Co., 1945, p.213
22 VW, *The Voyage Out* (Penguin 1992), p.196
23 VW, *Night and Day* (Penguin 1992), p.426

24 Ibid., p.90
25 Katherine Mansfield, 'Leves Amores', from *New Zealand Stories* (Oxford University Press, Auckland, 1997), p.20
26 VW, *Mrs Dalloway* (Hogarth Press, London, 1950), p.39
27 VW, *L*III, no. 1821, p.431
28 VW, *L*II, no. 1228, p.515
29 Katherine Mansfield, 'Bliss', from *Collected Short Stories of Katherine Mansfield* (Constable & Co., 1945), p.96
30 Katherine Mansfield, *The Journal of Katherine Mansfield 1914–1922* (Constable & Co, 1927)
31 Ottoline Morrell to Rosamund Lehmann, 28 May 1931, KCLC

Chapter 5 – Carrington

1 Julia Strachey/Frances Partridge, 'Carrington, A Study of a Modern Witch' from *Julia* (Phoenix, 2000), p.118
2 Ibid., p.120
3 Aldous Huxley, *Crome Yellow* (Flamingo Modern Classic, 1994), p.34
4 Ibid., p.11
5 Ibid., p.136
6 VW, *L*II, no. 798, p.124
7 Letter from Carrington to VB, n/d, 1916, KCLC
8 Letter from Carrington to VW, n/d, 1917, MHP Letters III
9 Letter from Carrington to VW, n/d, MHP Letters III
10 VW, *DI*, 12 December 1917, p.89
11 Ibid., 19 August 1918, pp.183–4
12 *Carrington, Letters and Extracts from her Diaries*, ed. David Garnett (Jonathan Cape Ltd., 1970), p.104
13 VW, *DI*, 24 January 1919, p.236
14 VW, *DII*, 23 May 1921, p.119
15 Ibid., 6 September 1922, pp.198–9
16 Ibid., 18 November 1924, p.231
17 *Carrington, Letters and Extracts from her Diaries*, ed. David Garnett (Jonathan Cape Ltd., 1970), p.434
18 Quoted in Jane Hill, *The Art of Dora Carrington* (The Herbert Press, 1994), p.17
19 Ibid., p.28
20 Frances Partridge, *Memories* (Gollancz, 1981), pp.79-81
21 Julia Strachey/Frances Partridge, 'Carrington, A Study of a Modern Witch', from *Julia* (Phoenix, 2000), p.120
22 Vita Sackville-West to Harold Nicolson, 13 June 1926, quoted in Victoria Glendinning, *Vita, The Life of V. Sackville-West* (Weidenfeld & Nicolson, 1983), p.163
23 *Carrington, Letters and Extracts from her Diaries*, ed. David Garnett (Jonathan Cape Ltd., 1970), p.139
24 Carrington to Lytton Strachey, 7 March 1928, British Library
25 VW to Clive Bell, *L*IV, no. 2330, p.294
26 VW, 'The Orchard', from *The Complete Shorter Fiction*, ed. Susan Dick (Triad Grafton Books, 1991), p.149
27 Carrington to Gerald Brenan, 5 May 1924, from *Carrington, Letters and Extracts from her Diaries*, ed. David Garnett (Jonathan Cape Ltd., 1970), p.228

28 VW to Quentin Bell, 11 May 1929, *LIV*, no. 2028, p.55
29 Carrington to Lytton Strachey, 28 July 1931, from *Carrington, Letters and Extracts from her Diaries*, ed. David Garnett (Jonathan Cape Ltd., 1970), p.473
30 Lytton Strachey to Leonard Woolf, 21 December 1904, quoted in Michael Holroyd, *Lytton Strachey and the Bloomsbury Group* (Penguin 1971), p.19
31 VW to Carrington, *LIV*, no. 2484, p.414
32 Unpublished letter from Carrington to Roger Senhouse, n/d, 1932, BC
33 VW to Carrington, *LV*, no. 2517, p.11
34 Carrington to VW, February 1932, from *Carrington, Letters and Extracts from her Diaries*, ed. David Garnett (Jonathan Cape Ltd., 1970), p.492
35 Carrington to George Rylands, n/d 1932, KCLC
36 VW, *DIV*, 24 March 1932, p.85

Chapter Six – Vita

1   VSW, 'Sissinghurst', from *Collected Poems Vol.1* (The Hogarth Press, 1933)
2   Quoted in Nigel Nicolson, *Portrait of a Marriage* (Weidenfeld and Nicolson, 1983), p.10
3   VSW, *Pepita* (Grey Arrow 1961), p.187
4   Nigel Nicolson, *Portrait of a Marriage* (Weidenfeld and Nicolson, 1983), p.24
5   Ibid., p.30
6   VSW to Harold Nicolson, 5 November 1910, from *Vita and Harold*, ed. Nigel Nicolson (Weidenfeld and Nicolson, 1993), p.16
7   Nigel Nicolson, *Portrait of a Marriage* (Weidenfeld and Nicolson, 1983), p.42
8   VSW, *Pepita* (Grey Arrow 1961), p.229
9   VSW to Harold Nicolson, 19 December 1922, quoted in Nigel Nicolson, *Portrait of a Marriage* (Weidenfeld and Nicolson, 1983), p.185
10 VSW to Harold Nicolson, 12 January 1923, from *Vita and Harold*, ed. Nigel Nicolson (Weidenfeld and Nicolson, 1993), p.119
11 VSW Diary, 22 February 1923, quoted in Nigel Nicolson, *Portrait of a Marriage* (Weidenfeld and Nicolson, 1983), p.185
12 VSW to VW, 16 July 1924, *The Letters of Vita Sackville-West to Virginia Woolf*, ed. Louise De Salvo and Mitchell A. Leaska (Virago 1992), p.53
13 VW, *LIII*, no. 1687, p.302
14 VSW to VW, 11 October 1925, *The Letters of Vita Sackville-West to Virginia Woolf*, ed. Louise De Salvo and Mitchell A. Leaska (Virago 1992), p.78
15 VSW to Harold Nicolson, 17 December 1925, from *Vita and Harold*, ed. Nigel Nicolson (Weidenfeld and Nicolson, 1993), p.134
16 VSW to VW, 21 January 1926, *The Letters of Vita Sackville-West to Virginia Woolf*, ed. Louise De Salvo and Mitchell A. Leaska (Virago 1992), p.98
17 VSW to Harold Nicolson, 28 June 1926, from *Vita and Harold*, ed. Nigel Nicolson (Weidenfeld and Nicolson, 1993), p.150
18 Ibid., 30 November 1926, p.175
19 Nigel Nicolson, *Virginia Woolf* (Weidenfeld and Nicolson, 2000), p.75
20 VW, *DIII*, 21 December, p.52
21 VW, *LIII*, no. 1735, p.532
22 Helen Dunmore, 'Virginia Woolf and Her Relationships With Women', *Charleston Magazine* Issue 23, Spring/Summer 2001, p.9
23 VW, *DIII*, 2 September, p.247
24 VSW to VW, 11 October 1927, *The Letters of Vita Sackville-West to Virginia Woolf*, ed. Louise De Salvo and Mitchell A. Leaska (Virago 1992), p.252

25 Ibid., 11 October 1928, p.305
26 Lucio P. Ruotolo, *The Interrupted Moment, A View of Virginia Woolf's Novels* (Stamford, 1986), p.144
27 Suzanne Raitt, *Vita and Virginia – The Work and Friendship of V. Sackville-West and Virginia Woolf* (Clarendon Press, 1993), p.66
28 Brenda R. Silver, *Virginia Woolf Icon* (University of Chicago Press, 1999), p.223
29 VSW, 'Sissinghurst', from *Collected Poems Vol.1* (The Hogarth Press 1933)
30 VSW, 'To any M.F.H.', from *Collected Poems Vol.1* (The Hogarth Press, 1933)
31 Evelyn Irons to VSW, 15 August 1931, BC
32 VSW, untitled poem to Evelyn Irons, n/d, BC
33 VW, *LV*, no. 3071, p.435
34 VW, *The Years* (Grafton 1977), p.276
35 VW, *Between the Acts* (Hogarth Press 1941), pp.51–2
36 Lillian Faderman, *Surpassing the Love of Men* (The Women's Press, 1985), p.368
37 VSW to Harold Nicolson, 8 November 1949, from *Vita and Harold*, Ed. Nigel Nicolson (Weidenfeld and Nicolson, 1993), p.391
38 Ibid., p.412

Chapter 7 – Ethel

1   VSW, 'Ethel Smyth, The Writer', from Christopher St. John, *Ethel Smyth, A Biography* (Longmans, 1959), p.245
2   Ethel Smyth, *Memoirs*, ed. Ronald Crichton (Viking 1987), p.196
3   Reminiscence by Sylvia Pankhurst, from Christopher St. John, *Ethel Smyth, A Biography* (Longmans, 1959), pp.153–4
4   Letter from George Bernard Shaw to Ethel Smyth, from Christopher St. John, *Ethel Smyth, A Biography* (Longmans, 1959), p.185
5   VW, *LII*, no. 1100, p.404
6   Ethel Smyth to VB, 22 June 1930, CP
7   Ethel Smyth to VW, August 1930, n/d, BC
8   Christopher St. John, *Ethel Smyth, A Biography* (Longmans 1959), p.223
9   Ibid., p.224
10 VW, *LIV*, no. 2204, p.188
11 Ibid., no. 2335, p.297
12 VSW to Evelyn Irons, 5 August 1931, BC
13 VSW to VW, 11 June 1933, from *The Letters of Vita Sackville-West to Virginia Woolf*, ed. Louise De Salvo and Mitchell A. Leaska (Virago, 1992), p.400
14 VSW, 'Ethel Smyth The Writer', from Christopher St. John, *Ethel Smyth, A Biography* (Longmans, 1959), p.223
15 Nigel Nicolson, *Virginia Woolf* (Weidenfeld and Nicolson, 2000), p.101
16 Ethel Smyth, 'Mrs Waters's Aria', from *The Boatswains Mate*, 1913–14
17 Ethel Smyth to VW, August 1930 n/d, BC
18 Ethel Smyth to VB, n/d, CP
19 Ethel Smyth, diary 1933, quoted in Christopher St. John, *Ethel Smyth, A Biography* (Longmans, 1959), p.223
20 Ethel Smyth to VW, 23 October 1931, MHP
21 VW, *The Years* (Grafton 1977), p.414
22 Ibid., p.410
23 Ethel Smyth to VW, 3 June 1938, BC
24 VW, *Between The Acts* (The Hogarth Press, 1941), p.72
25 VW, *DII*, 18 May 1920, p.39

26 Ibid., 29 April 1921, p.14
27 Ibid., 1 November 1924, p.320
28 VW, 'The String Quartet', from *The Complete Shorter Fiction*, ed. Susan Dick (Triad Grafton Books), 1991, p.139
29 VW, *D*III, 21 February 1930, pp.291–92
30 VW, *D*IV, 4 February 1931, p.10
31 VW, cancelled passage quoted in Mitchell A. Leaska's *The Pargiters: The Novel-Essay Portion of The Years* (The Hogarth Press, 1978), p.27
32 Ethel Smyth to VW, 11 August 1930, BC
33 Ibid., 31 August 1930
34 VW, *The Waves* (Oxford World Classics, 1998), p.133
35 Ibid., p.134
36 VSW to Harold Nicolson, 2 May 1938, from *Vita and Harold*, ed. Nigel Nicolson (Weidenfeld and Nicolson, 1993), p.300
37 VW, 'A Sketch of the Past', *MOB*, p.72
38 Ethel Smyth to VW, 5 February 1941, quoted in Christopher St. John, *Ethel Smyth, A Biography* (Longmans, 1959), p.237
39 VSW, 'Ethel Smyth The Writer', from Christopher St. John, *Ethel Smyth, A Biography* (Longmans, 1959), p.246
40 VSW, 'To Ethel', 8 May 1944, from Christopher St. John, *Ethel Smyth, A Biography* (Longmans, 1959), p.xiii

Chapter 8 – Virginia

1 VW, *LIV*, no. 2222, p.202
2 VW, *Orlando* (Oxford World's Classics, 1998), pp.218–19
3 VW, *APA*, p.124
4 VW, 'A Sketch of the Past', *MOB*, p.141
5 VW, *APA*, p.142
6 Adrian Stephen's Diary 1909, Ad 13, MHP
7 Quentin Bell, from transcript of *Omnibus* programme, n/d, MHP
8 VW, *D*III, 4 May 1928, p.183
9 Letter from Cecil Woolf to the author, 2001
10 Dirk Bogarde, *A Particular Friendship* (Penguin, 1990), pp. 114–15
11 E.M. Forster, *Virginia Woolf – The Rede Lecture 1941* (Cambridge University Press), p.41
12 VW, *D*II, 18 August 1921, p.133
13 VW, *D*III, 28 September 1926, p.112
14 Nigel Nicolson, *Virginia Woolf* (Weidenfeld and Nicolson, 2000), p.156
15 Michèle Barrett, *Virginia Woolf on Women & Writing* (The Women's Press, 1996), p.123

Afterword

1 Violet Dickinson to VB, April 1941, n/d, CP
2 Vita Sackville-West to VB, April 1941, CP
3 Ethel Smyth to VB, April 1941, CP

Index